"This is a brilliant book gleaned from decades of experience. It provides a clear and practical blueprint for approaching the complex and unpredictable challenges of leadership, usable in the heat of battle. The stories and anecdotes bring the model to life and make this book a pleasure to read."

—**RAMEZ SOUSOU**, founder and cochair, TowerBrook

"Working with David and Carol opened my eyes. I saw leadership in a new way."

—**HISAYUKI "DEKO" IDEKOBA**, CEO, Recruit Holdings

"A savvy playbook for navigating the troubled seas real leaders face."

—**DANIEL GOLEMAN**, bestselling author, *Emotional Intelligence* and *Primal Leadership*

"Carol and David not only helped me better prepare for unexpected and complex leadership challenges, they also helped me understand why I have acted the way I have in the past. It is a great guide to help one continuously grow as a leader in an ever-changing world."

—**GERMAN HERRERA**, US Managing Partner, Egon Zehnder

"David and Carol beautifully illustrate how to become a successful change-maker in all situations. I will keep referring back to this book as I continue to evolve as a person and as a leader."

—**BYRON JONES**, cornerback, Miami Dolphins

"When the stakes are high, we're easily hijacked by old reflexes that keep us from being the leader we want to be and the leader others need. This practical and timely book offers a step-by-step playbook of MOVEs you need to master to bring your best to these critical moments."

—**HERMINIA IBARRA**, Professor of Organizational Behavior, London Business School; author, *Act Like a Leader, Think Like a Leader*

"The MOVE model unlocks major opportunities while simultaneously managing risks. David and Carol draw on their world-class coaching experience to show how a great strategy can build character in leaders and unlock the potential of others."

—**NICK STUDER**, CEO, Oliver Wyman

"David and Carol have something fresh and invaluable to say about leadership today that will resonate for years. Any current or future leader would greatly benefit from reading this book."

—**DARLEEN CARON**, CHRO, Siemens-Healthineers

"*Real-Time Leadership* gives you specific, usable actions to expand your leadership range. Whether in the private or public sector, it helps you create new options to navigate any big opportunity or major threat."

—**BRUCE HEYMAN**, former US ambassador to Canada

"This book is amazing. And the timing cannot be better. The tools are exactly what any current or aspiring leader needs to be ready with a dynamic real-time response to whatever the world throws at us. I apply the MOVE framework to my own continuous development."

—**HASSANE EL-KHOURY**, CEO, ON Semiconductor

"*Real-Time Leadership* is a master class in high-stakes leadership. Highly cohesive and on-point practical from the first to the last. I couldn't stop taking notes. Superb!"

—**WHITNEY JOHNSON**, CEO, Disruption Advisors; *WSJ* bestselling author, *Smart Growth*

"The MOVE framework provides not only the fuel to act with urgency but also the guardrails to reduce risk by considering potential blind spots and biases."

—**TODD ABBRECHT**, co-CEO, Thomas H. Lee Partners

"Consistent, high-quality decision-making in the highest-stakes, highest-risk situations is the ultimate test of leadership. Carol and David show that it's a skill that can be learned. *Real-Time Leadership* is essential reading for those who want to outperform at the very highest level."

—**JOHN-PAUL PAPE**, Global Practice Lead, CEO Transformation, Accenture

"This breakthrough contribution to the art of leadership is a must-read, with an original framework applicable to any career. Noble and Kauffman provide timely, relevant, and precise master moves for today's changing world while also delivering a fun and insightful read."

—**JONAH BOKAER**, international choreographer, arts leader

REAL-TIME LEADERSHIP

*FIND YOUR
WINNING MOVES
WHEN THE
STAKES ARE HIGH*

REAL-TIME
LEADERSHIP

David Noble | Carol Kauffman

Harvard Business Review Press
Boston, Massachusetts

Printed in the United Kingdom by TJ Books Limited, Padstow, Cornwall

10 9 8 7 6 5 4 3 2

The web addresses referenced in this book were live and correct at the time of the book's publication but may be subject to change.

Library of Congress Cataloging-in-Publication Data

Names: Noble, David (Writer on industrial management), author. | Kauffman, Carol (Writer on executive coaching), author.
Title: Real-time leadership : find your winning moves when the stakes are high / David Noble, Carol Kauffman.
Description: Boston, Massachusetts : Harvard Business Review Press, [2022] | Includes index.
Identifiers: LCCN 2022034367 (print) | LCCN 2022034368 (ebook) | ISBN 9781647823931 (hardcover) | ISBN 9781647823948 (epub)
Subjects: LCSH: Leadership. | Decision making. | Executive coaching. | Success in business.
Classification: LCC HD57.7 .N57 2022 (print) | LCC HD57.7 (ebook) | DDC 658.4/092—dc23/eng/20221025
LC record available at https://lccn.loc.gov/2022034367
LC ebook record available at https://lccn.loc.gov/2022034368

ISBN: 978-1-64782-393-1
eISBN: 978-1-64782-394-8

The paper used in this publication meets the requirements of the American National Standard for Permanence of Paper for Publications and Documents in Libraries and Archives Z39.48-1992.

*To our families, who made space
to embrace this book as well as us.*

CONTENTS

M O V E : **Validate Your Vantage Point**

M O V E : **Engage and Effect Change**

Move in a Big New Role

Move to Drive 10x Change

FOREWORD

David Noble and Carol Kauffman are two of the most accomplished executive coaches in the world. While many coaches call themselves "CEO coach," few have actually worked with top CEOs in major companies. David and Carol have decades of experience working with great leaders from incredibly diverse organizations. *Real-Time Leadership* gives you a fascinating "behind closed doors" view of what executive coaching is really like, based on their invaluable experience and wisdom.

The MOVE framework, detailed in this book, has been extremely helpful to me in my own coaching practice and in my own life.

> Be Mindfully Alert: I am a philosophical Buddhist and have studied Buddhism for more than fifty years. Carol taught me one question that, to me, captures the essence of Buddhism better than any I have ever heard. I share this question with my coaching and leadership development clients every day: *Am I being the person I want to be, right now?* The section on mindfulness captures the essence of how we can remain mindful and present in a world filled with seemingly endless distractions. On many days, I need this help more than my clients do!

> Generate Options: Busy leaders tend to be impatient. I am no different. We usually feel a need to quickly come up with a solution and move on. This section explains the value of carefully weighing alternatives before leaping into action. A little reflection in the beginning can eliminate a lot of grief in the end. Although I found this section quite helpful in my coaching practice, I found it even more helpful in planning my own life!

> Validate Your Vantage Point: Possibly the most unique section of the book. Our perception of *What is really going on here?* is often warped by factors outside of our awareness. Learning how our views can be distorted and how to overcome this distortion can be immensely valuable in a real-time leadership challenge. Every situation does not require the same degree of urgency or understanding.

Learning when a "high-def" view is needed—as opposed to when a "grainy" view is good enough—can help leaders save time and focus on what matters most. I have never had this concept explained so clearly.

Engage and Effect Change: The biggest challenge leaders face isn't understanding the practice of leadership, it's *practicing their understanding* of leadership. David and Carol provide practical advice on not only how to effect change but also how to scale change to create an impact throughout the organization. This section is especially important for entrepreneurs, who can be wonderful at creating the business yet terrible at scaling it.

David and Carol also skillfully apply their work to two major real-time challenges every leader faces. The first challenge is stepping into a new role. These chapters provide a new and valuable take on those first ninety days and beyond. The second challenge is surviving disruption, and more important, creating disruption—how to do it and how to use it to innovate and make a positive impact.

This book isn't just about being successful. It is about becoming an extraordinary leader and human being.

In a very positive way, *Real-Time Leadership* is a dense book. Some books can be criticized for being one chapter replicated fifteen times. Not this book! There is no filler. Each chapter provides fresh and valuable insights to help you face your biggest leadership challenges.

David and Carol are among the world's greatest leadership coaches. Very few people can hire them for one-on-one coaching (that is, their unique "two-on-one" coaching). Thanks to this book, we can all learn from them and immediately apply that learning—both at work and at home. This book has helped me. I am sure it can help you, too.

—Marshall Goldsmith

Why MOVE?

Anyone can hold the helm when the sea is calm.
—**Publilius Syrus**

• • •

This book is not about calm seas.

We devote this book to handling high-stakes, high-risk leadership challenges, the ones you have to manage in real time as they unfold, whether you need to face them this moment, this month, or over the long term. They're challenges that may be unfamiliar to you and that could lead to a prize, or to peril. Getting your leadership right in these high-stakes, high-risk situations could be the difference between winning and losing; between the company surviving and perishing; between your career accelerating and faltering; and between feeling fulfilled by your successes or experiencing only hollow victories.

• • •

The Gulfstream G650 touched down at Westchester County Airport in New York early on a clear March morning, carrying a single passenger. Matt stepped off the plane and into a waiting car for the short drive to Greenwich, Connecticut. A hotel suite was booked so that he could work with us—David and Carol—for the day without interruption.

Matt was a top executive in a *Fortune* 50 company. A new CEO would be named within the next week, and Matt had been the odds-on favorite candidate.

But he was in trouble and needed to talk. The previous day he'd bombed his interview with the board's nominating and governance committee (NomGov). Upset, Matt recounted for us how, as he made his pitch to NomGov, he saw doubt in the faces of the committee members. He doubled his efforts but only felt the tension increase, washing through the room like a wave. By the time the Q&A started, Matt could feel the committee's frustration and knew he was underwater. He left unsure of himself.

What Matt sensed was real, and he was right to be worried. He didn't know it at the time, but the committee had shifted to favor an external candidate with a well-known personal brand. That candidate had made a stronger case and gained an inside track on the job.

Matt had one more chance to make his case, in front of the full board the next day. The NomGov chair had called us in to help Matt make the most of his last shot.

• • •

If Matt had known our leadership framework, MOVE, he would have been able to scan through that committee meeting in real time and change the course of the situation. He would have been able to read what was happening and identify the best response to those tough moments. Better yet, he could have prevented the interview from taking a disastrous turn entirely.

We couldn't go back in time to fix the situation, but we were motivated and prepared to help Matt avoid a repeat the next day. You will read more about his journey below.

• • •

What challenges are you facing right now? Storms can kick up at any moment, within the company and outside, and sometimes both at once. In such fierce gales, facing rogue waves, can you hold the helm? A startup founder we worked with described the experience of his first funding round as "a tornado of fire and sharks." Can you keep standing through that?

You can. A good captain reads roiling seas well, remaining calm and determining an optimal path through the chop. Doing so requires constantly monitoring for changing conditions and adroitly ensuring the crew is aligned and operating at peak performance. This book will help you become that kind of captain so that you can remain even-keeled, acutely read the situation, move beyond your basic reflex, and respond in the best way possible.

To accomplish this, we need to help you create space between the challenges that are thrown at you and how you react. Making optimal choices in real time is possible. The key to doing it lies in the wisdom Viktor Frankl shared after surviving three years in four concentration camps during World War II. "In between every stimulus and response there is a space," he said. "And in that space is our freedom to choose."[1]

Every step of our framework helps you find, open, and use that space well.

Our evidence-based approach and decades of experience have shown us how the best leaders do this, and we've been privileged to join some of them on their journeys. We'll show you how to weather any storm by following our MOVE framework:

> **M**: Be Mindfully Alert. Find the space to be attuned to the Three Dimensions of Leadership so that you are clear about your high-priority goals, which character strengths and skills you want to cultivate as a leader, and how best to relate to others to accomplish your goals.

> **O**: Generate Options. You want at least four pathways forward and four ways to win and make either whip-fast or slow, thoughtful decisions in real time.[2]

> **V**: Validate Your Vantage Point. Check your take on reality and choose the best point of view.

> **E**: Engage and Effect Change. Do this first as an individual, then at scale, or all else is moot.

When it's your move, you MOVE. Get these four principles right, master this framework, and you'll succeed. This book is a crash course. You are going to meet many of the amazing leaders we have worked with, and experience how they successfully moved through the most challenging times in their leadership together with us, using this framework. People like:

- Stevie, who was tasked with transforming the core of her company to compete more effectively in the future, starting with a painful reduction in workforce

- Cheryl, who stepped in as CEO to grow a company ten times the size of anything she had previously led, by building out adjacencies in product lines and geographies, leading a digital transformation, and seeding potential moon shots

- Marcus, the brilliant, results-oriented head of a massive energy company, who was losing followership in his team and possibly compromising his recent appointment to the CEO role

- Akash, the analytical chief operating officer who almost micromanaged his way out of his job

- Amanda, a CEO who felt so pressured to grow her business that she almost went after an impulse acquisition that would have led to catastrophe

- Aria, the executive director of a nongovernmental organization who was on the verge of being pushed out by the board

- Leo, a scientist who was a subject matter expert and became lost when he was promoted to become a leader of leaders

And many more. While we typically work at the top of the house, the lessons we've learned apply to nearly everyone. Great leadership has evolved: It's flatter, faster, and more fluid than ever. Executives face waves of mega crises, and what worked yesterday doesn't work today. We designed our framework to be flexible enough to be of service to you no matter what your challenge is. It can be a lifeline for you when the stakes are at their highest.

Welcome to the private world where real-time leadership happens.

How We Help

We have taken our tens of thousands of hours of working with top leaders and distilled them into advice and coaching that can be helpful to you. Chapters 1 through 11 walk you through our overall framework as well as each of its four elements in depth. You'll see how to focus your efforts, find multiple ways to navigate your challenges, identify techniques to validate your choices, and implement best practices to effect change.

Then we take you on a journey we have taken with many newly minted CEOs and other C-suite leaders, guiding them as they stepped into a new level of leadership and faced more-intense challenges than ever before. In chapters 12 and 13 we show you specific ways to apply the MOVE framework when taking on a high-pressure new job. We go further and deeper than the "first 90 days" acceleration programs, which really just focus on table stakes. We show you how to apply the MOVE framework to grab opportunities and avoid pitfalls.

Once you have the job, big challenges follow. In chapters 14 and 15 we examine how you can tackle what we call 10x challenges. These are big, thorny goals that you set to supercharge the company's performance, perhaps greatly accelerating growth, completing a turnaround, or charting a path for achieving innovative disruption. We show you how to meet the strategic and execution challenges to create massive value while at the same time detecting and containing risks that could be fatal to your company and your career. Those 10x challenges can be scary stuff, but pulling them off with your team is what makes you distinctive as a leader.

Chapter 16 describes shortcuts that you can take in some situations by doubling down strategically on one or two aspects of the MOVE framework to drive peak performance. Finally, in our conclusion we help you get above it all so that you can lead in real time, all the time, and go from being a great to an extraordinary leader. We'll explore how to sustain and renew growth as a leader over the long term, which is a hallmark of all extraordinary leaders.

The executives we work with take pride in having a growth mindset and are always challenging themselves to become better.[3] They relish being at the edge of their expertise, becoming more agile and able to shift to new leadership styles as requirements change. It is easy to feel lost here, but transformation is always close at hand. When you are at the top of your game, it can be disorienting as you wonder *What's next? Can I really do this?* After all, you've never been in that place before. Yet that's what success feels like, and you must get comfortable with that feeling to stay at the top.

Quick question: How important is your personal development?

Quick answer: In a recent survey by Egon Zehnder of nearly one thousand CEOs representing a total annual revenue of $4 trillion, 90 percent said that personal transformation was necessary before succeeding in organizational transformation. In the same survey three years earlier, only 30 percent said personal transformation was key.[4] Times have changed and so must you.

In this book we share what we have learned, and we also pull back the curtain to bring you into some of the real-life coaching scenarios we've been through. Personal development and business acumen are intertwined with how you choose to lead. You'll see our leaders at high-stakes moments, and we'll take you into their heads and hearts as you hear our conversations. While we have shortened actual dialogues, we have faithfully maintained the intent of the speakers in all cases. But we've changed identifying details and at times merged two similar clients together to protect their privacy. The work we do with leaders helps them drive advantage in the marketplace, and no one wants to give that away.

MOVE is your playbook—dive in. It takes practice to master, but you can immediately apply some or all the principles. Go through step by step or just jump into what you need right now. Expand or contract it as you need, either at hyperspeed or through deep work over days, months, or even the rest of your career.

Truly immersing yourself in the MOVE framework will help you on your journey to sustaining peak performance and life satisfaction over the long term. It is our hope that you come back to it, again and again. And, it is our desire to help you become as successful and fulfilled as you can imagine.

Why Listen to Us?

We are recognized as two of the world's top leadership advisers and coaches. Together we bring complementary perspectives and expertise, offering a unique combination of insights and capabilities. For both of us, the best moments in our careers have been when we have helped others unlock and act on breakthroughs in how they view the world, their professional roles, and themselves.

David brings a rare trifecta of leadership, strategic, and operating lenses based on over three decades of experience as an operating executive as well as a consultant to senior leaders. He has been an executive at two of the world's best-run financial institutions, holding positions as varied as a head of strategy and the CEO of the world's first digital bank. He spent several years in leadership roles at two global strategy consultancies, followed by a decade as a senior adviser at Egon Zehnder, the world's largest private partnership devoted to leadership advisory and search, as well as other top firms. Thinkers50 has named him one of the world's top coaches. His personal purpose is to help leaders get to clarity and growth where and when they most need it.

Carol has trained thousands of psychologists, coaches, and leaders through award-winning programs she developed as part of the faculties of Harvard Medical School and Henley Business School.[5] She is a senior leadership adviser at Egon Zehnder. Thinkers50 shortlisted her as one of the top eight coaches in the world, and Marshall Goldsmith named her as the number one leadership coach globally.[6] She believes advisory work and coaching should be enjoyable, energizing, and a lifeline in times of need.[7] Her personal purpose is to be a conduit of joy and a sword of truth to care for and challenge the powerful, and to galvanize their goodness and become extraordinary.[8]

Our differences complement each other. David has a brain built on frameworks and models that he leverages and/or creates. Pattern recognition, logic, and deductive thinking inform his intuition. Carol comes from the position of an inductive and emergent thinker, with extensive experience in pattern recognition and decades of immersion in research and the scientific method. She uses theory and intuition to develop frameworks and models.[9]

Why Two Coaches with One Leader?

When a CEO calls for outside help with, say, corporate strategy, how often does one lone adviser show up? Never. Why should this be different when you are working on leadership issues at the top of the house?[10] While the two of us each have our own clients, we often team up because we've found that combining our particular strengths has an outsize impact.

We realized how powerful merging our experience and specific expertise would be, especially for the most complex leadership challenges, mostly by chance.

Carol was coaching Marcus, the new CEO of a *Fortune* 100 energy company, who was frustrated as his vision of shifting operating models to a single, global approach had met deep resistance. Regional heads were not only digging in their heels and defending their turf but also were working to undermine and upstage one another. Marcus and Carol had made great progress on emotion self-regulation and social intelligence to manage his frustration, but the team still wouldn't budge on supporting the strategy.

Meanwhile, David had been working with Marcus's team on their strategy. One day David passed by the glass-walled office where Marcus was sitting with Carol. She stopped the session and invited David to join. David asked how Marcus felt the transformation was going. When Marcus shared his frustration about the team's intransigence, David asked him how well he had articulated where he wanted the company to go, briefly mentioning the concept of leader's intent, which we explore later in the book. Marcus said he might not have explained his intent well enough.

David also asked him why he thought the strategy was the right direction for the organization. Marcus's answer showed that he had his strategic thinking down cold. But then David asked whether Marcus had clarity on how decisions should be made, who was accountable for what, and which milestones he had identified for verifying progress. David's awareness of what the team was feeling helped Marcus see that while he had taken the first step and nailed the strategy, he had done little to address these other important issues.

We immediately saw how we could coach Marcus together to further assist with his interpersonal priority, which was to get his team working with him, as well as with sharpening the clarity of his communication and instituting structures for executing the strategy and spotting any signs of bottlenecks or conflicts. Together we helped Marcus quickly bring his team into alignment, and as we continued to work with him and our other clients, we worked with each other to combine our experience in psychology, strategy, and operating roles to craft the MOVE framework. So effective has the combination of our experience been that even when we do one-on-one work with our separate clients, we consult with each other to make sure we're bringing the best the two of us have to offer.

What's Next

That's it. We're ready to start. Before we do, however, we need to be clear: One aspect of leadership that we know is crucial goes beyond success in the marketplace. We aim to help those we work with, and you as our reader, not only become more effective in managing even the toughest of challenges but also rise to a higher plane of leadership, characterized by curiosity, openness, kindness, and generosity. These qualities aren't just skills; they are part of you. Whether you realize it or not, they emanate from you and supercharge the impact of what you say and do as a leader.

Fostering these qualities not only fosters peak performance—it also leads to the highest levels of engagement, job satisfaction, and overall well-being for you, your team, and potentially everyone in your organization. Who you are is as much at the core of your leadership as what you do.

Some of you who just read that last paragraph felt it resonate with your hopes for yourself. You're eager to hear more about how we can help you reach that pinnacle. Others of you may have rolled your eyes at what you perceive as naive, feel-good mumbo jumbo. We've worked with many leaders who've expressed their view that leading through fear and scorched-earth aggression is the key to winning. We've heard "I don't just win, I destroy my competition" or "I don't get ulcers, I give them," and many similar sentiments. Sure, we've all read about, and maybe worked for, leaders who've achieved impressive success with that mindset. But we ask, at what cost? The cost is to their well-being, that of their teams, and often also that of their loved ones at home—as well as the additional cost of forgoing still grander achievements. We have seen that leaders can be ultracompetitive and demand extraordinary effort from themselves and others while at the same time being kind. We'll show you how these traits that you may be scoffing at now will make you a stronger and more fulfilled leader. We've also seen some of our most hard-nosed leaders transform, finding themselves just as successful but much happier.

Let's start working toward that now.

1

How to MOVE

If I'm an advocate for anything, it's to move. As far as you can, as much as you can. Across the ocean, or simply across the river.

—Anthony Bourdain

We're going to build out the MOVE framework in depth in the coming chapters, but it will help to give you a flyover here. This chapter will set you up with a general understanding and serve as a reference you can come back to time and again.

Let us walk you through our work with Matt, the CEO candidate from the introduction, and how it follows the MOVE framework.

M: Be Mindfully Alert

Mindful Alertness in high-stakes situations means being exquisitely aware of what is needed from you as a leader at this exact moment, so you can lead in real time. Mindfulness is about possessing calm awareness of what is around you, within you, and what you are feeling, as well as the capacity to accept this without judgment or bias.[1] Being mindfully alert implies being precise about and flexible with where you put your attention, like an elite athlete in a fast-paced competition. Achieving this requires facility in two core elements: overcoming reflexive choices and understanding that leadership is always a three-dimensional challenge. To begin your journey, your commitment to increasing your self-awareness and self-responsibility is paramount.

Many successful leaders have come to rely on their reflexes, honed by years of pattern recognition and skill development. They seem to know what to do effortlessly: when they see X, they know to do Y. Their reflexes can seem flawless when navigating known challenges or familiar circumstances. But operating in autopilot doesn't work well in high-risk, high-stakes situations where much is unknown or rapidly changing. In fact, it can be disastrous. Your instincts can cause you to overreact or underreact. Even if you can jolt yourself out of your default into real-time leadership by being mindfully alert, there is a steady pull back to your reflexes. Countering your habits that are hardwired, because they have worked so well until now, requires knowledge and practice.

Unlearning your reactive posture starts with understanding that any leadership challenge includes three inseparable dimensions. The dimensions are:

> External: Challenges, goals, and priorities in your role that come from your own aspirations for achievement and also from other forces, like the board, a colleague, or competitive pressures

> Internal: Challenges, goals, and priorities related to you as a person including character strengths, emotional regulation, values, purpose or your mindset

> Interpersonal: Challenges, goals, and priorities centered on helping others be their best through relationship skills, authentic connections, and social intelligence

Lock these three in. We will refer to them, again and again, as the *Three Dimensions of Leadership*. Every challenge you face involves some or all of these.

You can address your three-dimensional leadership demands with a well-thought-through strategy, one that over time can be honed into a new set of reflexes that don't fail you in real time. To develop three-dimensional leadership capacities, we will walk you through how to answer three key questions, each of which maps to one of the dimensions:

- What does a win look like for the goal you want to achieve? (External)

- Am I being the person I want and need to be right now? (Internal)

- Am I leading in the way others need me to? (Interpersonal)

The first question speaks to leadership's external dimension. External goals are specific high-stakes priorities that you want and need to achieve, like pulling off a merger, driving organizational change, making a successful decision, dealing with a conflict, or getting promoted to CEO. They include both goals that you choose and ones that are handed to you, like financial targets or making a reduction in force.

The second question maps to the internal dimension, developing your inner resources, what you expect of yourself and who you need to be as a person to meet those external goals.[2] Being who you want to be requires self-awareness, learning, self-responsibility, practice, and dedication. Especially when you are under high-stakes pressure that would crush others, you'll need to draw on your personal values, like courage, perspective, and compassion and put them into action. You'll also need to develop your character, strengths, and purpose.

The third question is the interpersonal dimension: Do you know how to create relationships that empower others and unlock optimal well-being and performance in them? Notice our question is how to lead in the way others need, not how to lead in the way that you'd personally prefer. In any interaction, a leader must have multiple ways to respond to unlock the potential of others. This applies not just to direct reports, but to the relationships up, down, and all around you.

Research is clear that simply pausing to ask these questions before you take any action is crucial to formulating an optimal approach to and achieving your three dimensional goals.[3] In the coming chapters, we equip you to both improve your Mindful Alertness and make it second nature. Once you do that, alarm bells will sound when you go off course. You will be able to see how your aim would have been way off by just reacting instinctually. It doesn't matter if you hit a bull's-eye if you are aiming at the wrong target!

• • •

Back to Matt, our leader on the cusp of losing the CEO succession race. He had, instinctually, aimed at the wrong bull's-eye. The NomGov chair told us, "Matt's the right guy, but he stayed in the weeds the entire time the committee spoke to him—he talked in paragraphs instead of sentences, with way too much detail. He came off like a robot, not connecting with any of us. We need someone who can elevate and be a real, strategic CEO. It's now a horse race between him and the external candidate."

As we sat down with Matt at 9:35 a.m., he glanced at his iPhone and said, "Stock's down 7 percent on opening. Wow. OK, we should get started." Clearly, he was better at managing his inner state than he was at connecting with the committee. His reaction to a stock dip showed he could stay calm in the face of stressful news.

David locked eyes with Matt. "What was your goal with NomGov? What were you hoping to achieve?"

Matt exuded tension, but immediately responded, "I needed to show them that I was on top of the business, with a command of the details and a clear plan for success. I know far more than any of the other candidates—even more important because of the company's difficult situation and with our stock price being all over the map." He sighed and looked down at his feet. "But the more I talked, the more the committee seemed frustrated with me. I didn't expect it. I know them all and I'm normally comfortable with them, so I thought I had it in the bag."

His disappointment was palpable, and David and Carol briefly commiserated with him. After all, we knew that judging the expectations for your leadership can be quite tricky. That can be just as true when you're promoted from the inside as when coming from the outside. From our conversation with the committee chair, it was clear to us that Matt had gotten his external, internal, and interpersonal goals wrong. He'd prioritized showing his knowledge of the business as an external goal, to prove he knew his stuff. But since the board already knew him quite well, this was off target. Additionally, we sensed that he believed his internal goal was to be rock-steady emotionally, which he saw as a great strength, and it was. But as a top leader, he would need to calibrate his emotions, show compassion, and give voice to his passion. His limited view of his internal priority, in turn, had distorted his view of his interpersonal goal in this situation, which was to show his full leadership range to the board.

We needed to confirm this hypothesis, so Carol asked, "If you think about your intangible qualities—your deepest strengths and your personal values—what matters most about how you show up?"

"I can't say I've thought this through," he admitted. "I'm normally so focused on financial goals, executing transformation initiatives, building employee engagement, and the like."

"That's understandable," Carol said. "Let's pause. Give yourself some space to think. What is really required of you as a leader to be the best CEO you can be? How can you convey what is most important to the board?"

"Being calm under any circumstance. That is exactly what we need right now since the company is in crisis."

David continued this train of thought. "So, what you're saying is that emanating a sense of calm is what matters most at this point. Being able to do that is crucial. What else might matter most now?"

"If I get the job, I will need to immediately make tough decisions. We have to transform our cost base, and that will mean thousands of jobs will be lost to save tens of thousands more. When I tackle issues this serious, sometimes my calmness can be mistaken for detachment. But the reduction in force will tear my insides apart. I wish others could see that I'm obsessed with doing the least harm possible."

Matt had perceived that some of his colleagues had seen him as robotic in past crunch times. He hadn't realized that to be the best leader he could be, he would need to address that perception of him. We have found that those who are truly good-hearted often fail to see that others don't automatically know it, so they don't always show it.

"So, being calm is crucial," David responded, "but people need to see how much you care and truly have their best interests at heart."

"I feel it. I guess I've been hiding that side of me."

* * *

Bingo! David and Carol were smiling now. With just a little reflection, Matt had improved his Mindful Alertness and begun to redefine who he needed to be as a top leader. It was going to be a struggle, but he realized "people need to see me as both calm and caring in order to feel safe."

Matt had just beautifully expressed one of the challenges of high-level leadership. We all have set images of who we should be, which form our basic assumptions of how we should act. In this case he was deliberately hiding the very part of him that would have won the board over.

With just a little more prodding, he remarked, "OK, here are my takeaways. One, show that I can get above the day-to-day fray with a strategic perspective and see around corners about what is ahead for us. Two, show up as a real person, not just an information dispenser. Three, focus on reading the room to find the best response rather than react to their comments based on my reflex."

We were delighted. In a relatively short time, Matt had locked in on his external priority to be more strategic in his messaging. He had also gotten clarity on his internal priorities of who he needed to be as a leader during this difficult time, and how best to interpersonally relate to the board. To win the board over, he had to stop trying to prove himself with his smarts. Instead, he had to show up as a leader who understood what those he was leading needed from him in that moment. To do that would be to win the NomGov committee's hearts as well as minds.

Matt was now mindfully alert—alert in three dimensions.

O: Generate Options

Knowing *what* to do must be followed by thinking through *how* to do it. That's what the mindfully alert leader must do next: generate options for moving forward.

Research shows that optimal performance requires not only willpower, but what has been called "waypower."[4] You may have all the will in the world, but for complex leadership demands, you need to be able to generate several different options to achieve your goals. Your automatic reactions and default approaches can become dangerous in new types of high-stakes situations. For anything important you need to be able to envision and act on at least four different pathways to win.

In chapters 6 through 8 we will walk you through our Options Generator, which is a powerful method for identifying at least four approaches to navigate any external priority; four ways to achieve your internal priorities; and four ways to act on your interpersonal priorities.

Here's a quick example of how to generate four options to win. You have probably heard the phrase "lean in," which means to have a highly active stance on resolving an issue. But there are three more stances, and these four together create a kind of template you can build upon.

Lean in: Take an active stance on resolving an issue.

Lean back: Take an analytical stance to observe, collect, and understand the data.

Lean with: Take a collaborative stance with others, focusing on caring and connecting to create an optimal culture.

Don't lean: Be still, discipline yourself to be receptive, and take in all that is around and within you so that creative wisdom can surface. (By the way, this is usually the most difficult stance for leaders to take, as you can imagine. But it is a necessary one to develop.)

Lock these in, too. Applying the Four Stances to your Three Dimensions of Leadership will be crucial for turning Mindful Alertness into options. Here's how we did it with Matt.

* * *

Since the board meeting was the following day, we didn't have time to take Matt through a complete Options Generator. Instead, we focused on helping him expand his leadership range by developing just one additional option for each of his three-dimensional priorities.

Under the pressure of the NomGov presentation, he had defaulted to and overplayed a lean-back stance. To meet what he mistakenly understood to be his external priority, he showed up as detached, analytical, and detail-oriented. To get the job, he had to be able to switch stances quickly. It was clear he needed to lean in by being crisper about how he communicated his priorities.

There was no time for us to be diplomatic. The clock was ticking. David pushed hard on Matt to help him get past his natural inclination to prove himself with cascades of information—an inclination that ironically masked his true leadership potential. We explored what the board needed from Matt, not how Matt could wow them with his mastery of detail. The better question was how many key messages the board could absorb: Two? Three? Four? Matt had to be calm and clear enough to be curious. Then he could look at himself through the eyes of the board.

For the next couple of hours, David and Matt crafted and practiced the crucial points that he would need to communicate to the board, no matter what. He needed to articulate his strategy in a single sentence to show two things: Yes, he really understood the business. And yes, he understood that the board needed both less and higher-quality content.

But Matt needed more than that. Carol worked with him to develop his inner game, including how to be more comfortable with who he was. He needed to build on his newfound understanding that hiding his caring side was not a winning strategy. "Since having compassion is clearly core to who you are, what gets in the way of you showing it?" she asked.

"It's just who I am. The bigger the challenge, the calmer I get and the less emotion I show. I'm also very aware of the importance of role modeling strong leadership. All my mentors were like this."

"In that way you're a good soldier, but is that the optimal way for you to be as a leader? If you were a ten out of ten as a leader, would you suppress this side of yourself?"

"I guess not. Honestly, I thought you had to take emotions out of the equation."

"That is an assumption you're making; do you think it's true?" Carol asked. And together they explored a new option of conveying both calm and compassion. He felt great about it, then as often happens when experimenting with something new, he worried he might pivot too far and be overly emotional in front of the board.

"Really? Do you think if you tried with all your might, you could come across as overly emotional?" Carol quipped. With that the tension evaporated, and we all had a good laugh. Now Matt was prepared to show his caring. This also provided him with a new option to meet his interpersonal priority. He could now lean with the board, infusing his humanity into his interactions.

V: Validate Your Vantage Point

Matt had his game plan. Now he had to give it a second look.

While it wasn't necessary to point it out to him at the time, what allowed Matt to change his stance to the board was the shift in his Vantage Point. During the meeting, he had assumed he knew what the board wanted and never thought to question his Vantage Point on the situation. From his position, it was crystal clear: *show how much I know, and I'll win.*

When we nudged him to look at things from *their* point of view, he could see he was drowning the board in details they didn't care about. With this new Vantage Point, he began to think about how much they could absorb, not how much he wanted to say. Vantage Point excellence is when you can see the world from others' points of view as well as your own.

Many factors can cloud our view of things, ranging from how we process information to how our biases lead to blind spots. In chapter 9 we'll unpack these, and we'll see how emotions, personality, and lived experience can sharpen or dull our view.

When we need to make judgments, we tend to connect the dots with our wishes or fears. This doesn't help. Those who see reality for what it is have a strategic advantage. If you get there first, you are more likely to win. But it will take a conscious effort to strip away as many distortions of the situation as possible. Chuck Jacoby, a retired four-star general and our thought partner, puts it plainly: "I fight the war I have, not the war I want to have."[5]

. . .

Matt had been fighting the war he wanted to have, and we were helping him fight the war he had instead. He was still torn up about being caught flat-footed by NomGov. He asked David, "How could I have gotten it so wrong? I felt so confident going into the meeting. I thought it was just a check-the-box exercise and I would get the job."

David told him it was about his Vantage Point. "You were looking at this from your current role and the Vantage Point associated with that, not your future one. It happens, and it's important to not beat yourself up about it. Isn't it possible that they have different expectations of a CEO than the leader of one of the biggest business units?"

Matt paused. "Ugh, I am so angry with myself. I was mired in the day-to-day, and most of my interaction with the board was to provide updates on my business. I missed the point about locating us within the broader industry and economy and focusing on the top issues that matter. That won't happen again."

While we agreed it was good for Matt to challenge himself, it was equally important for him to balance this with self-compassion. Blaming or shaming yourself doesn't lead to making good choices in real time.

. . .

Like Matt, when looking at your priorities, it is crucial to not exaggerate or discount opportunities and threats—or worse, completely miss the point. And when taking leadership options into account, you need to be realistic about which ones you can reliably call upon and not over- or underestimate your leadership capability.

E: Engage and Effect Change

Now it's time to activate the option that works best for the situation, while bringing along your team and organization. You do this by sending leadership signals, which are all the things you say and do as a leader as well as the qualities of your character that emanate from you. Start by communicating what we call your Leader's Intent: a clear vision of your top priorities, why they matter, and the way forward. For most high-stakes, high-risk priorities, formulating your Leader's Intent will be a highly collaborative approach with your team and others inside and outside your organization, to get the best data and insights available.

Once you have articulated your Leader's Intent, and know your people are in alignment, we encourage you to set up methods to effectively gather data with which to monitor both how your leadership signals have been received and whether any course corrections may be needed. We've found that leaders can have difficulty calibrating the strength of their signals, often sending weak signals that leave their team in doubt about how to proceed or intruding on their team's decision-making by sending overpowering signals. These are easy mistakes to make.

Matt's engage moment was the final board meeting—his last shot to impress on them that he was right for the CEO job. He had to send strong, clear signals that he had learned from the mistakes he made in the NomGov meeting. He knew he needed to communicate his Leader's Intent, which he had crafted with David. We also talked about how he could send well-calibrated signals to show his ability to remain both calm and compassionate.

As our time together came to an end, he shared one last concern with us. "I'm feeling confident about messaging to the board on what needs to happen with the company. And I think I have it in me to reveal how much the company matters to me and why. But it feels too fuzzy to say that I need to be able to respond in real time—and I'm still really worried about how I will react given all the possible curveballs the board could throw at me. How can I handle that?"

Just as he said this, he took another sidelong look at his iPhone. "Stock is down another 8 percent. Give me a minute." He stepped away to make some calls. Returning, he said, "OK, we're good. Let's stay with this."

We shared a glance with each other. Matt did not realize he had just shown us the exact behavior that was the answer to his question. This was how he should engage with any intense moments or nasty curveballs: Coolly. Use his calm as a strength. It would be a shield that would block anything the board could throw at him, protecting him from feeling self-doubt or from diving into a rabbit hole of excessive detail.

David said, "Matt, do you have ice water in your veins? Your stock is down 15 percent in a matter of hours, and you can calmly make a call and then switch back to me with your full concentration. That is a superpower. How about not worrying so much about how to respond to the board in the moment, and instead just set an intention, right now, that you will not let *anything* the board throws your way rattle you?"

Matt smiled. "I can do that. And I can show my warmer compassionate side, too."

And he did. Matt faced the board with a new strategy for his high-stakes moment, and he got the job.

How to Use the Four Elements of MOVE

Matt's story gives you a sense of how MOVE works generally, but know that you can tailor your use of the methods as you need them. We had one day with Matt, but often we'll work with leaders for months to help get them to the point that they're reading and responding with confidence in multiple situations. Others in crisis will use MOVE even more quickly than Matt did.

Reading this book will take you through an initial consideration of all the steps, and you might want to apply them to a current challenge you're facing as you read. As you do, reflect on when in the past you might have gone off course. The MOVE framework can help you unpack this. And do not overlook the reverse: Think back to your greatest successes. Can you use MOVE to now understand why things went so well? When you do, success becomes more scalable, you can repeat it more easily, and you can help mentor others as well.

But going forward, you may be in situations in which you want to focus on one or a couple of the steps. That might mean you'll primarily go through M, O, and E, with less focus on V. Other times V may be where you spend most of your time. You may decide to start with O or V instead of M, and so on. All four steps together will empower you in any situation, but when time is of the essence, aiming your attention at the most pressing problems can be vital. We'll share stories, for example, of leaders who faced career derailment with the challenges they had pursued, and who were able to get their execution back on track by drawing on just one of the steps.

That said, by getting the full grounding in MOVE that we provide in the following chapters, you'll find that you can quickly run through all the components in real time in any given high-pressure moment. Reminding yourself of MOVE will increasingly allow you to hone your performance so that you are able to reach and sustain a new level of peak performance.

Summary

When facing your highest-stakes, highest-risk leadership challenges, draw on the MOVE framework in real time to help you make the space you need to succeed.

M Is about Being Mindfully Alert

Remember first that leadership always has three inextricably linked dimensions: the external goals, the internal qualities needed to meet those goals, and the interpersonal challenges of connecting strongly with all your stakeholders and empowering your team.

To be mindfully alert, answer questions that map to your Three Dimensions of Leadership:

- **External goals:** What does a win look like for the goal you want to achieve?

- **Internal qualities:** Are you being the person you want and need to be, in real time? What inner qualities and character strengths need to be developed for you to be an optimal leader in real time?

- **Interpersonal challenges:** Are you leading in the way others need you to? How can you best relate to others to accomplish your goals?

O Is about Generating Options

For any type of challenge, whether it's external, internal, or interpersonal, you can step into one of the Four Stances. These show you four different ways to win. You will come up with different options for winning by using one of the Four Stances:

Lean in: Take an active stance on resolving an issue.

Lean back: Take an analytical stance to observe, collect, and understand the data.

Lean with: Take a collaborative stance with others, focusing on caring and connecting to create an optimal culture.

Don't lean: Be still, discipline yourself to be receptive, and take in all that is around and within you so that creative wisdom can surface.

V Is about Validating Your Vantage Point

You have your default ways of seeing reality, but you're not always correct. First double-check to see if you are seeing reality for what it is, not what you want or hope it to be or what you fear it can be. Be aware of your tendencies. Do you tend to look at things from high up or close up? Vantage Point excellence is when you can see the world from others' points of view as well as your own.

E Is about Engaging and Effecting Change

Start by creating your Leader's Intent. This is your vision and understanding of your top priorities and why they matter (drawing from M), possible high-level ways forward (leveraging O), and milestones along the way to know you're winning (V).

Refine or revise your subsequent leadership signals. Be highly aware of how your Leader's Intent is interpreted by others, and what you learn about how conditions are changing.

How to Use MOVE

MOVE is applicable to immediate challenges as well as longer-term challenges that you need to tackle in real time as they unfold. The framework takes some practice to master, but it can be helpful to you right now. Try it on an important leadership issue you are dealing with. Either scan through the entire framework, or if you feel one or two elements matter most in your situation, focus on those.

MOVE

Be Mindfully Alert

2

Create Space in Real Time

Between stimulus and response there is a space. In that space is our power to choose our response. In our response lies our growth and our freedom.

—**Viktor Frankl**

Stevie plopped down in the swivel chair and spun around twice. It was immediately clear where her nickname, "Powerhouse Pixie," had come from. She was tiny and sinuous, and her close-cropped hair and signature pink sneakers gave her an impish look. "I hate having to do this!" she said, spinning around again.

Carol and David had been brought in to help Stevie, the youngest head of transformation that her $40 billion industrial products company had ever named. As part of its cost-cutting digital transformation, the company was reducing its workforce, a task that landed in Stevie's lap. Her big heart would make it hard enough. Making it harder was the fact that she'd be working on it from transitional housing in Frankfurt, where she was still new, and that she needed to navigate complex differences in cross-border labor laws and practices. Doing this well would require being mindfully alert to all of the Three Dimensions of Leadership—external, internal, and interpersonal.

"I have about a thousand things to do and no time to do it." It came out as more of a groan than Stevie intended.

We wanted to help her define her most crucial external priority to get her on a mindfully alert track. "It's fine, just give yourself some space to think," David said. "What's the most important outcome for you?"

Stevie couldn't limit it to one and counted off all the outcomes on her fingers in double time. "We have to separate three thousand people. Keep our reputation intact. Manage the red tape with the work council. I have to get legal, PR, communications, and HR teams working together yesterday. It's a tough hill to climb; I've never taken on anything this big."

Stevie needed to slow down, so Carol asked her a question. "Let's step out of the fray for a moment. To get this done, what kind of leader do you want to be?" We were inviting Stevie to examine her internal dimension of leadership, being mindfully alert to how her inner state impacts her thinking, feelings, and actions in high-stakes conditions.

That question turned out to be a stumper. Stevie was someone who, nearly magically, got stuff done on determination and instinct. Her warm and friendly nature made people want to go all-out for her. She hadn't thought much about herself and the type of leader she needed to be.

"I don't really know," she said finally. "I need to stay strong in order to follow through. It's really hard. I know and care about these people. I also know that facing the council will be torture—they make every move a nightmare of details and endless cycles of reports." Stevie was now zeroing in on the third dimension of leadership—the interpersonal challenges.

David pulled her back to the internal challenges. "What can you pull on inside of you to get through this in a way that aligns with who you are?"

"I'm in overdrive. I have to finesse multiple layers of people and systems, especially with the work council, then get all the teams aligned. What do I need to do? OK, it's obvious, isn't it? Downshift!"

"Exactly right," Carol confirmed. The second dimension, managing impulses and regulating her bias for action, was the most important internal bar to get over if she wanted to stay steady for the long haul.

MOVE starts with M—being mindfully alert to what matters most.

Mindfulness is the capacity to be present, to separate yourself from distractions, to notice but not judge what is happening in your external environment, and to understand and accept how you are feeling.[1] If you are mindful, you will be aware, be centered, and have the capacity to be still and open. This acceptance of what is happening both outside and inside of you creates the space for you to choose your response to a high-stakes situation. You can and should cultivate the capacity to be mindful.

Being mindfully *alert* is more than that. It is the cross-section of mindfulness and the kind of intense concentration needed to win a Grand Slam tennis tournament. From our work with world-class athletes, we know they constantly try to improve their ability to be centered in the eye of the storm, intensely aware of what teammates or competitors need from them. They slow time down, seeing what to do in the present moment and when to pivot to win. They have teams of coaches and are constantly developing themselves, never content with their current level of play.

How does being mindfully alert apply to business leadership? Think of the benefits of being able to choose what you need to do under any kind of emotional or business turmoil. You can then clearly see what is happening, and just as you are about to follow your instincts, instead you can create space to stop and consider: Is your instinctual response the optimal one? This is how you shift into real-time leadership.

For example, Stevie is a courageous leader who always takes situations head-on. But now, facing a phalanx of administrators, she was staring down a threat that could easily undermine her if she didn't handle the reduction in force with finesse. The work council was notorious for moving very slowly, and if she pushed at the wrong times, the negotiations could stall and she could cripple the company as a result.

Being mindfully alert is about overcoming your instincts. If you automatically reach for your proven playbook in every high-stakes situation, you are not being mindfully alert. For example, you may have been using the same growth strategy for years, but when a disruptive technology arrives and starts attacking your core business, that strategy will fail. If you're not mindfully alert, you will keep reaching for that strategy over and over, taking suboptimal actions and implicitly refusing to address the threat. Mindful Alertness is not just about noticing a stimulus in your external environment or in yourself; it's about noticing the stimulus and then interrupting your reflex reaction, creating space to select the best possible leadership response.

In this book we will offer several ways to help you create that space to be mindfully alert so that you can make conscious choices that lead to the best outcomes. This is a foundational capability that we apply throughout the book and all aspects of the MOVE framework.

The Three Dimensions of Leadership

The first way to become mindfully alert is to be able to get clarity on, and name, your most important goals. Your external challenges, your internal challenges, and your interpersonal challenges. And these are inextricably linked. Clarity on the *external* demands of leadership is not self-evident. At times you are free to choose your priorities, but often they are imposed on you. Whatever the context, the question here is, What do you need and want to achieve? Throughout this book you will see examples of business challenges that aren't self-evident. A simple example: You may believe that the goal of a meeting is to make a decision, such as whether to make an acquisition. But it could be that the best approach is to collect more divergent opinions to open up the conversation and better inform a decision. Mindfully alert leaders can find these alternative goals in the moment.

Understanding your *internal* challenges and committing to your personal growth is key to successful leadership. Knowing which aspects of yourself to develop and deploy can be complex. However, if you can identify your inner resources, you are more likely to be able to harness them to help you meet the external and interpersonal challenges you face. These include knowing your values, strengths, and sense of purpose, while being clear on your limitations and liabilities. Perhaps you rev up too fast, overanalyze, or haven't thought enough about why you are on this planet.

Interpersonal leadership requires you to look beyond yourself. A typical error is to think that what you would want is what others want or need. For example, a die-hard extrovert trying to bring out the best in an intense introvert can lead to a comedy, or tragedy, of errors. The question is, What is the best way to connect with, collaborate with, or lead your stakeholders, one to one, in teams or through the culture of the organization?

All of the Three Dimensions of Leadership are intertwined. Mastering one or two is not enough. How many leaders do you know who specify goals and then tyrannically run over people to deliver results at any cost? How many leaders do you know who are caring and relate well to people but aren't clearly focused on delivering on targets?

Mindful Alertness also requires you to be aware of how your three-dimensional leadership priorities can shift, suddenly or gradually, based on changing circumstances and to adjust them accordingly.

The Four Stances

Mindfully alert leaders can call on any one of the Four Stances of leadership when they need to address an external, internal, or interpersonal challenge, not just the stance they instinctually default to.

We introduced the stances—lean in, lean back, lean with, and don't lean—in chapter 1. Peak-performance leadership means you can operate in any of these four ways, often switching between them in near real time.

Stances as we are using them are a metaphor drawn from the sports world, where competitors must have the right stance to be balanced and prepared for what comes next.

The concept also draws from basic evolutionary theory. We evolved to have several sets of reflexes and are hardwired to respond to danger in a few different ways: fight, flight, freeze, or befriend. You're probably familiar with fight and flight, and maybe even freeze, like a deer in the headlights. They are all easily understood. But "befriend" may be a new concept for you. Recent research has identified that this path is hardwired into our brains.[2] Sometimes it's called "tend and befriend." It's the instinctual response to protect others in danger (think of the parent who improbably lifts a car to save a child) and to lean on our social connections in high-stress situations.

In many ways, leadership is the ability to overcome and manage these reflexes in high-stakes moments. The Four Stances need to be available to you under pressure. The issue is we tend to default to a particular stance rather than assess what would be optimal for the situation at hand. But we can learn to shift our stance.

• • •

Stevie's transformation plan was going well, but there was a problem. "I should have expected it—we had an off-the-record discussion about the workforce reduction, and someone leaked it to the press," she said. "All hell is breaking loose. I know the colleague who did it, and I cannot believe it. What could she have been thinking!"

If this were you, what would you do?

Your instant reaction reveals your natural stance.

If lean in is your default, you will probably want to enter the fray, either overtly or covertly. You may be driven by aggression against the alleged perpetrator or protection of those affected by the leak. You will want to drive through the solution that you think is the best outcome.

If you want to lean back, you may feel the best tactic is to wait for things to settle while you steer clear, keep a cool head, assess the situation, ask questions, and collect the relevant information. Your analysis will guide your actions.

If you naturally lean with, you will be upset for those who are negatively affected by the situation. You will want to give emotional support and coaching and perhaps seek to understand the actions of your colleague. You will collaborate and take action.

Finally, the tendency to take a don't-lean stance means you are able to calmly watch the fracas unfold without taking action, a positive version of "freeze." You can be centered enough to question if the motives of the colleague who leaked the information were malicious, and also to see what else arises from your intuition. Now, no matter which stance is your default, is your default what you should do? Maybe not. But the only way to know is to create a space between hearing the inflammatory news and acting in response. This requires you to step back from what you would automatically do and take a moment, even seconds, to scan what is actually going on by considering how you could respond using each of the Four Stances. Visualize responses from each one. Following our example, you would then pick which stance will optimally serve you and your direct report. The goal is to have the control to be able to perceive and respond from any stance, any time. This is not easy.

You can practice, though. Start by being aware of your default stance, the one that is your most frequent go-to mode in day-to-day situations. Then think of the second most comfortable one, then the third and fourth, and come up with optimal responses for each.

Repeat this exercise, but this time think of the highest-stress moments you have faced. What stance did you take in those? You won't have the same go-to stance in every situation. One person can lean in most of the time but become dead calm or freeze, by not leaning, under the highest-stakes conditions. Or the reverse. Has your default always served you? Has it served your team or your organization, or even your family?

Here are ways Stevie could have been mindfully alert to her choices upon hearing the news of the media leak. You can use table 2-1 as a template for practicing yourself.

Our goal is for you to expand your view of what is possible in real-time high-stakes situations and to be able to evaluate the merits of different approaches. If you practice assessing the Four Stances for each dimension of leadership often enough, it can become second nature, even under pressure. With enough practice and coaching, you'll be able to create enough space to develop optimal responses in real time. We've seen it happen with our clients.

TABLE 2-1

Thinking up different outcomes for each stance

	Lean in	Lean back	Lean with	Don't lean
External goals	Confront the leaker.	Postpone engaging with the leaker until you're clear.	Understand the Vantage Point of the leaker.	Reflect on the experience.
	Jump into action to address the fallout, and begin damage control.	Analyze ramifications of the fallout and set a plan.	Make sure the team is OK, and then explore what to do.	Pause, and collect yourself and the team. Then proceed.
Internal goals	Have courage and manage feelings of being betrayed.	Have the capacity to be clear, take a good look, and have a balanced reaction.	Keep up the compassion for the colleague who leaked, but don't overdo it. Care for your team.	Get to calm before doing anything, and see what surfaces.
Interpersonal goals	Manage and strategize how to confront the leaker.	Get clear, and decide what stance is most ideal for the conversation.	Find a way to confront the leaker that can also restore the relationship.	Get to a calm place, so as not to overreact.
	Get the team back on track. Galvanize them, and optimize alignment.	Take stock. The team needs to debrief on what happened.	Invite the team to share their experience of the event, and help them feel safe.	Help the team slow down before they speed up.

The trick, of course, is being able to escape your default stance in those high-stakes situations when your body and brain are pushing you toward it. To do that, you need the highest levels of emotional regulation to create more space for you to choose. This requires learning the Five Cs.

The Five Cs

Being captured or swept away by your default stance limits your choices and can be dangerous. To pivot between stances and responses, you need to be balanced, to feel centered. No matter who you are, or what life you've had, you have a wise inner self and it is waiting for you to call upon it.

We've tweaked a framework originally developed by our friend Dick Schwartz to help you access this inner self and know what being centered feels like.[3] You know you've accessed this part of you when you feel the Five Cs: calm, clear, curious, compassionate, and courageous.

Let's take each in turn.

Calm: Despite the storm, you are steady. You have the ability to manage your physiological responses to danger. You can be at peace, be energized, and feel deeply settled. Or, in a high-pressure, difficult, or dangerous situation, you can lower your pulse and feel in control of your thinking and reactions.

Clear: Despite the fog, you can see. You can see things for what they are, no matter your proximity to the situation. Your thinking feels accurate, and nothing is obscuring your ability to assess your inner or outer world.

Curious: Despite the pull to have answers, you are open. You hold on to your desire to gather information, explore, and learn. It can manifest as a spirit of inquiry, fascination with how things work, or an omnivorous interest in what isn't known.

Compassionate: Despite the pull to criticize or judge, you put yourself in the shoes of another. You can empathize and put others' needs first. You have the ability to feel a deep sense of benevolence or to read a room and know what a group needs.

Courageous: Despite the pull to run, you feel the fear and face the challenge. You possess the desire and ability to stand up to challenges and speak truth to power. This goes beyond bravery; it's the determination to overcome setbacks and attacks. It can also surface as optimism, humor, and an ability to rally the troops.

You can develop your ability to access the Five Cs to create more space between stimulus and response. Then in the heat of the moment, even under great duress, you can more objectively assess your stance and choose the optimal approach to your challenge instead of instinctually reacting.

Mastering the Five Cs takes time, but practicing them can be key to your capacity to be successful (see chapter 7). As Rudyard Kipling famously wrote, you gain a massive advantage if you can "keep your head while all about you are losing theirs." To do this, your job is to access the inner-most, wisest core of who you are and to develop it. Start simply by taking a few minutes to reflect on where you stand with each of the Five Cs. Naming how you are feeling is a first step to being able to access high levels of all of the five under stress. If you can, find a quiet space to slow down your breath, and downshift your level of activation. This meditative breathing affects your neurophysiology, helping you to slow your mind and body and to realize you don't always need to have an instant, over-whelming reaction.[4]

Which of the Five Cs could best help Stevie right herself upon hearing the news of the leak to the media? For her, being compassionate came most easily, and she found she could draw on courage, too. But in this very high-stress moment, calm and clarity mattered most. She needed to fight the instinct to rage at the news and then recognize she was working with incomplete information and seek clarity.

As you get better at practicing the Five Cs, you'll be able to call on them at any time, not just when you're in a quiet space, and you'll be able to marshal them more quickly. With dedication, you can snap yourself into a more centered place in any high-stakes, high-pressure situation. This not only leads to personal fulfillment but also is an incredible advantage. One leader described breathing as her "secret weapon." At acrimonious meetings she would breathe diaphragmatically, lowering her pulse. When she did, she could more easily find that space between stimulus and response when deciding what her top external, internal, and interpersonal priorities would be. That's real-time leadership.

David developed a useful exercise for using the Five Cs in real time: In those moments when you feel things rising inside you, rate yourself on the Five Cs on a one-to-ten scale. Anything under, say, a five needs address-ing. Once, his client Samir was about to enter a contentious meeting and could feel his activation climbing. He did this exact exercise, telling David later that calm was a five, clear was a nine, curious was a seven, compas-sion was a two, and courageous was a ten.

Being aware enough to pause and name your feelings can be a powerful intervention.[5] It can create just enough space for you to consider alterna-tive approaches to your challenge. When Samir walked into the meeting and one of his leaders was nearly out of control, raving about some issue, Samir was upset. His default reaction may have been to roll his eyes, let it play out, and move on. Or, he might have tried to defuse his colleague's emotions with facts and data to counter his points. But Samir had done his scan and recognized right before the meeting that his compassion was at a two. So he forced himself to consider a compassionate response. To his shock, he got up from his chair, sat next to the leader, put his hand on his shoulder, and leaned with. The outcome was massively different from what could have happened: Samir's support helped the leader shift from being activated to feeling calm and included. Later, Samir told David that his approach "would never have entered my head or been an option for me, and it changed everything. With my whole team, actually."

A year after Samir's coaching ended, Carol asked him what he found most useful in his time with David. He responded instantly, "The Cs!" He was adamant about how life-changing they had been. "I do the exercise all the time. It helps me read situations so much better and come up with clear priorities on what my goals are and how I need to be as a leader." But it takes practice, he said. "I work every day to keep my calm above a five on the scale. Calm is usually the hardest for me."

"Really?" Carol asked, surprised. "Everyone sees you as great at that. They feel more settled and centered after talking with you. I can see that for myself."

"Calm!" he snorted. "Calm? I walk around here like a friggin' Buddhist monk, then go home and tear up shopping bags with my teeth!"

No one at work knew his level of stress. He credited his work with David on the Five Cs with helping him be centered, calm, and compassionate at work. As a result, his team stayed steady and successful. He still practices, and maybe one day the shopping bags will be safe.

The Ten-Out-of-Ten Approach

Mindfully alert leaders are able to identify and visualize ideal outcomes. One way to do this is to think about and rate possible outcomes on a scale from one to ten. The exercise below will help you do that. It's also useful for identifying and building strengths and capabilities you may not realize you possess, as well as for energizing you in high-stakes leadership challenges. Just asking the question, "If I achieved a ten out of ten with my goal, what would it look like?" is another way to make space by being explicit on what you actually want to achieve.

Pick one of your goals or priorities on any leadership dimension, and reflect on why it matters to you. Don't jump in and skip this step. Then ask these four questions:

Question One: If you achieved a ten out of ten on this goal, what would it look like?

Paint a vivid picture, describing what you would be doing to achieve your goal. What would you be thinking and feeling and if you were being filmed—what would others be seeing? What impact would you have? Positive visualization is difficult, so stay focused on it; it can be surprisingly powerful.

Laura Wilkinson, the Olympic platform diver, was injured right before the 2000 games, and for the six weeks before she competed, the only practice she could do was in her head. She visualized it over and over, going over each movement, each step. During the final competition, she hobbled to the diving platform—and won gold. Many replicated research studies have found that intense visualization of what you want to do is far more effective than just identifying a goal you want to achieve or a problem you want to fix.[6]

Question Two: With the ten-out-of-ten vision in mind, what would you rate yourself today?

Don't obsess about getting it perfect; just see what number comes to up in your head or in the mind of someone you are coaching.

When you begin doing this with others, and they give a number that is far off your assessment, put that to the side for now. For example, if they say seven and you think two, keep going. If they say two and you think nine, don't reassure them, just keep going. We're just setting up a starting point that can be a baseline, and that's enough for now.

Question Three: What are you doing right that puts you at the number you just rated yourself, and not a point lower?

Say you rated yourself a six.[7] What are you doing that makes it not a five? Answering this will not be easy at first. You may come up with some weak explanations. Keep going by asking yourself what *else* you did right. This is the art of positive confrontation. Look at what you have done right with the same intensity you would use if you were running a postmortem on a disastrous project, searching for the root cause of what went wrong. Keep asking "what else" until you have exhausted all ideas.

Question Four: What can you do over the next two months to get
from the number you're at now to a point higher?

Most people think the question is, or should be, What can I do to get to
ten? No. Change rarely means going from, say, a six to a ten in one step. If
you expect to make a sudden leap, it could overwhelm you, or even if you
somehow do get there, it is almost always unsustainable. Nascent behaviors are fragile, and it takes time for them to become embedded into your
new behaviors.[8] Change tends to be incremental and not linear. Look for
ways to bump up a half point. And then another half point. And another.
At some point it can become exponential where being mindfully alert and
at the top of your game in real-time becomes your new way of operating.

• • •

This is Mindful Alertness.

Real-time leadership to find your winning moves when the stakes are
high starts here: Know your Three Dimensions of Leadership; use the Four
Stances to create space in a high-stakes moment; practice the Five Cs to
center yourself so you don't default to your instinctual response; visualize
success with the Ten-Out-of-Ten Approach. You can think of this as the
3-4-5 and 10. We will continue to call on these throughout the book. The
3-4-5 frameworks are designed to improve the clarity and precision of
your goals, and the Ten-Out-of-Ten helps you to get traction for any goal.

It sounds like a lot to do in real time. But it can be done—we've seen
it. With practice, you will shift from being a good leader to being an effective, agile, great leader.

Mindful Alertness is so important that we're going to keep focusing
on it in the next few chapters, taking a deep dive into how it applies to
each of the Three Dimensions of Leadership—your external, internal, and
interpersonal leadership challenges.

Summary

Mindful Alertness is the ability to create space between a stimulus—a
leadership challenge—and your response to that stimulus, and then to use
that space to pick the best response. If you are not mindfully alert, you will
default to your instinctual response, which will not always be a good one.

Mindful Alertness is defined by four concepts, all of which help you to create the space you need:

1. **The Three Dimensions of Leadership:** All leadership challenges involve these three dimensions that you must recognize and manage.

   a. **External challenges:** Goals you set for yourself, goals given to you by others, and situations that arise, often unexpectedly, that you must lead through

   b. **Internal challenges:** Developing, understanding, and managing your values, strengths, and sense of purpose, while being clear on your limitations and liabilities

   c. **Interpersonal challenges:** Working with others to achieve goals and developing the ability to understand, empathize, and be intentional in leading others

2. **The Four Stances:** Being mindfully alert means having all four of these stances available for any high-stakes scenario you face.

   a. **Lean in:** Take action and manage a situation actively.

   b. **Lean back:** Observe, collect data, and analyze before acting.

   c. **Lean with:** Work with others to come up with plans of action and solutions to your challenges.

   d. **Don't lean:** Let a situation play out without intervening. Think of situations you've faced and how you've reacted. Also, think of a high-stakes scenario you may encounter, and imagine how you would react. The reaction that first comes to mind is probably your default stance. Your goal is to not always default to this. Use the template in table 2-2 to practice developing options beyond your default stance.

TABLE 2-2

	Lean in	Lean back	Lean with	Don't lean
External goals				
Internal goals				
Interpersonal goals				

3. **The Five Cs:** Developing balance and centeredness through knowing and harnessing these five emotions will help you create the space between stimulus and response you need to avoid falling back on instinctual reactions.

    a. **Calm:** Despite the storm, you are able to think clearly and operate normally.

    b. **Clear:** Despite the fog, you can see accurately and are not blinded by emotion.

    c. **Curious:** Despite the pull to have answers, you are open to learning and gathering more information.

    d. **Compassionate:** Despite the pull to criticize or judge, you can put yourself in the shoes of another and care.

    e. **Courageous:** Despite the pull to run, you feel the fear and face the challenge.

4. **The Ten-Out-of-Ten Approach:** The ability to visualize perfect outcomes in detail energizes you and helps you identify strengths and capabilities you may not realize you possess.

    a. For any challenge you face, imagine the best possible outcome, thinking about what it will feel and sound like, what others will say and think, and the emotions it will create.

    b. Score yourself on how you think you're doing on your challenge today. Don't worry too much about how accurate you are; just give yourself a score.

    c. List several reasons you got your score and aren't a point lower. Celebrate the things you're doing to get to where you are.

    d. List a few ways you can move up by half a point. Don't aim for a leap of several points—change tends to be nonlinear and incremental.

3

Know What You Want to Do

If the ladder is not leaning against the right wall, every step
we take just gets us to the wrong place faster.

—Stephen Covey

N
ow we do a deeper dive, applying Mindful Alertness to the Three
Dimensions of Leadership, starting with being clear on your top
external priorities—those with the highest stakes in terms of potential gains or losses to your organization and you. And you must continu-
ally monitor these; they can shift rapidly, as they did for Cheryl.

As CEO of a consumer packaged goods brand, Cheryl had built a spectacular track record, quadrupling her company's revenues to $1 billion in
four years. That got her recruited to become CEO of a brand ten times
that size, where she had a simple mandate: grow the business.

David had been Cheryl's coach at the previous job, and she retained
him to help tackle the step change in her leadership responsibilities and
accelerate her integration into the new company.

But just a few months in, the Covid-19 pandemic hit. Cheryl and her
team instantly pivoted from developing a growth strategy to entering survival mode. This is an example of a real-time leadership challenge that
many of you can relate to, and the way she handled it was pitch-perfect.

Days before the company's operations went into shutdown, Cheryl and
David held a coaching session on Zoom. David said, "Cheryl, what's coming up for you as your top priority for the next few days?"

"I think the team and I need to better align before I do anything else.
We tend to move superfast, jumping on problems and then going into
execution mode, which is great. But we have too much of a 'fire, ready,
aim' reflex under stress," she said, then paused. "Any reaction?"

Based on his understanding of how the team operated, David thought Cheryl was on the right track, and he prompted her to be more specific. "Tell me more about what you mean by alignment."

"So far, we have been having one-hour crisis meetings daily, but they have been used mostly for sharing information rather than for specifically agreeing on our top priorities and then making decisions as a team. It seems like we are managing through a tactical checklist of issues instead of stepping back to look at the big picture."

Finding the time to do this in the middle of a crisis is easier said than done, but it was essential. David said, "You know what you have to do, right? And there's not a day to waste."

"Agree. I've been reluctant to hold lengthier meetings because most of my team members' benches are weak, and I didn't want to separate them too long from their own teams. I'm calling for a meeting tomorrow, and we will go as long as we need to get alignment on our top priorities for the following days and weeks, as well as for the next quarter."

David thought that getting alignment on top priorities was the right first step, but he was concerned that the team would still have a tendency to go in different directions based on how they interpreted their individual roles in meeting the top goals. "Once the priorities get agreed, how about doing an explicit review of key interdependencies to make sure everyone's coordinated?"

Cheryl thought about it for a moment and then replied, "That's a good catch. Day-to-day we are OK at managing the links among supply chain, product manufacturing, and inventory management, for example. But when there's a big disruption, that constellation of functions needs to work in absolute lockstep. It's not happening right now."

"How about triaging the most crucial interdependencies that you and the team are most worried about? I think it has to be part of the priorities session."

Cheryl was on board. "Yes, I have two goals for tomorrow: get us aligned on our overall near-term priorities as well as on how best to manage our key interdependencies." Her instinct had told her that she needed to step back momentarily from the team's reflex to get more alignment on top priorities. Beyond that, the discussion with David helped Cheryl sharpen her goal to also make sure key sub-teams also were aligned regarding how they would work together in service of their collective goals.

• • •

Identify and Focus on Your Most Important External Priorities

The first step to being mindfully alert of your Three-Dimensional Leadership goals is to explicitly name your top *external* priorities—those with the highest potential gains or losses to your organization and to you. They can be short term, long term, or most likely a combination. These are your goals to achieve, not a to-do list. They fall into three broad categories:

- Problems to be solved, like how best to think about opportunities and risks facing your business

- Decisions to be made, like choosing the timing for a new product launch

- Actions to execute or implement, like rolling out a new performance management framework or creating the conditions to amplify others' impact

Sometimes priorities can be combinations of these, such as identifying a new market to enter (problem), deciding how best to enter it (decision), and then moving forward (action). Cheryl had an immediate need to align her team on priorities and deal with critical interdependencies as a first step in confronting her larger external goal of successfully dealing with the crisis.

Research shows that the more clearly you can articulate your destination, the more likely you are to reach it.[1] Be as specific and clear as possible about your most important external priorities by asking: *What? Who? When? Where?* and *Why?*

(*How?* will come later, when we generate options; for now, it's enough to specify the destination and not the route.)

Here is a straightforward example of a fully specified external priority. Josh, a head of corporate development, and his team were evaluating a possible bid to take over a large competitor. He answered our questions as follows:

What: To decide whether to recommend a major acquisition

Who: Me and my team together with the head of strategy and CFO, with input from key functional and business leaders

When: Within the next forty-eight hours because the target has a competing offer

Where: The executive committee

Why: Get to critical mass outside our home market; the target presents one of the few strategic opportunities to quickly acquire scale in three priority international markets

Here are two more examples of external priorities or goals that need no setup.

What: Building a culture of curiosity

Who: Led by my executive committee

When: Over the next two years

Where: Across the entire company

Why: Creativity and innovation have stalled

What: Increase alignment on our new strategy

Who: Me

When: In the next quarter

Where: Across finance, HR, operations, and IT, which are currently less aligned than the business units

Why: The company is embarking on a transformation program and we all need to be on board

Do this simple exercise for yourself. It pushes you to be deliberate and specific about what external forces matter most, creating space so you don't default to relying on your reflexes and end up spending time and resources on external challenges that don't drive maximum value.

Pressure-Test Your Priorities by Using the Four Stances

With priorities in hand, the Four Stances provide a way to evaluate what you believe you need to accomplish. *Lean in* to make sure you are setting the bar high enough on your goals when you have autonomy to choose them. An example would be electing to exceed your financial goals rather than just meeting them. Of course, in many situations priorities are imposed on you and you have no choice, as when you're confronting a crisis. In those cases, you can also lean in by accepting reality and getting on with things.

If you have time, *lean back* to scan the landscape. See what data is available, what is missing, and what additional insights you may need to gather before you can be confident about locking in your external goals. Leaning back is particularly appropriate, at least momentarily, when you are facing brand-new types of leadership challenges, like dealing with a hostile activist investor. Looking before you leap pays off.

You can *lean with* when you have the freedom to choose your goals by asking for input from trusted sources inside or outside your organization. Gaining others' wisdom is a great check on whether you might be exaggerating or discounting your priorities—or missing the point. It may result in significantly reshaping your goals. For example, you may initially believe that your goal is to immediately seek approval for an initiative you're sponsoring, but your peers might signal that the more pressing demand is to first hear all of their voices on the matter. And in cases where you have at least partial autonomy over a goal, you can lean with to negotiate it with others.

You can also *not lean*, if only for a moment. We often default to thinking *some* kind of action is necessary at all times, but sometimes it's worth taking a pause and asking yourself, What else do I know that I don't realize I know? Often insights are just beyond the periphery, and you know more than you think. As the thirteenth-century poet Rumi said, "There is a voice that doesn't use words. Listen."

Not leaning can be a physical exercise. Begin by focusing on your breath and taking a few deep inhales and exhales. See what arises from this; any number of things could come up. For example, lingering concerns or open questions that are in the back of your mind could emerge about that negotiation you're in. Or your hunches could surface and give you a new direction to take with your most important client. Overweight or discount your intuition based on how current your knowledge is and how well you believe you understand your situation. These are examples of how not leaning can work.

When you are facing uncertainty, there are situations where, after you examine your external goals from all of the Four Stances, you still aren't sure about what the external goal should be. Times when this can happen include a major disruption occurring in your operating environment (good or bad) or a sudden conflict arising with a longtime colleague. Don't let this stop you. Instead, come up with a "draft" goal that you can use to get started, and then refine it over time based on what you learn. If you perceive the goal as being primarily an opportunity for you, then play offense and frame the goal accordingly—for example, "Get a foothold in the B2B market." If you perceive the goal as primarily dealing with a threat, then play defense—for example, "Exit a client relationship to contain reputational risk for the company."[2]

Now that you have applied the Four Stances to your external goals, do the Five Cs exercise to see to what extent your feelings may have influenced how you identified your goals. Then take one more look to see if your goals need to be adjusted. For example, if you were not calm when formulating them, how might they change if you evaluate them from a place of greater calm?

Not all goals or priorities require this level of specificity or investigation. The higher the stakes, the more time you will spend on specifying and pressure-testing them before confirming them.

Priorities can shift rapidly due to changing circumstances, so be prepared to pivot by being mindfully alert in real time. Cheryl's priorities changed because of the sudden onset of a crisis. Other major events, like a surprise competitor move or a sudden loss of top talent, can prompt a rapid change in priorities. Beyond that, priorities can also shift as you detect more gradual changes to external trends such as the economy, consumer demand, and technology, as well as internal trends around things like employee engagement and productivity.

We started this section by saying you need to prioritize your top external goals. It's possible you'll prioritize so many of them that you find yourself overwhelmed. If that is the case, lean back to identify the top few. You can also reframe them by breaking them down into phases, identifying what the next best step would be for each, and assessing whether you can sequence them so that not everything has to be done all at once. If what you have on your plate after that is still beyond your personal leadership capacity and available resources, then you need to signal this to the appropriate stakeholders and gain alignment on how best to proceed.

Visualize a Ten Out of Ten—What Does Great Look Like?

Now that you've identified your top goals, use the Ten-Out-of-Ten Approach by visualizing perfect outcomes for each top goal. For example, if your goal is to develop a strategy, what would a ten out of ten look like and feel like to your team, and what would others be saying about it? As a service provider you can ask, "If we achieved a ten-out-of-ten outcome for you, what would it look like?" Or, if your top near-term demand is to recruit a chief marketing officer, what would a ten out of ten look like for their background and capabilities, and what would a ten-out-of-ten recruiting experience feel like for you and for top candidates? Paint as vivid a picture as you can.

You can take your *What?* answer to each priority and visualize a ten outcome for it. From our first example of an external priority above:

What: To decide whether to recommend a major acquisition

Ten/Ten: What would great look like? If you were to make the ideal recommendation, it would be supported by:

- A solid financial case showing the acquisition will be accretive to earnings per share within three quarters

- High and low scenarios to pressure-test the base-case forecast

- All known material risks would be identified and disclosed, ranked by likelihood and severity

- All key internal stakeholders would be supportive

- The board would say this is the best-argued case they have ever seen

Of course, you don't need a ten on everything. Think this through: for each external priority, what is an acceptable outcome for you that you would still consider to be a win? Some goals only require a seven out of ten. Or different components don't all have to be tens. In the example above, for instance, it may be OK to not have unanimous support from all stakeholders.

* * *

Cheryl convened her team for the all-day meeting. She decided to ask David to facilitate so that she could lean with the team as a participant to help drive overall team cohesion. We named this the "slingshot" meeting. We'd go slower than the team's normal speed to gain alignment on their most important external priorities and get clarity on how to tackle the most crucial interdependencies. By creating space to choose, they'd be able to execute faster and more efficiently later. It proved to be a galvanizing moment because every member of the team put aside their personal agendas to focus on how best to deal with the crisis.

They named their top external goals; each was a *What?* Next, they listed them according to priority:

1. Immediately launch initiatives to safeguard employees (action).

2. Decentralize decision-making to reduce bottlenecks and speed up (decision-making).

3. Radically shift customer service resources to call centers to support more digital sales (decision-making + action).

4. Raise debt capital to have a funding cushion (decision-making + action).

5. Begin to transform the cost base to be able to sustain lower sales for a prolonged period (problem solving + decision-making + action).

Then the team built out each of these goals beyond the *What?* with the *Who? When? Where?* and *Why?* When they specified *Who?*, the team drilled into their interdependencies and got more individual role clarity. After that, they jointly identified what a ten out of ten would look like for each goal.

For the next six months of crisis management, the team focused on these five external priorities and executed well across the board. After two quarters of crisis management, customer demand began to rise again, and the business started to show signs of recovery. Mindfully alert to changing conditions, Cheryl took the opportunity to shift back into a growth mindset.

"It turns out there was a silver lining to the pandemic cloud," she said. "We have a newly streamlined cost base. And we decentralized decision-making, which went amazingly well in terms of getting things done faster and better. On top of that, we caught an unexpected break because some competitors had been forced to shrink their operations or went bankrupt. Another surprise is that we spotted several new unmet needs in our customer base."

With a new context—recovery—Cheryl and her team worked out a new top external priority in the action/execution category. It looked like this:

What: Double annual growth in revenue and profitability compared to prepandemic plan

Who: Leadership team

When: Over a three-year time horizon

Where: Companywide with higher growth targets in international markets than in the United States

Why: Take full advantage of favorable changes in our competitive operating environment

Cheryl pulled together a plan with her team and got enthusiastic board approval for their new targets.

Be Alert to Risk

Being mindfully alert to external priorities requires recognizing that complexity and unknowns are an inherent part of the process of goal setting. The operating environment and your day-to-day leadership are rife with chance, especially in fast-moving situations. Almost every decision you make will happen with imperfect information and will have hard-to-predict upside opportunities and downside risks. Chance becomes even more of a factor in winning the further out you go in time with your external goals.

It's helpful to illustrate this so that you can internalize the important idea that probability is at play here. Let's assume the outcome of any external goal can be described by a normal probability distribution, as in figure 3-1.[3] This is a gross simplification of a situation, because we don't actually know the underlying probability distribution for most cases, but it is useful to illustrate a point.

The eEP is the expected outcome, the base case of your external priority. Most leaders have a single-minded focus to do their best to achieve the expected outcome, to be safely ensconced in the middle of the x-axis, at the "expected" and most likely point of the external goal. A great example of this is leaders who are focused on hitting their plan metrics.

But the nature of risk tells us that our attention shouldn't be placed solely on the base case. We also need to look to the left and to the right on

FIGURE 3-1

Outcome of external priority

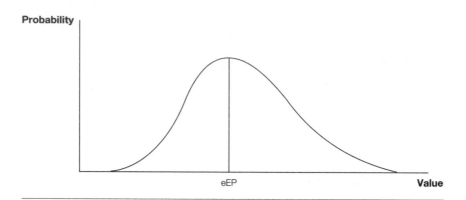

the curve. Explore what might happen as well as what you think will happen.

Take time to foresee what could result in you landing to the left of the expected outcome, in a bad place, or to the right, with better-than-expected performance. For example, if your external goal is to grow revenue by a certain amount, perhaps you have a recently launched product that could drive even better performance, or you may have an implementation failure or an adverse macroeconomic environment that creates a worse-than-expected outcome.

You should go even wider than this, though, and look at the edge cases at both ends of the curve. Every high-stakes external goal carries potentially extreme positive and negative results in the tails of the distribution, which are literally 10x outcomes.[4] (We'll explore this in detail in chapters 14 and 15.)

We find that few leaders pay adequate attention to the extremes, whether good or bad, with the exception of leaders with responsibility for life-and-death outcomes, like those in the military or public safety. As for the positive tail, those who keep their eyes there include founders with big visions. Figure 3-2 shows where those extremes are.

The tails represent the extremes of imaginable unknowns.[5] At these extremes, we are in the literal realm of 10x outcomes, where the right tail of the distribution has a small chance of delivering a spectacular outcome and the left tail has a small chance of delivering a disastrous outcome. Take a close look at the distribution. If there is a very wide dispersion

FIGURE 3-2

Outcome of external priority, with extremes

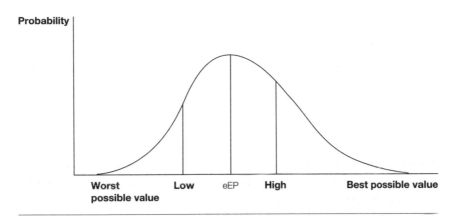

around the expected outcome, you have a low level of confidence about your base case. You will therefore need to invest more time in understanding what the high/low cases and the tails could have in store for your external priority.

We believe that all leaders should spend at least some time "in the tails."[6] For your most important external priority, identify the high and low, as well as best and worst, possible cases based on what you currently know. Consciously naming these heightens your sensitivity to the factors that could result in a more- or less-favorable outcome. As a result, you can be more mindfully alert.

• • •

Cheryl's company had developed a base case and low and high versions of a plan for revenue and EBITDA growth, but had focused almost entirely on the base case when managing the day-to-day. The team had not developed any hypotheses on best- and worst-case outcomes. Although it was impossible to predict a pandemic, they could have developed scenarios that anticipated major shocks in demand as well as major disruptions in the supply chain and used these to create contingency plans. Once they saw the worst case beginning to unfold, they could have activated those contingency plans. Instead, they had to scramble from scratch.

After working through the crisis, Cheryl started to put in place more of an emphasis on longer-term thinking along with more scenario planning. "I never want to find us in this position again," she said.

• • •

Cheryl responded well to the sudden pivot in her external priorities, from developing growth plans to containing the crisis, and then she found her way back to be able to concentrate on growth again.

Being explicit and thorough about your external priorities, constantly updating your information, and recognizing the upside and downside risks associated with your goals helps keep you laser-focused on what matters most. You increase your capacity to be mindfully alert and your ability to create the space you need to make optimal, informed choices.

Summary

Name your top external priorities. Being explicit interrupts your autopilot and keeps you clear on what the bull's-eyes are for your most important short-term and long-term goals.

- The clearer you can be about your destination, the more likely you are to reach it. Build out your priorities by naming the *What? Who? When? Where?* and *Why?* of each external goal.

- Apply the Four Stances (lean in, lean back, lean with, and don't lean) to see if they change your thinking.

- Do the Five Cs exercise to see if your current feelings have unduly influenced how you frame your top priorities.

- Once you have locked into your external priorities, use the Ten-Out-of-Ten Approach to visualize the best outcome for each, both what it looks like and what it feels like. If for any reason a ten is not possible to achieve, name the range of acceptable outcomes that you would still consider a win.

- Recognize that uncertainty is inherent in goal setting. Expand your focus beyond your base-case expectation for the goal, and also think about high, low, best-case, and worst-case outcomes.

4

Name Who You Want to Be

Knowing yourself is the beginning of all wisdom.

—**Aristotle**

W ho you are is key to what you can do. To lead in real time, you need to be as mindfully alert with your personal growth goals as you are with your external business challenges. You are already successful, but as your role expands, who you were before may not be enough now. The survey of one thousand CEOs that we mentioned in the introduction clearly shows that personal transformation is key to organizational transformation.[1]

In this chapter we help you create a map of your inner landscape to increase awareness of the types of personal development goals you might choose. We will help you understand who you are now, who you want to be, and how to learn the language of strengths.

It is important for you to be able to identify who you are at your best, your ten of ten. Then you can more accurately target the personal skills you need to develop. Those are your internal priorities. Becoming mindfully alert to these priorities will help you become the person and leader you want to be. In essence, this is about defining your personal vision.

Marcus, whom you met in the introduction, was a successful leader of an energy company's largest geography when the CEO job opened up. He threw his name in and went through an intense, high-stakes interview process. Marcus was on top of his game. He knew the key functions and stakeholders, and he had the numbers and the strategy down pat. He was certain he'd get the job over several highly qualified external candidates. And he did.

On one condition: to become CEO, Marcus had to agree to one year of coaching with Carol.

Marcus was shocked by the condition. He was about to take on a huge stretch role as a first-time CEO of the largest company of its kind in the world. He had reached the top; he believed he had nothing to learn.

But Marcus didn't know what he didn't know. He had been so focused on business success, and on his ascent, that he hadn't paid attention to developing his leadership. He was known to dismiss those he didn't respect, he lacked patience, and he created dysfunction within his team. He'd alienated his team and peers.

Marcus had heard feedback on these points before but had never taken it seriously. The board's directive got his attention, but he wasn't happy about it. So, he stalled.

After four months of dragging his feet, Marcus finally connected with Carol in his office. He graciously offered her a seat across from his desk. He leaned back in his chair and looked bored. The desert sun blasted through a window and shot directly into Carol's eyes, making Marcus a dark silhouette to her. After flicking a quick glance at his Patek Philippe watch, he sighed. "How long is this going to take?"

"We'll figure it out together," Carol said. "Coaching should fit the needs of the client, not the client fitting in with the coach."

Carol would later learn that Marcus was surprised that she was not defensive, which came from developing her own internal Mindful Alertness. For her, compassion had become a default. It made perfect sense to her that Marcus wouldn't want to be forced to talk to a stranger in order to step into the role he'd been working toward for twenty years.

"OK," he replied. "Then what should we be doing?"

Carol shared some options, then simply asked, "How could I be of the most service to you right now?"

Marcus was silent for a second before he leaped into describing, rapid-fire, what was going on with the company. He talked and talked. He rattled off high-stress issues that were top external priorities for him: the need to reset strategy, reorganize, cope with volatile markets, and fix one region after another as the company globalized its operating model.

He also talked about his interpersonal challenges. "I am heading the top group, and I want to get the most effective outcomes and hone the nuances in how I lead that will help me make the most difference."

Carol had read the feedback on Marcus: brilliant, competent, and thirsty for knowledge but also dismissive, obstructive, bad at listening, and prone to rejecting information that didn't conform to his opinion. This was going to require more than honing nuances.

Marcus kept going: "I can overdo things, but I don't want to lose people with potential. I might be doing things that disconnect people. But I have to get the slower members of the team engaged. If I don't lead boldly, things won't happen. Like at the last team meeting, we had a big decision to make, so I had to lean on people, hard."

"What happened?"

"My most valuable guy quit." For the first time in at least fifteen minutes, he stopped talking.

"Would you like that to not happen again?"

His head snapped up; he was all attention.

Find and Focus on Your Most Important Internal Priorities

In his march to the top, Marcus hyperfocused on his external leadership challenges. Now he needed to work on himself for the board to feel he could truly occupy the role of global CEO. He would not be seen as a viable leader if his leadership caused top talent to quit.

It didn't take much for Carol to see what Marcus's internal development priorities needed to be: empathy, emotional regulation, and humility. He needed to downshift his intense pace, increase his capacity to take in what others had to say, and manage his arrogance.

But you can't just tell someone, "These are your internal challenges." The goal was for Marcus to see this for himself so that he could begin to work on them.

For Marcus, and for all of us, we need to know where we need to grow.[2] To do this, we must be clear on our current state, the nature of our strengths, and where our gaps lie. Then we can map out what matters most.

A Look in the Mirror

When Peter Drucker challenged us to manage ourselves, he immediately pointed to knowing our strengths and getting feedback from others.[3] Most of us take our top strengths for granted and assume that most others share the same strengths. *Isn't everyone like this? Doesn't everyone know how to . . . ?* The answer is no. Explicitly knowing and naming your strengths create access to greater internal resources that you can harness and unleash.

Consider what aspects of your inner self you want to develop. What comes to mind? Can you "map" your inner world? There are several ways to do this. You can, for example, rate yourself on a scale of one to ten on the Five Cs we introduced in the previous chapters (calm, clear, curious, compassionate, courageous). Anything above a five is a strength you can choose to develop. Anything at or below a five is probably something you need to work on. These are not static, but shift according to the nature and level of challenge you are facing. However, many of us tend to be better at some of the Cs than others.

Developing and practicing these qualities increase your emotion regulation skills, allowing you to downshift or upshift depending on context. You'll be able to connect with yourself and others and balance compassion and acceptance with courage and confrontation.

TABLE 4-1

Personal strengths mapped to the Four Stances

Strengths of leaning in	Strengths of leaning back
I am highly determined and committed to excellence.	I am curious, open-minded, and organized, and I can see things from multiple angles.
I am enthusiastic and have a sense of zest and joie de vivre.	I have sound judgment and am able to be prudent when necessary.
I am optimistic and undaunted by difficult challenges.	I'm seen as wise and understanding; people come to me for advice.
I have the confidence and courage to speak truth to power, and a bias for action.	I stay rational under stress and approach challenges in a logical manner.
	I tend to be fair and see the long game.

Strengths of leaning with	Strengths of not leaning
I am seen as compassionate and caring; people come to me for support.	I am calm and centered; deep reflection comes naturally.
I am able to read a room and know what will be most useful to people.	I have a deep appreciation for and connection with nature and art.
I deeply believe in people and naturally see their potential.	I am humble but also have a deep sense of confidence.
I notice how others feel and it matters to me.	
I listen and see things from multiple perspectives.	

You can also list your inner strengths (and weaknesses) and map them to the Four Stances to get a sense of which stances you may need to improve on. For example, Marcus is a highly determined leader, committed to excellence and generally viewed as courageous. This maps clearly to leaning in. But he also struggles with being compassionate and caring for his team—and whether he can read a room or not, he often doesn't try to. Those skills are associated with leaning with, an area for him to develop. Table 4-1 shows a few more strengths mapped to each stance. You don't have to have all these traits to map to that stance, but you will have some of them. You can add your own as well.

A core aspect of your inner self is having a strong sense of purpose.[4] Why are you here; what is the value you bring anywhere you go? Knowing this allows you to be steadier under fire and keeps you in alignment with your deepest values.

There are any number of personal qualities for you to evaluate and work on. A coach can help surface many of them, but table 4-2 has a list of some that you may want to evaluate and, if you are weak on them, learn to develop. As you read this list, consider which ones serve you and which will create problems if you overlook them.

These qualities all inform your identity. They're the *you* behind what you do. Most crucially, they're not inherent; they can be developed. Doing

TABLE 4-2

Personal qualities to check and develop

Emotional regulation and intelligence	Open to new ideas when I don't agree
Open to change	Being less judgmental
Self-compassion	Being conscientious
Kindness	Generosity
Patience	Fairness
Forgiveness	Spirituality
Confidence in self	Confidence in others
Growth mindset	Humility
Gravitas	Authenticity
Sense of meaning and purpose	Independence of thinking
Wisdom	Perspective
Temperance	Prudence
Humanity	Transcendence

so will help you achieve your business goals and allow you to make wise choices about how best to connect with others.

We Are Human Be-ings

In teaching leadership, Harvard Business School uses the framework "Be. Know. Do."[5] Success as a leader depends on the "Be" element. This includes your identity, character, inner strengths, top values, and sense of purpose. You need to be able to call on this self-knowledge even in real time, during the most fraught moments, to guide your decisions as a leader. But how?

Try this: At a moment of choice, don't just ask yourself, *What should I do?* Also ask, *Who do I want to be right now?*[6] This can be a transformative, real-time inflection point.

For example, say it's the end of the day, you're maxed out, and you discover that a direct report dropped the ball on something. You can feel frustration rising, and it would be easy to lose it on this person. You are deciding what you should do. Now, stop yourself and ask, *Who do I want to be right now?* Do you want to be the person whose frustration gets the better of them? Or the one who can create a little space and choose the most effective response?

What if it's the opposite challenge? Say you realize that you've made a stupid and possibly serious mistake. Do you want to be the person berating yourself? Do you want to hide the error? Or do you want to use the Five Cs to metabolize the noxious wave of emotion and shame and figure out who to call in to help?

We've seen many people apply this concept beyond their leadership to develop themselves as people. Imagine that you're stuck in a traffic jam, the car ahead is going too slow, and your blood pressure goes up. *Who do you want to be right now?* Do you want to be that person who is activated and furious at something you can't control?

The simple but powerful question emerged when Carol was thinking how banal New Year's resolutions often seem. What was an alternative? The question that surfaced in her mind was *Who do you want to be right now?* The *right now* is key—that's the real-time part. Change happens in the now. There are opportunities to apply this question in the many micro choices we make every day that often fly by unnoticed. Carol tried asking it of herself many times a day, and it became her primary way to create a space that massively increased her capacity to choose how to be. You can use it to shift how you navigate your internal landscape.

Carol shared how this question had helped her in one of the meetings with a group of CEOs led by legendary executive coach Marshall Goldsmith. Marshall stopped one meeting and announced that he'd read hundreds of books on Buddhism and felt this was the best description of mindfulness he'd ever heard. He called it the "Carol Kauffman question" and started asking it of everyone, every week.

Leaders in the sessions started sharing how the question helped them. One CEO of a tech company said, "I was drained and bored, it was the tenth meeting of the day, and I was just waiting to get through it and get away. Then that question popped into my mind—*Who do I want to be right now?* It opened a split second of time, and then I realized: the least important meeting of my week was the most important meeting of theirs. That realization created an instant change in my mindset, and I could feel the impact of that on the entire room." Others shared similar experiences; the CEO of WD-40 turned it into a poster where it was in clear sight all the time. There is science behind the question. Articulating an intent makes it something you can strive for. There are dozens of research studies on what is called intentional change theory that show how this is the optimal question to launch your journey.[7]

Pause a moment. When you think of your day, how much of it would have gone better if you'd asked yourself this question and let it inform your response? Try it today, and ask the question of yourself a lot—say, twenty to eighty times. How often are you choosing who to be?

• • •

There are so many other questions you can ask yourself to develop your sense of your inner self and begin to improve it. We divide the questions into three categories. Table 4-3 has a sample of some of the questions you can ask yourself. See which catch your attention, and use them to develop a clearer view of where you want to go.

As you can see, it's not so easy to identify and be clear on who you are and who you want to be. It takes real self-reflection and honest dialogue with yourself and others to go through these and other questions. Confucius said centuries ago that naming things is the beginning of wisdom.

TABLE 4-3

Questions to ask to develop your internal strengths

Questions you ask yourself/A look in the mirror	Questions that come from what others have told you/ Reflective feedback	Questions that come from what you admire most about others/ Aspiration

What are you like at your best?[1] At your worst?	What can you learn about yourself from positive feedback you've received from others? Consider:
	
	• The compliments you've received that meant something to you
	
	  – Why those comments?
	
	  – What resonated with you?
	
	  – How do they help you identify who you are and who you want to be?
	
	• The positive feedback you've received in your professional life
	
	• The positive feedback you've received in your personal life
	
	• What you have heard from mentors
		Who are the most important people that you admire and respect? Why?
		
		What attributes do they have? Calm, courageous, selfless, ambitious, generous, a powerful legacy?
		
		What does that tell you about who you want to be?

Scanning through your day, when do you feel energized or deeply engaged?	What can you learn about yourself from negative feedback you've received from others? Consider: • The negative feedback you've received in your professional life • The negative feedback you've received in your personal life • The feedback you've received that hit you hardest – Why? From shame? A sense of failure because you didn't live your values? • What is the worst thing someone could say about you? • If you were your very worst self, who would you be? What does this tell you about who you do not want to be?	Who are the most important people that you do not admire and respect? Why? What attributes do they have? Selfish, inconsiderate, mercurial, poor communicators, lack of awareness? What does that tell you about who you want to be?

TABLE 4-3 (*continued*)

Questions to ask to develop your internal strengths

Questions you ask yourself/A look in the mirror	Questions that come from what others have told you/ Reflective feedback	Questions that come from what you admire most about others/ Aspiration
Think of three leadership experiences that you are most proud of. What do these three experiences have in common— perhaps achievement, discovery, creativity, or service? Who were you at those moments? What qualities are you most proud of? Which do you wish you had?	Looking around, what do you see to help you know who you most want to be? What feedback have you heard about how others saw your strengths and values that resonated with you? What surprised you? • What can you learn about yourself if you reflect on your performance reviews? • What feedback have you ignored that you should revisit? • When you think back, what are the compliments you've received that really mattered?	Thinking about role models, both positive and negative: • Who are the people who have brought out the best in who you are (not what you achieved)? • If you've had good role models, what was it about them that you most valued? • If you have not, what would the ideal role model look like for you? • If you have had someone try to tear you down, what aspect did they go after? • What attributes of your role models do you wish to emulate or avoid?
Think of the three toughest moments of your life. What got you through them? Was it grit? Your capacity to analyze? Were you able to rise above the experience and not lose the bigger picture? Did you connect with others to support you or to support them? What qualities are you most proud of? Which do you wish you had?	What feedback have you received from mentors or colleagues about how you handled these intense real-time challenges?	Who have you seen manage crucible experiences in a way that inspires you to be even better?
Ask yourself how truthful you are being with yourself. Overly rosy? Overly critical? What do these considerations tell you about who you want to be?	What have you heard from others to help reflect on these questions?	Who do you think embodies having a balanced, realistic view of themselves?

1. Linda Orkin Lewin, Alyssa McManamon, Michael T.O. Stein, and Donna T. Chen, "Minding the Form That Transforms: Using Kegan's Model of Adult Development to Understand Personal and Professional Identity Formation in Medicine," *Academic Medicine* 94, vol. 9 (2019): 1299–1304.

Use the questions above to articulate qualities you have and want to develop. Research shows that stepping back and getting beyond a subjective view of yourself leads to maturity.[8] It also shows that being able to bring language to these intangible qualities helps you access them.[9] We need to be able to harness the best of who we are and deploy it in ways that serve our teams and our organization. Just as we can map out what we need to accomplish with external challenges, we can learn to map out which aspects of ourselves we need to develop to rise to the occasions we face.

Many of our leaders have skyrocketed through their careers, and these questions got left behind. However, many things can block you from actually knowing the "real you." Messages from your family, teachers, bosses, or society can drown out the still, small voice in your mind. Perhaps you've heard you're not good enough, or you're better than everyone, or you need to be a doctor, or you're not as smart as your sister. As children we absorb these messages without question. When they no longer apply, we don't unnecessarily unlearn them.

• • •

"People feel they don't know the real Ilanya," the CEO said to Carol, referring to one of her executives, "and it is eroding the capacity of her team and her peers to trust her. People see her as arrogant and withholding. But it's not actually true. In my conversations with her she is genuine and humble."

Our coaching quickly uncovered that Ilanya had been fiercely trained by her family to say absolutely nothing personal at work. She couldn't talk about what she did over the weekend, much less that she'd had an amicable divorce. Carol asked her where these beliefs came from. Ilanya traced it back three generations, to when a grandparent had done things the family members felt they had to hide. "In a way, you've been brainwashed," Carol said. "We don't even know how private the real you is."

Ilanya agreed and began to test the range of what she felt comfortable sharing, running through many of the questions above. To her surprise, she was willing to share more than she'd expected, and opening up a little led to her team warming to her. This made her more comfortable, and a positive spiral was created. Her CEO is delighted with the progress, and Ilanya is now one of the few on the CEO succession list.

Asking yourself the questions above can help you transcend the messages you've been taught but perhaps haven't questioned. Your internal demands should be your own, not inner demons thrust upon you.

Closing the Gap

We've spent much of our chapter helping you identify your strengths, but we can't stress enough the importance of agility. Strengths today may be liabilities tomorrow. Abilities you use in one situation may not apply in another.[10] Overuse of our inner strengths and stances can contort them. Leaning in, when overdone, can lead to being seen as a bully. Your inner strength of curiosity may be good for a lean-back exploratory project, or it could be seen as analysis paralysis while you're on a tight deadline. When caring and concern eclipse other aspects of who you are, you can be seen as too soft. If being centered, calm, and able to not lean takes over too much of who you are, people can misperceive you as being passive, absent, or even neglectful.

Examine yourself and see if you are overusing one aspect of yourself. Then work on expanding your repertoire and begin practicing applying different inner strengths to match the current context.

Personal development is not easy! It requires us to acknowledge that in parts of our lives, we are at war with ourselves. We want to do one thing but find ourselves doing another.[11] At those moments your inner challenge is to tolerate the "burn" this experience creates and to understand what is happening. Say you've decided that your top internal priority is to be more patient. You remember that—yet you keep watching yourself do the opposite. Just acknowledge the struggle and keep trying.

When there is a disconnect between who you are and who you want to be, how can you identify what might be going wrong? You may need to back up and get an overview of what could be draining your energy. If you can identify that, it may point to a different set of internal priorities you need to meet before tackling the one that you're going after and missing on.

You may want to be patient. That will be harder if you feel your basic needs of survival, security, and social attachments have not been met.[12] For example, if your impatience is due to overreacting to a possible business failure, your internal challenge may be to notice that you are feeling a threat to your survival at the company. At those moments, call to mind the Five Cs and notice if focusing on one of them in real time will help you create the space you need to stay grounded.

Know What Really Motivates You

Knowing what motivates us and others helps to identify how we can create the conditions for us and others to thrive. Extrinsic motivations are those that push us—money or fame, for example. Intrinsic motivations are those that pull us, that we want to do for their own sake. These range from achievement to meditation, creative pursuits to sports. You need both types of motivation, but we want to create the conditions for intrinsic motivation as much as possible. Hundreds of studies show that intrinsic motivation unlocks performance in remarkable ways.[13] There are three factors—autonomy, relatedness, and competence (ARC)—that help us identify when we are intrinsically motivated and create those conditions for others:

Autonomy: This is the internal state of feeling free, able to choose what to do or how you do it. You feel a sense of ownership over your life, actions, and how you work.

Relatedness: This is the state of feeling psychologically safe, connected, and the joy or satisfaction of belonging and inclusion. You feel energized and open to others.

Competence: This is a sense of mastery, an ability to grow and achieve. You are not thwarted and feel unleashed to do your best.

While choosing your internal priorities, these ARC factors are important considerations. As a leader, it is your responsibility to know yourself and how your personal transformation is core to your organization's transformation. The highest internal goal is self-actualization, when we are intrinsically motivated to be our ideal selves with a sense of meaning, purpose, and direction.

• • •

Marcus had overlooked the internal dimension of leadership and was taken aback when it threatened his dream of becoming the CEO. The biggest complaints about him were about his interpersonal leadership (more on that in the next chapter). But for him to shift the way he related, he first had to shift himself and become mindfully alert of his internal challenges. If he couldn't, his top talent would keep leaving.

Marcus was a powerful and passionate leader, but his passions often managed him rather than the other way around.[14] He was smart and confident, but his overuse of these strengths led him to be too certain of his correctness, and thus he came off as arrogant. While he was a good guy at heart, people found his behavior intimidating and his micromanaging demotivating.

He was also intensely curious and data-driven; he respected and listened to teachers more than anyone. So Carol put on her professor hat and used an evidence-based approach to help him shift his mindset.

"Can I give you a short tutorial?" she asked.

"Sure!"

"People have psychological needs that need to be met for them to be at their best and be engaged."

"They do?"

Carol talked about the importance of helping others be self-determined. She described the three top needs of autonomy, relatedness, and competence. "You can remember them with the acronym ARC."

"That's great, but what if they can't have autonomy? We are in a free-fall crisis here!"

"Will that last forever?" she asked.

"No," he said, sounding surprised.

"Can you let them know it's temporary?"

"I could. Yes, that makes sense. You think psychological needs really matter so much?"

"That's what the data says."

"What do I do to help with the safety part?"

"What do you think?"

"I know I'm not great at listening, and I take over."

He was on the right track; few things increase psychological safety as much as truly being seen and heard by another. If he could develop one of the Five Cs to listen and help himself create a space between a stimulus and his tendency to take over situations, it would be game-changing.

"What would it take for you to slow down?" This was a lucky question. It turned out Marcus was dedicated to meditation; he'd just never thought of bringing that aspect of himself to work.

"If you were able to pull on that side of you, what kind of impact could it have?"

Marcus was a quick study. "Got it. If I can calm myself down, I won't jump in and take over so quickly." He leaned forward so fast that it startled Carol. "This changes things! I have a board meeting coming up, and the entire team is going to be there. I'll step back, give them more autonomy. After all, we'll have prepped, and I'll more or less know what they are going to say."

Well, that's a start, Carol thought.

Summary

Internal challenges and priorities are necessary to develop and can lead to breakthroughs in your leadership. You can develop clarity on what areas of personal growth are your highest priorities.

To learn your inner strengths and weaknesses, you can apply several techniques:

- Scan the Five Cs, rating yourself on each on a scale of one to ten. Anything above a five is a strength and anything at or below a five is an area to work on to increase your emotion regulation skills and allow you to downshift or upshift depending on context.

- List your inner strengths and weaknesses, then map these to the Four Stances. Which stances are more common in your strengths list? Your weaknesses list? Focus on developing the ability to access the stances associated with your inner weaknesses.

- Scan table 4-2 to reference other qualities you may find to be strengths or weaknesses, and decide where to focus on improving.

Develop the habit of asking yourself this question throughout the day as you make decisions and have moments when you feel yourself becoming agitated, upset, impatient, or something else you don't like: *Who do I want to be right now?*

Probe further by asking questions in the three columns of table 4-3. The answers will point you to where you are strong internally and where you want to develop. Being intentional about this process is the point.

Research shows that doing so makes you more likely to develop your inner strengths.

Be agile with your strengths, because a strength in one situation may be a liability in another. Understand that overusing our inner strengths may contort them. Even if you're good on curiosity, for example, having too much of it in a situation that demands action will result in analysis paralysis.

Seek intrinsic motivation, fostering the ARC qualities in yourself and others:

Autonomy: Being able to choose what to do or how you do it

Relatedness: The state of feeling psychologically safe, connected, and included

Competence: A sense of mastery and an ability to grow and achieve

5

Get Smart about People

To handle yourself, use your head. To handle others, use your heart.
—**Eleanor Roosevelt**

You know your external priorities. You're working on your internal challenges. The third factor in Mindful Alertness is the interpersonal challenges—learning how you can best connect with others depending on what they need and what the situation requires, while shifting in real time as needed.[1] Interpersonal challenges may occur with one other person, your team, or even an entire organizational culture. The overarching interpersonal goal is to be mentally alert to which stance is appropriate and to be able to shift quickly and seamlessly. It's the heart of leadership.

This makes sense.

As a leader, 80 percent of your time can be spent in meetings and interacting with others—reports, peers, bosses, stakeholders, investors, customers. How much have you thought about how effectively you interact? Do you listen well? Do you follow when it's necessary? Can you influence and lead people?

Relationships Are the Greatest Stumbling Blocks for Leaders

In the introduction, we shared the results of a CEO survey that show nearly all leaders agreed that their relationships were their Achilles' heel.[2] They excelled at strategy, execution, getting results, and most of the first dimension of leadership outcomes (external). The overwhelming criticism they received was how they related to their teams and their boards.

Analysis of the data coalesced around three common behaviors where CEOs fall short:

- Not listening

- Talking too much

- Being impatient

We saw this with Marcus. Whatever success he had, his interpersonal behaviors tracked exactly to these three shortcomings. The major derailers for many powerful leaders are they are good at winning minds but not hearts and they are good at the what and not the how.

In some ways, it's understandable. Pressures are crushing, and you are being challenged to deliver yesterday. What's more, the qualities that are now needed are the very ones leaders have had drummed out of them. CEOs are now often "comforters in chief," required to create inclusive, psychologically safe, and even healing environments while still pleasing Wall Street. Command-and-control leadership is what they are taught. But how you relate to others can make or break your career.[3] Hundreds of research articles describe how having high-quality relationships in the workplace carries huge importance, beyond just engagement and work satisfaction scores.[4] It often goes to the bottom line: Fostering safety and inclusion increases trust and leads to positive emotions at work. This leads to faster cognitive processing, greater innovation, a wider range of resources, more resilience, and good organizational citizenship. In other words, optimal performance.

Do you know how to set the tone and create the best interpersonal environment to accomplish what needs to be done?

In our work with leaders, we teach the maxim that you need at least four ways to win. Nowhere is this more paramount than in how we connect with others. And it's hard. Carol developed the four-ways approach many years ago and used it consciously for the first time during a coaching session with Max, the COO of a well-known media giant.

• • •

Max was usually calm and clear. Not today. His former good friend was now the CEO and his boss. Their relationship had gone to hell.

"I can't stand it anymore!" Max fumed. "I used to love working with Gemma. Now, I schedule her at the end of the day so I can immediately get out of here. Jim has a vodka martini waiting for me at home and insists I drink it before he'll talk to me!"

He was agitated, and without realizing it Carol had caught his energy. Max described how Gemma had changed after being elevated to the top job, saying it was as if she had molted. His former friend was now in continuous command-and-control mode, micromanaging him to death. Worse, she'd commandeered resources he'd fought for months to obtain and used them for one of her pet projects.

Max's typical stance was to lean back. In the rare cases he felt betrayed or under attack, he'd flip into a lean-in stance. Now he and Carol were working to form a battle plan.

As they strategized, Max interjected. "What's even weirder is that halfway through the meeting, after hazing me, she suddenly got all nice and cozy, confiding in me, telling me things that are confidential, and asking for my advice."

Carol felt alarmed. Flipping from attacker to confidante was a classic manipulation technique. But just as she was about to point that out, it hit her. She'd gotten swept away and forgotten her own advice: four ways to win! She slammed on the brakes, closed her mouth, and slowed down her breathing to become calm, clear, and curious. As Max's coach, Carol had to stay mindfully alert to not slide into an aggressive-protect mode, which she had almost done, but just in time she'd been able to lean back. Max didn't know, of course, but she was practicing the same real-time leadership you're learning here.

"Let's hit the pause button and get some perspective," she said. "What's the bigger-picture view of what could be going on?"

After taking a minute to slow down, Max said, "There is a lot going on at the top of the house." As he thought aloud, a new picture emerged. "The board chair has Gemma under a tight leash and is questioning her every move. Like she's doing to me, actually. There are two new activist investors on the board. No wonder she's stressed out. But that doesn't make how she's acting OK."

Carol agreed but noticed they were both a lot calmer and clearer. They'd interrupted the spiral of getting sucked into their natural lean-in stance. They were now mindfully alert and freer to identify other ways of relating to Gemma. As things cooled, Carol pulled strongly on the Five Cs.

After a quick internal scan, Max felt that curiosity felt like the right resource to explore. This led Carol to consider what a don't-lean point of view might uncover. As often happens, nothing came to mind right away. Carol relaxed to get to a calmer, more receptive state and waited to see if something new came to mind. It did! She rolled her eyes at herself and wondered why this always seemed surprising to her. Similarly, if you can slow yourself down under stress, it creates space for intuitive or creative insights to emerge. Often these are fully formed and create an aha experience.

The new train of thought was a bit tricky to communicate. It could land the wrong way easily. "Max?" she began tentatively. "In the end, don't you almost always wind up getting what you want pushed through? I mean, you found some workarounds and even got your funds reinstated." He nodded. "OK. So why even let this bother you?" she asked, with a bit of lean-in in her voice.

Max looked out the window for a few seconds. "Well, that is true. I hadn't thought of it that way." Carol felt like she could see new thoughts flickering through his mind as he considered not leaning and letting things go. That was an improvement, but Carol still sensed his unease.

There was one more stance to try: would leaning with be helpful? She tried another tack, not feeling terribly optimistic. "OK, Max. What would it be like if your entire goal in the meeting was to have Gemma feel better by the end of the hour?"

Max looked up, startled. Then a new expression came over his face—he looked energized. "Yes, that feels exactly right! We've been friends a long time before this. She is pretty much being persecuted right now, and that *has to* be a big part of what is driving this. I'll try it. No matter what happens with her, this feels right to me."

For a couple of months his relationship with Gemma improved significantly. Then it got much worse, and nothing he did helped. Max felt he'd done his best and began accepting calls from recruiters. When an incredible offer came his way a few quarters later, he took it.

• • •

By making space in the coaching session, Max moved from attack stance, to analytical, to reflective, and finally to a caring and collaborative stance. Four ways to win. In this case, leaning with felt optimal, but which stance is ideal changes all the time. The goal for the coach is not to tell leaders what to do, but to get them to create that space to create options and then pick one they feel good about. Carol typically tells leaders, "I don't care which choice you make. I care that you have the capacity to make any of them."

Know Your Defaults to Get beyond Them

Here's what we mean by finding four ways to win for interpersonal interactions. Know your default stance—we covered this in previous chapters. Then identify your less developed stances and become mindfully alert for when you need to call on them. Max tended to be adept at all four. He was famous for being calmly analytical and collaborative. The many reorganizations he led went smoothly. He leaned back first, accompanied by an understated leaning with. His people felt a high degree of safety and inclusion. When the executive committee went into an aggressive mode, he had the ability to not lean and observe. He used this skill to come up with innovative solutions to problems, and when he spoke people listened. This level of agility was supported by an active meditation practice that helped him lower his blood pressure at will.

Max is an all-star leader, yet even he could be rattled when something triggered a fight/flight reflex. Thus he was unprepared when an interpersonal challenge threw him off balance and catapulted him into a lean-in stance.

It will take time, but you should strive to be like Max. How wide is your range, and how flexible can you be? Before you can effectively find four ways to win in the moment, you need to increase your awareness of what your interpersonal goals are in the first place.

Be Clear on Your Choices

How clear are you on the best way to unlock the talents of your reports, to connect well with your peers, and to relate effectively to your line manager or board? Interpersonal excellence is being able to shift stances and expand your awareness of all the choices you have. It's important to know what stance is most likely to snare you, to respect its power, and to stay mentally alert, because your automatic responses may not be the wisest.

Are you aware of what percentage of the time you operate from each of the Four Stances?

For many of you, the stance you use with others the most, by far, is lean in. You needed it to get where you are. That's how you became a leader at the top: you delivered. When it works, you are highly engaging and determined.

But you can overuse it with others, and when you do, there are clues all around you. People quiet down when you enter a room; they don't disagree or argue; you hear rumors that people are afraid of you. Do not discount this feedback simply because you know (or at least feel) it isn't objectively correct. It's others' perception of you, and that perception is as real as your feeling that it's wrong. If this is the story people are telling about you, you need to go on alert and think about shifting to a different stance and begin seeing and creating a different story.

Those leaders who lean back with others may be baffled when their rational argument falls flat or logic seems irrelevant to others. These are clues you need to identify a different stance.

It might seem self-evident that those who primarily lean with have the best interpersonal relationships, and they often do. Those who lean with are more likely to create safety, and their people will feel cared for. But that doesn't mean those leaders always get it right. Overuse of leaning with can limit the interpersonal choices available to you in certain contexts. Say you need to have a tough conversation or hold someone accountable. Leaning with isn't always going to be as effective there. There are kind ways to confront, and it isn't good for you to avoid the conflict. In the long run they need to hear the truth of how they are seen.

Those who don't lean are comfortable with silence and long pauses in the moment. (They are also rare. Most of us find it quite difficult to "don't just do something, sit there!") However, overreliance on this approach may cause blind spots when people need active intervention. You can be seen as laissez-faire or neglectful if you rely on this approach when someone or some team needs help now.

Again, the key is agility, having all stances available in the moment. Here is one example of how to approach a common challenge—giving feedback—from different stances. Jen, the chief revenue officer, is taking up too much airtime in meetings and needs to understand that. Here's how to approach that feedback from the Four Stances:

> "Jen, you've helped us hit our numbers, and that's great. But I need to let you know you are talking too much in meetings.

People feel you're taking over, and the team finds it demotivating." (Lean in)

"Jen, I have noticed that you are speaking more than others in meetings about 40 percent of the total time. I usually orient around equal time for all, so I'd aim to take 10 percent to 20 percent of the airspace. Try decreasing your word count." (Lean back)

"Jen, you are such a great member of the team and have so much to offer. I feel, though, that you are overusing your strengths of wanting to teach others during meetings. My sense is it would help the group if we had a bit more white space. It's hard, but we need to let them learn from their mistakes." (Lean with)

"Jen, I'd like you to reflect on how you contribute to our meetings. Take some time to reflect, then tell me if something comes to mind about how you see your role and where you want to grow." (Don't lean)

When you can pause and identify what good looks like for each stance, then you are much more likely to carry it through once you have chosen the optimal stance for the situation. Can you see the ten-out-of-ten outcome behind each of these responses?

Bring Your Inner Strengths to the Game

It's not just the stance you pick with interpersonal challenges that matters, it's how you implement it. Pairing the right stance with your internal resources is the key. Doing so can even alert you that you have picked an incorrect stance and allow you to adjust.

Let's say that you've explored "Who do you want to be right now?" and that emotion regulation and fairness surfaced as the greatest internal priorities for you to develop. You may have picked lean in as the appropriate stance, but if you have a lot of work to do on self-regulation, you may want to consider another choice. Once you have confirmed which stance would be best for the situation, you can continue to bring your internal qualities to take your leadership to the next level. If you choose to lean in, emotion regulation empowers you to titrate your intensity. You want to adjust it based on the needs and preferences of the other people involved in the situation. Some need intensity to be inspired. Others could find it intimidating, and a lower-key approach will encourage their greater engagement. Being alert to your commitment to fairness will help you notice disparities in how you are connecting with members of your team. You can apply this to any stance, infusing it with any of the inner qualities you want to develop to hone your leadership skills.

In our decades of working with leaders, we've uncovered some prevalent myths when it comes to interpersonal leadership challenges. Let's discuss them now.

The Golden Rule Is Wrong

To unlock the potential of others, forget some good advice you've gotten in the past: the Golden Rule. Treat others as you'd like to be treated—right?

It's not bad advice on its face, but as a leader, you must go further to understand when that won't work. Step up to what we call the Platinum Rule: treat others as *they* would like to be treated, which might be very different from what you would want for yourself.[5] Step beyond your automatic reactions and assumptions of what is best.

If you've been developing yourself and are creating space between the stimulus and response so that you don't simply reflex and react, you are on your way to living the Platinum Rule. In that space you can stop to think about what others need, just as we did above when we looked at the stances in reference to leading others.

Waiting to Speak Up Can Be Suboptimal

Confronting someone usually comes after an accrual of behavior reaches a critical mass. Perhaps it's their chronic lateness, constant interrupting, or any number of behaviors. Most of us will excuse it (*It's not that bad* or *They don't really mean it*) for a long time, until we can't stand it anymore and feel like we'll explode if we don't say something.

We find it's more effective to say something when you first start noticing that a behavior is bothering you. The interpersonal goal here is to take care of the relationship by saying something when the stakes are low. Look for signs that the relationship is becoming suboptimal, and decide if you want it to be better. What should catch your attention is if you notice you are withdrawing from the person or if being with them starts to feel difficult or inauthentic. This is an alarm bell for you to be mindfully alert and make a space to decide how to meet this interpersonal challenge. Think through what you might do or say from each of the Four Stances to expand your range. Then choose. But the key is not to wait until the situation is fraught.

Your Leadership Isn't Just What You Say and Do

Leadership is something you emanate. Your private attitudes and emotions are detected by others and people react to them. At times they are contagious. Our brains pick up subtle sensory input signals from people; for example, we process facial expressions that are too quick to see. Some slightly scary research makes the point: Imagine that you are hooked up to monitors measuring physical responses like skin conductance and pulse.[6] A frightening image flashes on a screen. How long do you think it takes your brain to react enough to send signals for other parts of the body to react? Under thirty-three milliseconds. Another startling study showed that a scary face flashing on a screen activated the amygdala of people who were cortically blind. Our brains are shockingly attuned to seemingly invisible signals.

Remember, every interaction is neurological. There are two basic systems in the brain, reward and threat (parasympathetic and sympathetic). The question is, What part of the brain do you want to activate in the other person with the signals you emanate (even ones that aren't obvious)? Research shows that compassion, a growth mindset, and positive emotion activate the reward center of the brain; this is the physiological basis of the ten-out-of-ten question.[7] By visualizing success, you're activating the reward center. Focusing on the problem or on where you're weak does the opposite.

So, when working with others, notice what is right with them. Use a warm tone of voice, and show enthusiasm if that matches their style.[8] These emanations have real, palpable effects on your relationships with others.

Don't force this too much. If you need to give hard feedback, this may feel like a way to deliver the proverbial s*** sandwich—a positive signal followed by a corrective message and then another positive signal. It's hard to do this well. Even if they don't consciously know it, the person getting the sandwich will pick up on the lack of authenticity through all these nearly invisible signals you emanate. If you've heard of the Pygmalion effect, this is what we want to pull on.[9] Your authentic belief in another person's capacity to grow improves their performance.

• • •

The three dimensions of Mindful Alertness are inextricably linked. But truly great leadership is contingent on being excellent in the internal and interpersonal realms. Whether it's creating a high-potential team, winning a transaction, or meeting your numbers, your being a ten out of ten in how you relate is much more possible if you have paid attention to your personal growth. Identifying and choosing to develop key areas of the second dimension, your inner world, increases your capacity to identify and meet your interpersonal goals. Excellence in the third dimension, how you relate, makes any goal more attainable. In turn, when you are aware of what truly matters to you and have worked on your resilience, you can be more successful at the business goals you need to win in the market.

You have the power to create a virtuous cycle in which your development in professional, personal, and relationship priorities can augment one another and help you to be of the best service to you and your organization.

• • •

Marcus, the energy company CEO, was learning this. While he was always great at the numbers, his increased awareness of his need to manage himself and relate in a more positive way with others was shifting his impact.

It was two weeks after the coaching session he'd started with, "How long is this going to take?" Now, Marcus was animated and looking forward to our second session. After our first one, he'd decided to radically shift how he prepared for the board meeting. Carol was curious about how that had gone for Marcus.

"Unbelievable! The board said it was the best meeting ever. What stuck with me was the ARC thing and people wanting to be self-determined. I decided my new goal was to help the team have more autonomy, relatedness, and competence. In the interest of having better relationships and empowering them, I realized I should step back and let them shine. I told them it was their meeting, and they did great."

"Wow, what did you do?"

"I made sure to listen better, so they felt valued. Then, what you said about people having psychological needs really hit me. We were standing around the table in the boardroom. I made myself just stop and take a long look at each one of them. I've known them for many years. Suddenly I had this image in my mind. I pictured each one as a ten-year-old, and who they were as a child was standing in front of them looking at me. It hit me—that child needs to feel and be safe. And that's part of my job."

"That's amazing! How did you do it?" To say Carol was taken aback was an understatement. Marcus's transformation at this speed was unlikely but rewarding. On reflection, it made sense. He was famous for his capacity to deliver whatever he put his mind to. He'd identified goals that previously had never come to mind—now his execution strengths had a new target.

"I wasn't sure what to do at first," he admitted. "But I took each one aside and said, 'Don't worry about the board meeting. I'll be there and no matter what, I'll have your back.' None of them have ever had a leader say that to them before. One of them even cried. And it led to an amazing outcome."

Speechless. This guy who was repeatedly labeled as emotionally unintelligent and capable of inducing fear in others now had team members crying from his support. With very little input he was able to access a skill in interpersonal relationships that had always been there, but that he had not tapped into at work.

Needless to say, he's still the CEO.

• • •

We have now explored the Three Dimensions of Leadership: what external goals we must achieve, how to step into our ideal selves, and how to become highly aware of what people need from us. What is required of us as leaders shifts, often suddenly. Like the elite athletes we know, all of us need to be on our toes, able to read what is going on around us, inside us, and with our teammates.

These are skills and qualities you can develop and use to lead in real time when the stakes are high. Next, we will examine what you can do now that you're deeply, mindfully alert. You can quickly read the situation, but how do you react and create the best options for your next move?

Summary

Meeting interpersonal challenges is key to your leadership growth. By far the most common shortcomings leaders have are in the interpersonal realm, and the top three are:

- Not listening

- Talking too much

- Being impatient

You can work on these and other interpersonal challenges if you:

- Identify your interpersonal priorities and your default stance.

- Develop the capacity to identify four ways to win by using all Four Stances in situations that involve other people.

- Get clarity on which stances are strengths and which need to be developed.

- Practice noticing when you default to a stance and experiment with shifting to another.

- Identify how to bring your inner resources, like caring and curiosity, to interpersonal challenges. Sometimes they will be useful, sometimes they may create friction in the relationship. Learn to shift your inner resources to match the situation.

- Learn three myths of interpersonal leadership and how to overcome them:

  - The Golden Rule is wrong. Your aim is not to treat people how you want to be treated, but to treat them as *they need* to be treated. We call this the Platinum Rule.

  - Waiting to speak up is suboptimal. We often intervene with others when we can't take their behavior anymore. A better approach is to be attuned to when someone starts a behavior and to intervene early, when the stakes are low. Before intervening, game out how you could do this using each of the Four Stances.

— Leadership isn't just what you say and do. You emanate signals, subconsciously, that others pick up on. They are neurologically aware of how you bring yourself to interpersonal situations, even if they don't realize it. Be cognizant of your tone of voice, facial expressions, and more, and be aware that people pick up on authentic communication. You can't fake the signals.

MOVE

Generate Options

6

Find Four Ways to Win

We are our choices.

—Jean-Paul Sartre

Mindful Alertness is the first step in managing those high-stakes situations you're going to face. You've created space to deliberately name the Three Dimensions of Leadership, covering your external, internal, and interpersonal priorities. But now what? How can you achieve what you want, be who you want to be, and bring out the best in others? It's optimal to have multiple options available to move forward. In this and the following two chapters we'll share how you can generate different pathways forward for each dimension of leadership. Here we focus on the first, finding at least four options for achieving your external goals.

From Willpower to Waypower

You could be mindfully alert to your three-dimensional priorities, think of a way forward, and act— but that's going to limit your success, no matter how much willpower you have to make it happen. We advocate with our executives to develop what is called *waypower*: the capacity to come up with several viable ways forward.[1] The research is clear, and our experience is even clearer: having multiple options makes success more likely.

Sometimes this is a hard sell with the executives we work with, because they've become used to a default approach to leadership, as you may have. One of our high-powered leaders, with whom we were trying to explore these principles, said, "I always win. I go fast and make key tactical moves. Together they make my biggest priorities happen. With the inner game, I just rely on being able to tough it out. I go over, under, or through any wall in my way. And I get your idea of four different stances when dealing with people, but leaning in is what always works best."

This is a very narrow path (and you can see this leader wasn't being mindfully alert), which unnecessarily constrains options—especially in high-stakes situations, when we're most likely to stick to our default settings and become exaggerated versions of ourselves. Eventually this kind of leader will meet a wall that doesn't break and that they can't get around. At some point they may not be able to tough it out. And they may not even know how much they've lost by relentlessly sticking to default settings and putting people off.

Another leader had the reverse challenge. He had the lean-back groove down and was an incredible delegator with legendary calm. This worked well until a crisis surfaced and his team was stunned and lost. He remained steady, confident in his default style, telling people, "Just stay calm, I have a lot of confidence you will figure it out." They didn't figure it out, and he hadn't generated other options for responding.

The groove became a rut he couldn't escape. A more mature leader would have a lean-in stance as a secondary option that was developed enough to be second nature, and available to be called on as needed. That person would have heard his team and understood his organization was screaming for him to be actively involved. He would have sprung into action to guide his team.

Dozens of research studies spearheaded by the late American psychologists Rick Snyder and Shane J. Lopez and their teams demonstrate how people's capacity to reach their desired goals can be increased by conceiving of multiple possible pathways.[2] It is a combination of willpower and waypower that drives successful outcomes. They called their research instrument the hope scale.[3] In our favorite study, the researchers used scores on the hope scale to predict that female marathoners with high willpower and high waypower would come out in front, and they did, very strongly.[4] The studies have been replicated with groups of people from all walks of life and show that that combination of willpower and waypower adds resilience and persistence to a person's efforts and reliably increases chances of success.

The research suggests that, ideally, you will have four or more pathways forward for each external, internal, and interpersonal priority.

Creating Pipelines of Possibilities

Surfacing all of these new options is an art as well as a science, as Akash discovered.

Akash worked his way up in his massive apparel company and eventually became COO, responsible for sourcing, production, inventory, distribution centers, and all of IT. To cover such a disparate range of responsibilities, he insisted on heavy governance and reporting mechanisms so that he would always know the status of key issues. The dashboards he implemented were granular and a burden for his team, but his approach seemed to work, because he always delivered results.

Then, rather suddenly, several of the green lights on his dashboard turned red, especially for inventory management, and he started to miss his targets. At the same time, functional leaders were pushing back hard on his governance model.

Akash sought out David for coaching. "I've never had this level of criticism. I'm not delivering, which is painful enough. On top of that, I've been told I saddle my teams with too much governance."

David asked what he was now hearing that he hadn't heard when his group was hitting its targets. "I talk too much, I don't listen, and I'm too directive. This is all news to me. My confidence is shaken. It can't be true." He looked at David. "Is it true?"

"I understand how hard that must have been to hear," David said. "Try to separate the sting you're feeling from the way the feedback was delivered. If you can do that, how much of this has any merit?"

"I guess I have blind spots like everyone else. The shock is more about the sheer number of messages that came out at the same time!"

David wanted to help Akash find a way to reset his equilibrium. He couldn't take on every criticism at once, so David asked where he wanted to start.

"I'm really struggling with the feedback on governance."

Akash had picked the right thing to address. David knew from discussions with Akash's team that this was the big problem. A typical comment he heard was, "He loves his decks and dashboards, and it feels like we spend more time on reporting and compliance than we do on operating the business."

Akash went on. "The CEO told me, 'Governance is necessary. But do it *light*.' What is that supposed to mean? Strong governance is so core to my leadership playbook. That's what I always do to tackle my priorities. I don't know what 'do it light' means."

• • •

Akash knew what he had to tackle, but he needed options for how to tackle it, just as you will once you name your priorities. Here is how you can create your personal Options Generator to come up with additional ways to tackle your three-dimensional priorities.

Start with an exercise of answering these either/or questions to explore different angles you could take to approach your high-stakes external priorities.

Should I . . .

- Be strategic or tactical?

- Be risky or conservative?

- Move fast or slow?

- Make big moves or small?

- Be rational/data-driven or feelings/intuition-driven?

- Strive for 100 percent perfection in due diligence, or go for an 80/20 solution?

- Be innovative, or go for what's proven?

- Be conceptual or pragmatic?

- Use a top-down framework or bottom-up?

- Apply extensive governance and reporting or light?

These questions are a starter kit for options generation and are designed to stop you from instinctually reflexing to your default approach. If you add an in-between alternative to each of the ten choices in the list, then you have even more options to consider. Add your own set of choices to this list based on what you think might work for your priorities.

You can also use the Four Stances to unlock more options. First, lean in and come up with a long list of options for your external priority. When you think you are done, lean back and ask yourself "What else could work?" so that you can add to the list. Then lean with by consulting with others about what they think the options are to meet your external priority. Finally, don't lean and see if anything else pops into your consciousness.

Now run through the Five Cs to help you get into an objective and centered state of mind and scan your list. Circle those words you are instinctually most attracted to—they describe your default approach. For example, you may be drawn to taking risks, inclined to always come up with an innovative new solution, and driven by hunches and subjective emotions. Or you may typically opt for a more strategic route, moving slow but making big bets based exclusively on data.

If you are mindfully alert, you won't immediately choose the option that matches your default approach. Instead, ask yourself if your default is the most viable way to achieve your external priority. If it is, great, but you still should go through the list again to name at least three more options, in case that approach doesn't work or the situation changes. If your default doesn't seem viable upon reflection, identify four more options. Once you've done this, not only will you have made the space you need between stimulus and response, but also you will be prepared to use that space well and not simply do what you always do without thinking.

• • •

David asked Akash—a lean-in guy if there ever was one—to elaborate on how he would typically approach his external priorities.

"Bulletproof governance comes to mind first. Also, I insist on a lot of due diligence before coming to a decision, and everything I do is driven by data, not intuition. My gut is to take small steps where I can and only move big when I have no other option." Akash's default angle for his external priorities is summarized in the list below:

- Heavy governance

- Heavy due diligence

- Data-driven

- Small steps

Now that Akash had been explicit about his default, David could help him identify more options by leaning back to think about the variety of high-stakes situations he faced. "You have so many projects going. They don't all have the same impact and risk, right?"

"Right."

"So, let's parse your initiatives into low, medium, and high risk. What are some lower-risk situations you are facing?"

"I think our strategic sourcing function is well managed with experienced leaders, and things are pretty much in hand."

"How do you handle governance with them?"

"I specify goals and then assign roles and responsibilities for each key person."

That was still lean in. Akash specified the goals, and Akash assigned roles. But this was a low-risk area; maybe leaning back would work here. "How about asking the team to do this instead of telling them?"

"I would have to stop myself because it's automatic. But of course I can do that."

"What next?"

"Well, once you have roles and responsibilities, you need to look at decision-making criteria, metrics and reporting structures, reporting frequency, and so on."

David pushed further, hoping Akash could see how a lean-back stance might fit a lower-risk situation. "Could you imagine your involvement ending after the team told you what the roles and responsibilities are?"

Akash took a long time before he finally responded. "Maybe. For things that are very low risk. For other things that are a bit higher risk, but not mission-critical, I could maybe have less frequent check-ins than I would normally insist on." New options were emerging.

"Great. How about in cases where your team is very confident—could you also ease back your standards for due diligence, and let them rely just a little bit more on their experience and intuition?"

Laughing, Akash said, "Now that you put it that way, yes, I can handle that! While we're at it, I could even envisage a few bigger moves. It's making me think I should have given more weight to my inventory team's input. They feel we need to be bolder. That's probably why we are way behind in our timeline to show proof of concept for our new inventory transformation model."

For lower-risk initiatives, Akash now had a new option, which was the *opposite* of his default:

- Light governance

- Lighter due diligence

- More intuitive than data-driven

- Selectively take bigger steps

Still, David knew it was in Akash's best interest to identify more options. "So, now we've got some situations where you can implement light governance. How about situations when we could do *lighter* governance, between light and heavy?"

Akash was warming to the possibilities, and new ideas started flowing. "I think I can get there for some medium-risk initiatives. I could double down on our due diligence for selection of our new inventory management model, and that would give me more confidence to let go a bit on governance. And I can maybe move bigger on some initiatives if I come up with a lighter but more nimble form of governance that lasers in on identifying and mitigating risks. I guess I could emphasize having more early warning signals in place than I had before. For that, I perhaps need closer to three metrics rather than thirty, with simplified daily reporting, rather than having ninety-page decks every month."

Another option, an in-between model for medium-risk initiatives:

- Lighter governance, a midpoint between light and heavy, focused on early warnings

- Heavy due diligence

- Double down on data

- Selectively take bigger steps

David was pleased Akash was getting to more options that he would normally be comfortable with. He could imagine Akash's team greatly benefiting from downshifting on reporting. But David was still concerned about what Akash might do under stress. He thought there were additional options for high-risk situations, where Akash would typically double down on his default stance. He hoped that even then Akash could create space for himself to make new choices.

For the highest-risk situations, Akash said, "I must keep my standards for governance. But I could consider trade-offs for the other aspects. You know I love data, but we have had some pretty strong hunches on some fairly big initiatives that we could take. We've been holding off until we get all the proof points, but we are already 95 percent certain. I could probably rely on our collective intuition and just go for a few of these—but not all. I can go bigger for these as long as I can still shut them down if things start to go wrong."

Akash now had his fourth option for certain types of higher-risk initiatives:

- Heavy governance

- Heavy due diligence

- Mix of intuition and data-driven

- Selectively take bigger steps

• • •

Here are some steps you can take to get to where Akash did.

Don't Limit Your Options to What's Immediately Accessible

If you are primarily an action-oriented leader but being a strategic leader makes the most sense for a situation, realize that you don't have to be outstanding at everything. You can leverage the strategic skills that reside inside your organization, hire a strategic adviser, and build your personal capacity for strategic insight. Think about risk-taking—either increasing your personal appetite for risk or reigning yourself in—as something to tackle with your internal priorities.

Size the Options

When new options call for a large step change compared with your current capabilities, that doesn't mean the move isn't viable. You can always get started by right-sizing the challenge into a manageable goal. Find a goal that you are more confident about achieving, one that stretches but doesn't break you.

Rank the Options

Write down and rank your options from most preferred to least preferred so that you can figure out which one to start with. Then fill in alternatives in case your first choice doesn't work out. How you rank criteria will vary depending on the external priority, but you could include considerations like:

- How much time do you have to achieve your priority?

- Is the option reversible or not?

- How much leadership time and resources does the option involve? What is the benefit-to-cost ratio?

- What are the second- and third-order consequences of the option?

- Is the option within the organization's tolerance for risk?

You don't have to do the ranking all by yourself. You could involve your team, your boss/board, peers, or other trusted advisers.

Keep building your options-generation muscle by tracking how you are doing relative to your top external priorities. How many times is your default option the ideal one for the situation? How many times have you tried new options, and what was the result?

When Outcomes Are Highly Uncertain, Generate More Options

We noted in chapter 3 that your external priorities can result in a range of possible outcomes due to risk and uncertainty. But you can develop options to influence the outcomes, and by acting on these options you can change the probability curve—both where the most likely outcome is and how far away other possibilities range from the center.

Scenario and contingency planning (which is a form of options generation) can help you respond more effectively to external volatility.[5] Take a snapshot of factors that could significantly affect the outcome of your external priorities, for better or for worse. These include: fluctuations in macroeconomic growth, inflation, geopolitical flare-ups like trade wars and armed conflict, supply chain disruptions, regulatory developments, technology, cybersecurity risks, strategic weaknesses you may have in your business model, and operational risks in executing your strategy.

Some of these are out of your hands, while others you can influence. Whatever the case, if you devote some leadership time to anticipating these possibilities, you can create space to develop options for dealing with them in advance—contingency plans—that will help you react faster (and feel more in control) when they arrive.

For each of the most important risks to you (upside as well as downside), develop a series of "what if" scenarios by assessing how vulnerable you are and what the consequences would be for your external priority at various levels of severity for the potential risk. Make sure you cover the full probability distribution, including best imaginable case and worst imaginable case in addition to high and low cases. As an example, if your priority is to achieve a target level of earnings, how would different paces of macroeconomic growth affect the outcome? What if your cost transformation initiative fails to deliver? What if your new product launch is far more successful than you anticipated?

Rank your risks according to likelihood and severity. For the highest risks, you should have contingency plans that can spring into place as needed. This is the "what's next" that follows "what if." These include business continuity plans, convening war rooms for cyberattacks, and having backups for your primary suppliers in case they go offline. Other options could include taking a minority stake in or buying out startups that pose a medium- to long-term threat, or making plans to quickly scale up delivery capacity when needed.

Beyond contingency options, you can decide to cultivate new foundational capabilities, like implementing MOVE in your personal leadership or growing your organization's capacity for innovation or operational excellence, which generate new options and can positively affect the likelihood of achieving your external priorities.

This kind of future-looking options generation helps you make the most of favorable developments and contain the impact of unfavorable developments. Mapping it on the distribution shows how these actions reduce risk, shifting the expected outcome of your external priority (eEP in figure 6-1) to the right, and narrowing the range of possible outcomes.

Remember Cheryl from chapter 3, the CEO of a consumer packaged goods company whose growth plan was interrupted by the pandemic? She decided to invest heavily in scenario and contingency planning. It changed the leadership team, a team that was used to living quarter to quarter.

FIGURE 6-1

Shifting the outcome of external priority

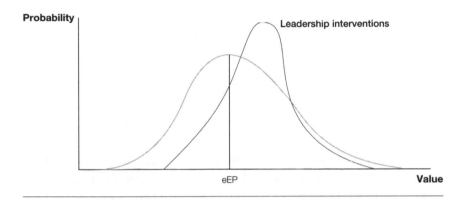

"The team is increasingly comfortable thinking beyond three months and looking three years out," she said. "In fact, we've gamed out several different scenarios, both positive and negative, and developed plans for them if they play out. A major part of this involves making more of our cost base variable than fixed. And after being burned by the pandemic, we are examining more extreme scenarios than we have in the past."

Cheryl was determined to be more on the front foot when the next surprise rattled the company. "I want us to be in a position to pivot seamlessly as needed from offense to defense and back again."

Pay Special Attention to Worst-Case and Best-Case Outcomes

Some downside risks are so severe that you can't survive them. In those cases, create options to contain your vulnerability. For example, if a single customer accounts for 30 percent of your total revenue, you may need to have a diversification policy in place to focus more resources on growing other customers and perhaps even limit how much new business you land with heavily concentrated relationships. Similarly, if you are intolerant of market volatility, you will want to put asset allocation guidelines in place when investing in equities, fixed income, and alternative investments. Or if you place a premium on consistent, steady growth in revenue, then you may delay entering a frontier geographic market that has wild swings in GDP growth.

On the plus side, paying attention to the best imaginable case helps you to dream big. And once you do so, you can begin to think about what your first steps might be to get on a path to a 10x outcome. (We'll explore those later.)

• • •

You can start to see how being mindfully alert leads to good options generation. If you're not mindfully alert, you won't have the space or ability to break free from your instinctual reactions to situations, from your subconscious playbook.

But once you can be aware and live in that space, you will find you're generating many good options for how you can respond to external challenges. You'll be planning for the longer term and be more prepared for sudden shocks and shifts. Remember, willpower is good, but waypower is key. Where there's a will, there should be at least four ways.

Summary

- You can expand your leadership repertoire by creating waypower for yourself.

- Waypower comes from generating at least four options to achieve each of your external priorities, so that you don't always have to rely on your default, instinctual approach to win.

- Use the Four Stances to come up with a comprehensive list of approaches for tackling your priority. For example, you could be strategic or tactical; move fast, medium, or slow; or make big, medium, or small moves.

- Scan your list and see which option you are instinctively drawn to—this will be your default option.

- Check if your default could work for the situation you are facing. If it could, great, but still identify three additional options. If your default isn't viable, come up with four new options.

- Rank the attractiveness of the options.

- In highly uncertain environments, look at high, low, best-case, and worst-case possibilities. Based on these, expand your set of options even further by doing robust scenario and contingency planning to give you more ways to act when reality turns out not to track your base-case expectations.

7

Be Who You Want to Be

Physical qualities such as strength and agility are highly trainable;
mental qualities such as joy and calmness are also highly trainable.

—**Chade-Meng Tan**

You've learned how to generate options for the first dimension of
leadership when the stakes are high. Now we explore doing it for
the second dimension—being the person you want and need to be.
While these goals are less tangible, we'll guide you in to how to develop
options to grow yourself. We think of this as your internal development
plan.

• • •

Gwen was truly shaken. Her 360-degree report was eviscerating. She
read some bits aloud to Carol: "Arrogant and contemptuous? I have
sacrificed everything for this team, and we had a successful turnaround.
We've met our numbers for the first time in five quarters! And yes, I'm
a bit intense when people aren't doing their best or trying even half as
hard as I am."

True, Carol thought. Gwen's biting remarks had become urban legend.
One of her reports drummed up the courage to confront her, telling her
that he felt she was a bad listener. She snapped back, "I'm not a bad listener. You're boring." Another said, "She comes down the hall and people
dive back into their offices."

HR had given up. When they approached Gwen, she showed no interest in "discussing my shortcomings."

Carol had been called in and did not expect to meet a diminutive and perfectly coiffed executive with a ready smile. To start the coaching process, instead of adding to the cascade of negative feedback Gwen had received, Carol asked, "If you could be the leader that you most wanted to be, what would it look like?" Note, she began with the ten-out-of-ten question. This is a good default when beginning a coaching session, especially with a tricky leader.

"Well, I don't want to lose my edginess and drive, but I don't want to blow people out of the water either."

"I don't think people are asking you to lose those parts of yourself, but they do want you to be in control of them. Putting that to the side for now, who do you want to be? What kind of leader and what kind of person?" Carol knew working on the second dimension of leadership would be most important for Gwen. She didn't just need to become mindfully alert to this part of herself; she needed options for better ways to move forward.

"I just want to be a better person," Gwen said.

Options to Find Options

There are many paths to becoming your best self. To create an internal development plan, first get clarity on who you want to be. You took time in chapter 4 to prioritize which inner challenges are most important, and then focused on what you'd like to develop in yourself. Now identify a plan that matches your current capacity and motivation in order to access a "flow" state, of optimal experience.[1] In essence, create a smart strategy for yourself. Options that are too small will be boring and bring only tiny change at best. Options that are too big will overwhelm you and make it hard to develop your internal priorities.

Use the Ten-Out-of-Ten Approach and the Five Cs that we first explained in chapter 2 to start implementing your plan. With practice you can develop each of the Five Cs as part of your inner development plan:

> Calm: Work on meditative breathing and staying in the moment to put your challenge into perspective.

> Clear: Practice concentration exercises and note what tilts you to confusion.

Curious: Ask one more question than you normally would. Then ask another. Notice what others are asking.

Compassionate: Describe to yourself, what is the other person's point of view? Their story might feel strange to you, but it makes sense to them. Figure out their why.

Courageous: Make one more point than you would naturally, one more step.

However, be aware of overusing any one of the Cs in an overly self-protective or defensive way. You can be too calm (passive), too clear (laser focused but missing emotions or intuition), too curious (asking, absorbing but not deciding), too compassionate (losing your story when you hear another's), or too courageous (foolhardy or taking on unrealistic risks). You can also use the exercise described in chapter 2 to simply rate yourself on where you stand on each of the Five Cs and notice which may have fallen too low.

When you do go into action mode, measure progress and keep yourself accountable. This doesn't need to be hard accounting. You can even do it with the most intangible goals. For example, you can measure progress with questions like "Did I do my best to be authentic?" or "Did I do my best to live my values?"[2]

Finally, you need to factor in failure. Even if you've picked the appropriate-size goal, you won't be successful all the time. Any innovative process requires you to develop your plan, experiment, and then iterate as certain things work and others do not. Once you've been successful in one area, identify the next to work on.

Gwen Elaborates on Her Goals

"I want to be a better person. I still want to drive results, but also leave people feeling good about themselves. I'd like to be an empowering mentor and coach and have a more positive mindset," she said.

The starting point of change is to identify and own a need to change. Gwen had done this. Now she needed to translate the intention into something tangible and actionable.

"What else does being a better person mean to you?" Carol asked.

"Not hurting people and not having them see me as arrogant and dismissive."

As they went over the Four Stances, Gwen knew her default was lean in, and in certain situations she could lean back. Leaning with was not her forte, to say the least, though she did say there were situations outside work where she felt she could lean with. "I'm much better with my family, we have a lot of fun together. And I'm pretty good with my community advocacy work with women. They see me as an inspiration and advocate and mentor."

"Sounds like you have a lot of capacity but you haven't brought that part of you to work."

"There isn't the pressure to perform there—at work it's do or die." Gwen's intensity escalated just talking about work. "I always have to be the driver; my team isn't taking ownership and pushing the ball forward, and it feels like it's all on my shoulders. I'm sick of it!"

"I can see how it gets to you. Let's walk through what actually happens. Can you give me an example of what you just talked about?"

Gwen described a recent incident when she'd held in her frustration but finally snapped at a team member. "I told him that, yet again, he didn't perform up to standard. I just couldn't stop myself. Then I said he should have known what to do, it's basic stuff, and I was sick and tired of picking up the balls he dropped." As Gwen related all this, she looked at the floor. "Not my finest moment."

Many leaders are caught in this exact cycle, unable to access or work on their internal priorities. Under high-stakes and high pressure they can find themselves just leaning in harder and harder, exacerbating the problem.

"How often does this happen?" Carol asked.

"Honestly," Gwen said, "it happens multiple times a day."

Developing any kind of internal strength requires that you find the right level of difficulty to start. From what she'd seen so far, Carol knew they had to start small with creating options for Gwen. Carol suggested they begin with "mini activations" and work up from there. Gwen was drawn to this approach, so they explored how to raise herself a point on regulating her activations over the next few weeks.

Gwen's initial internal goal was vague: be a better person. We needed to define that more specifically if we were to generate options for reaching her goals. It wasn't that Gwen didn't understand or believe in the Four Stances; she even recounted times she had used them in other parts of her life. She just couldn't access them when it came to work, where she felt tremendous pressure. Gwen would need significant amounts of self-regulation to become someone who could lean with, which would help her lean in more skillfully.

Carol and Gwen went over the Five Cs as a path in. Gwen assessed their relevance and decided her best option was to work on calm. They built a plan that included diaphragmatic breathing for moments when she noticed a mini activation. This would help neutralize Gwen's physiological fight reflex by reducing the cortisone that rushed through her system.[3] She also decided to restart yoga to be in more control of her stress levels.

Keeping the development plan conscious is crucial. Gwen was taken aback when Carol suggested journaling every hour. Seeing Gwen's expression, she smiled and said, "Relax, it's not that bad. Just some numbers. Jot down how many times you were activated that hour and give yourself a plus or a minus score if you did your best to manage it." Notice that Carol suggested Gwen rate herself on whether she did her best, not if she *succeeded* in being calm or not.[4] That would come later.

Through this process, Gwen was able to manage her activation level. As she described it, "I used to go into the red zone; now I go into red alert and deactivate." This was one of those small wins in her internal challenge to be able to lean with. She could now create other options for increasing her internal capacity to "be a better person."

Ten-Out-of-Ten Approach: Working on Your Inner Development Plan

Over the next few weeks Gwen developed a short list of other options for her internal challenges beyond being calm, which included being less judgmental, increasing confidence in others, having compassion, and having a growth mindset. When she looked these over, she felt like being less judgmental was a good one to work on because it would unlock her capacity to be successful with the others.

To work on being less judgmental, we used the Ten-Out-of-Ten Approach. Here is a condensed version of how that went, which can help inform how you use this method when generating your own internal options.

First, Carol asked, "Why does being less judgmental matter to you?"

Gwen listed two reasons. "I'll be more effective. I'll be a better leader of my team." Carol noticed these were extrinsic motivations—success at work. She pressed on, looking for intrinsic motivations, and eventually Gwen offered some. "I'll create a better atmosphere at work, and people will feel better around me and at work. We'll have better team dynamics." And for the first time it occurred to her: "I'll feel better, too, about myself and about them."

Then Carol asked, "What would a ten out of ten of you not being judgmental look like?"

"I would be calmer. I wouldn't get triggered when someone didn't meet my expectations. I'd give them a second chance. I wouldn't jump to the conclusion that they weren't trying. I'd try to see where they are coming from and step into being curious about what help or resources they needed to succeed. They would be less afraid of me. We would develop mutual trust, and there would be a more relaxed and positive energy in the team. I'd know more about their private lives."

They continued to walk through the process. Gwen's homework was to notice and name when she was being judgmental. As we've said, you first have to truly see it and name what you want to do, then practice your options. In the next session, Carol asked, "How have you been doing? On a scale of one to ten, where would you say you are on not being judgmental?"

"I think I'd give myself a four."

Now the key question to get Gwen to focus on positive things she's done: "What are you doing right that you're not a three or a three and a half?"

"I am able to think through what they might need to succeed. Now that I'm calmer, I'm not snapping as much. I've been telling them I'm working on myself, and I've apologized when I'm harsh. I can sometimes see things from their point of view. I'm asking more questions. I've been listening better. When I catch myself being judgmental, I'm trying to reverse my focus to what they've done right. I am asking them about their weekends."

This was a very good list for someone who knew they had so much work to do; Gwen could visualize positive steps she'd already taken. "So, what can you do to raise yourself half a point?" Carol asked.

"When we meet as a team, I can make sure not to interrupt them. When I see something that makes me think they are off base, I can pause and be open to the fact that there may be more to the story than meets the eye. I've been postponing having a team offsite; I think I will follow through with it." Gwen ended with: "I'll keep asking myself the question we talked about—'Who do I want to be right now?' If I could be more proactive and less reactive with them, that would probably help a lot."

Notice how many options she was able to generate to become less judgmental through this exercise. And, as we've observed often happens, the process of identifying those options pointed to the next internal challenge to work on. A few sessions later, Gwen began exploring how she could be more open and vulnerable with the team. At the next team offsite, her reports were stunned as she shared the story of her coaching, her understanding of how much she needed to change, and how sorry she was for hurting them in the past. The team is still healing, but they share more trust and people are no longer avoiding Gwen.

A Different Stance on Stances: Four Ways to Work on Your Challenge

Gwen was creating options for improving her internal capacities in the hope of learning to overcome her reflex to always lean in, and hard. She wanted to learn to lean with. At the same time, the Four Stances can be used within this process to identify different ways to approach how you develop the quality you want to work on.

To illustrate, let's pick a very different kind of goal. Imagine you need to increase your gravitas and you were generating options to achieve this. You could lean in, taking an active, hands-on approach. You might sign up to make a presentation at the next all-hands meetings, putting yourself out there and getting feedback on how it went.

A lean-back approach creates different options. You could observe, even study, people known to carry themselves with gravitas. You might start with some self-help books or read biographies of those who overcame challenges similar to your own. You might collect data on how you come across to assess what specific behaviors will help you achieve your goal.

A lean-with approach could lead you to interview others who have developed their gravitas. You might join a group whose members are working on similar challenges. Inspiration to develop might come from knowing how your gravitas could help you be a better advocate for your team.

If you don't lean, you might simply reflect on the issue, perhaps assigning yourself a writing exercise where you think about gravitas and jot down whatever comes to mind. You might be led to work on values that you could draw on to help unlock your ability to be a more active but grounded presence.

Building Bridges from Your Strengths

In many ways, James was the opposite of Gwen.

He dreaded the fact that a conversation scheduled for later that day might end with him having to fire one of his reports. "I'm not ready for this," he told us.

His boss and peers all joined in to "encourage" him with advice like, "You need to be assertive" or "Claim your space." When he heard this, he felt whatever energy he had drain away. "There is no way I can do that," he told Carol.

"That's because those options are just the wrong ones for you," she replied.

James perked up at this. Carol knew that the advice he was getting was coming from people whose strengths were different from James's. In fact, they were giving him advice that played right into his internal weaknesses: lack of comfort with assertiveness and power. Fortunately, there was another category of options to draw on, ones based on his natural strengths rather than shoring up his weaknesses.

Carol had developed an exercise called the strengths bridge.[5] First, we identify a leader's top strengths. In James's case, they were love of learning, fairness, and optimism.[6] These three qualities were resources he could use to help create options for approaching this conversation.

"Think of having that tough conversation as being on the other side of a ravine," Carol said. "You are on this side, and getting over the gap to the other side feels impossible. You need a bridge to cross over it. Now, you've already figured out that the two options you heard aren't going to do it."

"I'd fail badly," James sighed.

"So, let's create more bridges. If you were to think of this conversation as an opportunity to use your strength of love of learning in a new way, what would that be like for you?"

"That's a good question. So instead of doing the power thing, I could step into a teaching headset and frame it as lessons he needs to learn?" James kept talking with a new paradigm in his head—how he could think of the conversation as a chance to shine a light into the issue. And he was off and running.

That option clicked quickly, but he also thought through how to use his fairness in a new way. After all, it was only fair that his report knew the truth of what people were saying about him. Then James's optimism could kick in as he could help his team member see how things could change for the better.

By harnessing these three strengths, James found three new options. He felt more empowered to have the conversation in a way that felt right to him. He wasn't into being assertive or using power, so those suggestions didn't help. Performing out of alignment with your strengths and values is draining and can make you feel de-skilled or lost. Choosing options that instead are in alignment with your core self can allow you to find your own path forward, one that taps into your sense of meaning and purpose.

Summary

Finding and working on your internal challenges require you to generate options for continuing your personal growth to be a more effective leader. You can do this through identifying and working on an internal development plan.

- Notice when you are, and are not, able to access the inner qualities you'd like to develop.

- Do a step-by-step analysis of what either helped or hurt the outcome. You can see things a bit more clearly if instead of going through from the beginning you start at the end point and work your way backward to identify each decision point where you could have made a different choice.

- Don't leap into action; find the best next steps first.

- When you have a specific quality to work on, try daily or hourly journaling where you simply put down one number to note how many times you were faced with your internal challenge. Mark a + or – for each time period, based on whether you did your best with the challenge.

- Use the Ten-Out-of-Ten Approach as a template for creating your inner development plan.

- Use the Four Stances—and use them in a new way, to identify different ways to work on your challenge.

- Use the strengths bridge exercise—which matches the strengths you identified in chapter 4 to the challenge you have before you—rather than trying options that don't match your internal strengths.

- On this journey, balance compassion and challenge as you work on developing yourself.

8

Unlock Talent around You

A good leader gets great results from great people. A great leader gets great results from ordinary people.

—Charles O'Reilly, Stanford Graduate School of Business

Great leaders tailor how they connect to and unlock skills and followership in their stakeholders. It's not easy, or everyone would be a great leader. Remember that in the survey where one thousand CEOs were asked about the most frequent feedback they received, the number one response was that they needed to work on how they related to others.[1] Only 46 percent said they were fully aligned with their executive team, and fewer said they were with their board. Thus, a core development goal for most leaders is to learn to relate authentically and skillfully, to inspire people and lift performance.

To do this you have to be flexible, agile, and willing to meet people where they are—not where you want them to be, and not where you think they will be. You need many options for any given interpersonal challenge. Here's how you generate them.

Know the Many Pathways to Connecting with Others

"No one can do the job as well as Jack, but he is a universe of perfectionism and pain for others," the CEO told Carol and David when they were called in to help prevent another team disaster.

In our first meeting with Jack, we explored the three dimensions of leadership and the Four Stances. Jack said, "I'm not a political beast. I practice humility and understanding, but there is no accountability here. We have to catch up. When I know something and the team thinks differently, I'm like, 'Hey, we have a lot to do, can we just move on?'"

"What's a win for you?" David asked.

Predictably, Jack pointed to accountability and beating the competition.

"What about on the leadership front?" David asked.

"I don't know, I've not really thought about that."

"What's the argument for challenging yourself to start thinking about it?" Carol asked.

Jack reflected. "I had one fiasco a while back. The guy who wanted my job wound up reporting to me. To prove myself, I thought, *It's time to earn my stripes by getting a lot done fast.* I was 100 percent wrong and alienated the team for three months. I should have been listening more." He was right; he'd steamrolled his direct reports by leaning in too much.

David pressed forward as it became clear Jack was taking the conversation seriously. "What's in your toolbox? If you were a ten out of ten on being a good leader, where would you start?"

"That's easy—start with the team, get people in the right roles, stay out of the way."

"But what would you be doing differently?" Carol asked.

After a long moment he replied, "I haven't given it any thought. I see where you're going. I should be more flexible. But to be honest, is the squeeze worth the juice?"

"How about giving yourself some space to figure that out?"

"I will, but when people don't think the way I do, it goes sideways, and I move on and don't care."

David suggested Jack start with just one direct report: over the next two weeks, he should try changing that relationship. Jack was up for it and decided to try leaning with more.

What Carol and David had done was help Jack find a new option besides leaning in. In our next meeting he shared his realization: "I've spent so much time preparing for the content part of meetings. I've never prepared for the people part."

When he worked on listening more and issuing fewer directives, people were more engaged.

"It works when I remember, but it's too easy to forget when I get triggered." To handle that, Jack created a new goal to "ask a question versus blow a fuse" when he could feel himself about to derail.

With his newfound insight, he found that even more options opened up. He slowed his pace, acknowledged others' strengths, and sanded down the edge in his tone of voice. At the outset of a meeting, he'd force himself to think, *What's my intention?* and set his phone to buzz a couple of times during the meeting to remember.

Jack started with one interpersonal option and only one stance: lean in to drive people forward. Leaning with helped people to feel included, and with success it opened the way for him to develop even more options.

Waypower in Action: Discern in Real Time Which Stance Is Needed

Your stance needs to match the needs of the people you are with. In any interaction you should have all of the Four Stances available to you. That means you'll start with four options.

A stance isn't fixed; sometimes it varies moment to moment, and you need to be ready. Let's say your team is setting a goal. You have many options for how to get them to perform, but different situations will call for different stances, and you'll have to reset your options often. One team may do best if you don't lean to create a space for their blue-sky thinking. Later, they may need grounding, so you lean back to help them sum up and synthesize their thinking. To make the shift to execution, leaning in can get them energized, and leaning with can help them feel safe by knowing you'll support them if they fail.

You need to be able to develop these options for interpersonal challenges with people who aren't on your team—customers, say, or other stakeholders you need to support your cause, buy your product, support your acquisition, or even decide to hire you.

Omi-san, a senior partner in a professional services firm, faced four stone-faced figures across the table. He'd just quoted them the price for a proposed consulting project. The air was sucked out of the room. Let's look as he deftly deploys all of the Four Stances in real time with his prospective customer.

Leaning in, he said, "This is what it takes to be successful at scale." His eyes flicked to the left as he saw his challenge land well with one person, who sat up a bit straighter and gave a short nod. The others were unmoved.

Leaning back, he commented, "Our studies reliably show that the project will pay for itself in two and a half years." Another one of the four looked more engaged, but two still looked blank.

Leaning with, he suggested, "If we all pull together, this will transform the culture and make this organization the best place to work in the business." Nothing. The two holdouts kept silent.

Not leaning, he decided simply to wait a moment and see what would happen. The two whom he hadn't reached looked down and seemed anxious. At that moment an idea sparked and he leaned with again. With a warm voice tone he asked, "Who is going to make the final decision?"

"Our chief financial officer, and she won't be happy with us," one of the two said.

Omi-san smiled. "Then let me help you find a way to make an argument that will make her happy." The tension ebbed as all five got on the same page and started working together.

It seems like magic here, but Omi-san used his practice and skill with the MOVE framework to be so agile. We've seen this kind of scenario play out with less-agile leaders. The minute they see resistance, they lean in harder, or they lean with too aggressively. Creating options for knowing which stance is best requires keen observing skills, like Omi-san's. Remember the Platinum Rule to treat others as they would want to be treated. Notice nonverbal signals, stony eyes, or physical tension. Listen closely to what people are saying; don't discount concerns that seem minimal to you. Be courageous enough to let silence happen.

Before you can learn the nuances of how to deploy each stance, you first need to develop a sense of which stance to choose. Table 8-1 provides a starting point for developing those observation skills. As you read through it, think of how you could choose different options when working with others.

Building Your Options to Call on All Four Stances

Let's push up our sleeves now and build more options to excel at applying the Four Stances. As we go through each stance, first consider these steps to assess your starting point.

TABLE 8-1

Interpersonal challenges: Generating and choosing options

	When to use it	When not to use it
Lean in	When people seem rudderless and passive, it may help them organize themselves and focus their efforts. You want to energize them but not trigger fear. When change is highly rapid and chaotic. When the world turns upside down, being directive can be stabilizing.	When you notice that people quiet down when you enter the room. When you notice that your questions are met with silence. When you notice that people aren't interrupting you or offering counter opinions. Chances are you need to downshift to a stance that is more supportive or that allows them time to think.
Lean back	When people need to feel informed. When emotions are running high and more data will help ground and calm the team down. When you are working with introverts who respond better to data than inspirational rhetoric.	When the team has gotten to an asymptote and more input doesn't lead to more knowledge. When people seem over-whelmed with data and it is not leading to clear thinking.
Lean with	When morale is low. When your people are extroverts and connection is the currency of choice. When you notice how a smile or an affirming remark energizes someone.	When you notice that someone needs space to think. When a team is operating well on their own skill and expertise and doesn't need support. When people are wanting to feel independent.
Don't lean	When you sense the team needs to work something out on their own, your presence may intrude or slow their growth. When the team is frenetic and needs a break, you can help them center by calling time-out, injecting calm, and slowing things down.	When the team needs to step into planning or action mode. When a crisis hits and people are looking to you for guidance.

- Rank-order how comfortable you are in each stance when working with others.

- What percentage of the time are you in each one in a team setting?

- Do you have one preferred stance in all situations?

- Do you have a default stance, and can you shift if the occasion calls for it?

- Which stance do you most need to develop to generate more options in interpersonal situations?

We'll go through each stance and share variations in how to tailor it to meet the demands of the moment. For each, we'll give a detailed description and discuss how you can adjust the intensity level, the emotional tone, and pull on the Five Cs and your strengths. Then we'll offer suggestions to either dial up or dial down your use of each stance.

You've decided to lean in—what are your options?

When you lean in, you are highly engaged, often intense, and action-oriented. Here are a few options for how to lean in:

deciding	doing	directing
galvanizing	inspiring	creating
guiding	challenging	confronting

Intensity: Calibrate the degree to which you lean in, depending on context. For example, you could lean in with the force of an Olympic shot-putter. Or you could lean in with the grace of a dancer.

Emotions: The tone you choose for how you lean in informs your impact. You can lean in with excitement and optimism, or with calm, or with aggression.

The Five Cs: There are many ways to "be"—which options can you choose? You can lean in while being calm, clear, curious, compassionate, and courageous, or lean in while being agitated, confused, close-minded, critical, or fear-driven and ferocious.

Strengths: You can lean in with love of learning, wisdom, creativity, or any of your character strengths or values, as well as any strengths you have chosen to work on as part of your inner demands.

If you need to lean in more often: Use one of your strengths in a new way. For example, if curiosity is a strength, push yourself to ask one more question of your team than normal to keep them engaged.

Imagine that a colleague made a snide remark during your presentation. Normally you may not default to lean in; you might privately stew about it or just try to let it go. But leaning in may be a good way to cut this behavior off at the pass. Once you decide you want to lean in, you have options for how to do it. You could ask a question: "I noticed you had a concern with my presentation. Is there anything I can do to address it?" You could lean in a little more forcefully: "I didn't feel comfortable with your tone. Please don't do that again, especially in public." Or you can lean in even harder: "If you have a problem with me, talk to me, don't go sideways." Or: "Don't do that again—do you not realize how that hurts your brand more than mine?"

Any one of these could be a valid approach, depending on the context. More forceful leaning in should be reserved for the most piquant situations. The key is to build up your capacity to create these options for yourself *before* you react in your default way.

If you don't lean in enough, answer these questions as a way to name the behaviors you want to develop for your interpersonal challenges:

> If you were great at leaning in, what kinds of things would you be doing?
>
> How are you doing now?
>
> What are you doing right?
>
> What are a few things you could do to improve?

If lean in is a default and you need to dial it down: Overreliance on one stance reduces your capacity to generate more options. If you're hearing that you are too action-oriented, tend to talk too much, don't listen well, are impatient with others, or are experienced as aggressive, step back.

You can track your word count to make sure you are not speaking too much. Listen with the goal of understanding, consciously catching yourself when you realize you're thinking about how to respond when someone is talking rather than listening carefully. After someone has stopped speaking, take two breaths before you reply. Impatience can be detected by others, and it shuts them down. Moderating your tone of voice and downshifting your energy can help you get out of this stance.

You've decided to lean back—what are your options?

When you lean back, you tend to be objective and data-driven. Here are options for how to lean back:

analyzing	assessing	wanting data
pulling back	delaying/avoiding	detaching
inquiring	studying	perspective
worried	cautious	fearful

Intensity: Watch for the line between analysis/inquiry and over-analysis/too much scrutiny. Cross it and you create stress for people. If you keep collecting more and more information, you can confuse and dishearten others. There are ways to review facts, synthesize them with perspective and wisdom, and create a learning environment.

Emotions: You can emanate a settled energy, as pilots do during the safety check before takeoff or when calmly informing passengers about a possible incident without creating panic. Lean-back options you would want to avoid are those where you interact from a place of anxiety, fear, or risk avoidance, where you can be seen as dithering or having analysis paralysis.

The Five Cs: These offer you five options for how to help yourself relate well under pressure. If you sense yourself avoiding a tough conversation, you can choose which inner resource to harness and deploy. If stepping into courage isn't natural, but is needed for this interaction, remind yourself of when you've done this well—pull on that memory. Note that lean-back courage looks different from lean-in courage, as it is often based on being calm, clear, and curious.

Strengths: Generating options within this stance derives from choosing which strengths you would like to harness. These can be from your top strengths or those you use less often. Leaning back when creativity is your top strength would likely involve sharing novel ways to approach an issue. In contrast, someone strong in prudence would easily identify the risks and ramifications of a course of action.

If you need to lean back more often: Downshift your energy, and pull on being clear and calm to create a moment of space. Modulate your action orientation by forcing yourself to ask more questions before springing into action. Slow down to connect the dots for others, even if you've already connected them for yourself, as quick thinking may come easily to you but leaves others in the dust.

If lean back is a default and you need to dial it down: Collect some data on yourself. Scan through the past week to reflect on the number of conversations you avoided or times you didn't say what you thought. In retrospect, would a different choice have served your team or your organization better? Look through the list of lean-in or lean-with behaviors. Which can you develop to offset your propensity for objective analysis?

Being overly objective can blind you to other sources of data, including subjective experience, hunches, or emotion-based data. One of our leaders ignored their "irrational" feeling that a direct report was dangerous. He needed to deliver some tough feedback. When he did, the report became threatening and explosive and stormed out. The irrational feeling turned out to be quite instructive.

Pull on your ability to be calm to manage the anxiety of moving too quickly. Instead of holding back on speaking up or making and sharing a decision, ask yourself what the benefits could be of leaning in or leaning with versus staying back.

Observe the impact of your lean-back stance. Is your team engaged, with bright eyes of alertness? Are they drowning in data? You may win minds with analysis, but you can lose hearts. People don't work through the night for an idea, but they will for an inspiring, caring leader.

You've decided to lean with—what are your options?

When you lean with, you are nurturing and supportive and people feel connected to you. Leaning with includes showing benevolence and social intelligence.

Here are several ways of relating associated with leaning with:

connecting	compassion	supporting
inclusion	collaborating	encouraging
coaching	consulting	rescuing

Intensity: Leaning with can create a warm and psychologically safe team. Your belief in others can create a Pygmalion effect.[2] Many studies have shown that when a teacher or leader believes positive things about another, they tend to rise to the occasion. As a leader, reasonable high expectations paired with belief in the other's potential leads to improved performance. Some prefer this interpersonal intensity; others find it overwhelming. Developing an overall sense of benevolence and kindness is more effective with some, and less compelling for others.

Emotions: Hundreds of research studies show that experiencing positive emotion at work increases business outcomes.[3] It builds trust and has been shown to reduce race bias.

The Five Cs: Harnessing the Five Cs can help you match your style of caring to what people need. Some thrive when caring is paired with calm, others when it's connected with clarity or curiosity and compassion. Courage comes from the French word *coeur*, meaning heart. Caring and courage help others take risks and harness bravery.

Strengths: Factor in the strengths and default stance of the person or people you are with when deciding how to lean with. You'd connect differently with someone who defaults to leaning back— possibly drawing on curiosity—than someone with gentler strengths of temperance or humility who tends to not lean, in which case you might draw on compassion.

If you need to lean with more often: Some leaders can have a great deal of difficulty leaning with, because they are "all business." Driving results, they believe, is what makes them a good leader. Feeling empathy and compassion for the team is either superfluous or is even seen as a weak or ineffective strategy. If you personally don't need affirmation, or even find it patronizing, you may miss that others find it necessary. Remember the Platinum Rule: Treat others as *they* need to be treated, not how you want to be treated. Scan through the past week to look for opportunities where emanating warmth or belief might have been useful.

High-quality relationships at work are a powerful predictor of high performance. One organization we know measured support and performance.[4] Shockingly, one kind and supportive interaction with a boss, just one time a month, increased engagement. A little goes a long way.

If lean with is a default and you need to dial it down: Note that this stance can also cause you to avoid tough conversations or to accept poor performance because you "care." You should watch for when your desire to help becomes counterproductive.

Support is different from protection. Scan the past week and think about how many times you overlooked a performance issue because you feared it would hurt the other person's feelings. Did you praise your team when you should have been pushing for something more, because you feared how they might react? As a leader it can be painful to watch someone struggle to find their feet, but should you help? When a baby chick tries desperately to break open its shell, you can't help it. If you do, it will die. The thrashing around inside the shell is how it strengthens its leg muscles. Without the struggle, it won't be able to walk to get food.

You've decided to not lean—what are your options?

When you don't lean, you are being reflective, stepping into a meditative and open awareness. Options include:

being mindful	contemplating	visualizing
observing	mulling	visioning
centered	nonreactive	receptive
creative	attuned	dreaming

Without doubt, this is the toughest mode for most of the leaders we coach—leaders who are brilliant at winning, solving complex issues, and rallying the troops. However, while you may not call on this mode often, it needs to be an option in your repertoire. When in the fray of fast decision-making, the ability to get your team to pause and settle down can help you avoid expensive mistakes.

Intensity: Don't lean can be a state of inner concentration where you screen out the world to find an answer to a serious business problem. Or it could be seconds of pausing to center and absorb what is going on around you, so you can create a space to decide what to do next. Many achieve this state when running, meditating, or just sitting in nature and not directly thinking about the problem. Some have had these don't-lean eureka moments in the shower when the answer to the challenge hits them, fully formed, seemingly out of the blue.

Emotions: A don't-lean stance can be calm and pleasant, like a reverie or a sense of oneness with the world. However, you can be driven into that stance by fear, when a shock causes you to tune out rather than experience something disturbing.

The Five Cs: When members of your team are agitated, you can use this stance to create calm. Being clear and curious can help bring your team to a more reflective space. Accessing compassion by tuning into what your team needs or finding the courage to stop the moving train are ways to access this more receptive mode.

Strengths: Don't-lean strengths tend to be those that temper our gut reactions. When you need to be less activated in the way you are connecting, pull on self-regulation, forgiveness, temperance, humility or prudence to help get you out of your reflexive need to act now.

If you need to not lean more often: You've heard the phrase "Don't just sit there, do something." Reverse it: "Don't just do something, sit there." This mindset allows you to be attuned to subtle or even subliminal information and access inductive and intuitive thinking, where solutions suddenly emerge.

If don't lean is a default and you need to dial it down: It's not that common that this is a default stance, but some people are overreliant on it in high-stakes situations. They shut down under threat. That leads to errors of omission. Scan your calendar and consider if there were times when you did not respond to others or tuned out their concerns because they might have raised your stress level. Have you actively ignored a situation, like a difficult team dynamic, in hopes the problem would somehow solve itself or others would solve it without your participation? If you are susceptible to this type of behavior, work hard to notice when it's happening, what it feels like, and what other stances you might take.

A dangerous leadership style related to this stance is being overly laissez-faire. While actively believing in your people to operate independently can be good, being passive and assuming they will sink or swim on their own is taking that stance too far. You may need to work around it by getting more support or by partnering with someone who has a different default style.

• • •

We can often develop agility in our stances far more than we realize.

Warren slouched over the gigantic boardroom table, exhausted by a team workshop that just ended but needing to debrief. "What the hell am I supposed to do?" he asked Carol. "I can't help that people are afraid of me." Or could he? He was a master at leaning in or back, but leaning with was foreign to him.

He scared people and didn't know why. Like several of Carol's leader clients, he had some superhuman strengths. He was brilliant and lightning-fast. Someone would send him an eighty-page white paper, and in twenty minutes they'd get it back, edited and with a critical analysis leading to substantial improvements. Why this was intimidating baffled Warren. (Carol's first—and very simple—intervention was a no-brainer: Don't send it back so quickly!)

Warren's journey needed to begin with self-awareness, with understanding his impact on others and mapping out what a lean-with stance might entail in interpersonal situations. The coaching uncovered that he listened well and he was respectful, or at least he thought that's how he came across. It also uncovered blind spots. He had no idea his silence and piercing gaze were unnerving. Without meaning to, he emanated signals that created fear in nearly everyone he worked with. Carol helped him practice emanating warmth and appreciation. Sending such positive signals increases interpersonal trust. That would help people feel safer and more connected to him.

"Here's the problem with that," Warren said. "How do I convey emotions I don't have? I don't really have feelings. My wife comments on that regularly." It was true, he was a walking, talking execution machine with a huge brain. He also flew jets and helicopters and was calm even when things went horribly wrong. Carol's first suggestion was for Warren and his wife to go to a museum and find paintings of portraits for them to guess what the person was feeling. "She will love that!" he said, and by the next session he went twice. "I'm not very good at this," he said.

But there's always a way. "Let's try an experiment," Carol suggested. "For two days, when your hand is on the doorknob and you are ready to open the door for your next meeting, stop. Make yourself think through three things the person waiting for you has done well or that you respect. Hold it in your mind and focus on it until you feel even a slight uptick of energy. The instant you do, open the door, smile, and put some enthusiasm in your hello. Let's see what happens."

He did, and it worked to a surprising degree. Being affirming jumpstarted his team. He kept it up, and over time people were not as tense when he walked into the room. They started talking more. Even though he wasn't very emotional, and it would never be his default stance, leaning with was now an option for him.

Summary

To be successful and form optimal relationships, you need to generate options for your interpersonal challenges—often those with your teams, but also with customers, bosses, even strangers. By having multiple options for working with others, you will become a leader who can bring out the best in yourself and in others.

- Keep in mind that relationship challenges are the most common derailers for top leaders, so developing options is a key leadership development task.

- Understand that you can not only develop options, but also develop them in real time and shift between them, even in just moments. To do this, become a keen observer of other people and yourself. Notice body language, tone of voice, eye contact, and reactions to what you do and how you move. Review situations that went wrong in the past and what cues you may have missed that could have altered the interaction.

- Learn when each stance is likely to help or hurt when dealing with other people. Refer to table 8-1 for examples of good and bad uses of each of the Four Stances in interpersonal situations.

- Rank-order your comfort level and percentage of use for each stance.

- Pick which one(s) you'd like to build and use more.

- Identify the style for each stance that fits you best:

  - What is your intensity with the stance?

  - What emotional tone will you take in this stance?

  - How can you use the Five Cs in this stance?

  - What are the strengths of this stance for your interpersonal relationships?

- Make small experiments to notice, and develop the stance that is most difficult for you.

- Review the tips on what you can do to either use a stance less, if you rely on it too much, or use it more, if you don't call on it when it may be helpful.

MOVE

Validate Your Vantage Point

9

Check If You're Right

Each era has the fatal hubris to believe that it has once and for all climbed to the top of the mountain and can see everything as it is, from the highest and most objective vantage point possible.

—Eric Metaxas

As a leader, you need to be adept at understanding your Vantage Point for any given challenge or priority so that you can do an internal check on it. Ask yourself as you look out at the landscape: Am I right? Am I seeing clearly, or is anything interfering with my point of view? What if I looked at this situation from someone else's point of view? True alignment means you fully appreciate others' perspectives and use them to challenge or validate your own. If you look around at your team or board, do you know what enhances or blurs their take on reality? Understanding your inner and interpersonal landscapes is a necessity.

When we explain our MOVE framework, Vantage Point (V) comes after being mindfully alert to your leadership priorities (M) and generating options (O). In real time, it's not always so linear. In fact, Vantage Point validation is part of a continuous practice woven through all of your choices. It may take seconds, or it may need thoughtful study. Many forces—external, internal, and interpersonal—can tilt our Vantage Point. Our default stances can also have an outsize impact on what we believe we see, as can our wishes and fears. It's our job to catch ourselves when this happens and know how to rebalance.

But this is a worthy pursuit, because having the right Vantage Point, and finding it quickly and accurately, is a competitive advantage.

Amanda's story captures the value of validating that you're looking at your challenge from the right Vantage Point, and the price you can pay if you don't. Amanda had been recruited to turn around a *Fortune 250* company and engaged Carol and David to coach her on pressing strategic issues and some trouble spots with her team.

"I'm under tremendous pressure by the board to grow faster," she started. "I feel railroaded to do something, and I've concluded that the only way forward is through a major acquisition. It's my obligation under securities law to tell you that I'm now making you insiders."

We both thought that her very first comment of being railroaded indicated she may still be activated. Although it wasn't the right time to point it out, we simultaneously made mental notes that the Five Cs would be useful at some point. Our sense for now was that Amanda was pushed into a lean-in stance, perhaps too quickly.

We both nodded. "Understood."

Amanda continued. "One large public player could be an excellent strategic fit. It would extend our geographic reach and add two adjacent business platforms. Valuations will be uncomfortably high, but I feel I have to engage with them to demonstrate progress. I'm instructing my CFO to run some models to assess the financial impact of acquiring that company."

At first glance, it seemed she had clarity on her first dimension, the external challenge. But initial projections showed the acquisition wouldn't be accretive to earnings per share for years, and she had upbraided her CFO, saying, "You're being way too conservative. You can do better." The revised model showed earnings per share to be accretive within eighteen months. We became concerned that she was leaning in too much and not metabolizing the pressure being put on her; this could be affecting her judgment.

Amanda met with Carol and David just as the revised projections hit her inbox, and she was elated as she shared the results.

David was concerned that the arithmetic just wouldn't add up. Selling prices were high in a frothy M&A market, and the stock price of Amanda's company traded at a discount compared with its competitors'. So, he decided to launch a gentle probe: "Your excitement about finding a way out of the growth trap is understandable. How much confidence do you have in the projections?"

Amanda's smile evaporated, and she inhaled sharply. "Damn, I'm doing it again—seeing things as I want them to be rather than as they are. I should know that by now." We noticed that, like many great leaders, Amanda was not reacting defensively to David's challenge. She was open to feedback and could pivot immediately to identify and correct her Vantage Point where it had clearly gone off course. She could lean back, put it in the larger context, and see how it had been a challenge to her in the past.

She continued, "Years ago, I got an incredible job offer when I was trying to leap out of a toxic organization. So, without due diligence or looking under the surface, I grabbed it and swung from a frying pan right into another fire." She chuckled, "You'd think I would learn my lesson. But I so badly wanted to talk myself into these projections. I need to take a harder look."

"Let's be even more realistic and think through some alternative growth plans together when we next meet," David said. His goal here was to invite her to lean back and reassess her goals, and perhaps find an entirely new Vantage Point for her overall challenge.

Later, Amanda went back to her CFO and said, "I need earnings per share, not 'yearnings per share.' I shouldn't have pushed you so hard. Wishful thinking is not a strategy, and this acquisition is not right for us."

Here we see her strengths in her internal and interpersonal dimensions of leadership. She could use her insights to slow down. She took accountability for having pressured her CFO and created the conditions for them to analyze and decide next steps together.

Carol opened our next session by saying, "You showed a lot of courage by facing reality and deciding to not proceed with this, given all the pressures you are facing."

"Some CEOs would go after an acquisition at any cost because of ego or just to demonstrate decisive action for its own sake," David added. Both of us were naming and supporting how she'd identified her inner challenge and met it.

"After sleeping on it, I think you're right that I need to create better options for growth," Amanda said. "I'm going to scour the earth for organic growth opportunities by setting up some 'tiger teams,' and I'm going to build up our corporate development capability so that we are better prepared for future acquisitions. I'm also not ruling out smaller acquisitions where we won't have to bet the company. And I'm hoping that eighteen to twenty-four months from now we can revisit making a large acquisition, because our stock multiple won't be this low forever."

Your Reality Check: Validate Your Vantage Point

The overarching question now: Are you seeing your challenges and opportunities clearly and properly? If not, then you risk hitting a bull's-eye with exquisite skill only to find out you aimed at the wrong target. Whatever your level of certainty of the way forward, it always pays off to pressure-test your Vantage Point. If you don't, worst-case scenarios can become reality.

Let's first put this in the context of the MOVE model and the 3-4-5 we've mentioned previously. We have many things to validate: First, you need to see each of the Three Dimensions of Leadership accurately and know if something you need to do or develop has eluded you. Second, you need to reflect about whether the options you've identified to move forward are based on reality. There are many forces that lead you to over- or underestimate your challenge and your capacity to meet them. Pulling on the Five Cs is a good foundation. We will help you develop an optimal Vantage Point by building up your self-awareness, understanding of others, and ability to read the external environment and then use that to your advantage.

Perfect Vision

An ideal, ten-out-of-ten Vantage Point has four qualities. We'll use a vision metaphor to describe those qualities. A good Vantage Point is:

- Clear, like 20/20 vision

- The right resolution, neither too detailed nor too vague

- The right scope, neither too wide nor too narrow

- The right level, neither too high up nor too close to the ground

Let's take each in turn.

Clear, like 20/20 vision

You're in trouble if your vision is blurry, distorted, or tinted, and as a result you misperceive what is being required of you or what the best path forward is. If you sense that you are not seeing clearly, there are ways to correct it. You can triangulate with someone to take in their perspective, letting theirs inform your own. You need a clear, unobstructed view of the future as well as of the present or past. For example, despite her history, Amanda initially kept her rose-colored glasses on when exploring her options to grow her company.

Check yourself: Are you being nearsighted and not seeing far enough ahead, or farsighted and not seeing what is under your nose? For example, the inspirational vision of one of our brilliant and farsighted colleagues blinded her to the fact that she had been a victim of extortion, right under her nose.

The right resolution, neither too detailed nor too vague

Think of this as density, how many pixels per square inch are necessary to validate what you see. Sometimes you need a high-definition view; other times a grainy image is sufficient. Think of all your priorities: do you need to pay scrupulous attention to the fine-grained detail for all of them?

Your attention budget is finite, so spend it wisely. Overspending on data collection and in-depth analysis can drain you and your team. Going off on tangents can also deplete resources.

However, if your Vantage Point is based on a grainy gut feeling, that can be deadly, too. Despite being urged to take measures to risk-proof her supply chain, one of our favorite leaders in retail took a very low-resolution Vantage Point on the situation. She had the basic details and felt, from her Vantage Point, things would be fine. When the supply chain experienced a major disruption, she was unprepared and paid the price.

The right scope, neither too wide nor too narrow

For some endeavors you need a wide view to scan the entire horizon, read the field, to know where best to invest your time. Others could require something narrower. For example, your Vantage Point on the best option to deal with a colleague's behavior probably doesn't require such a broad view. Creativity is best served by a wide-angle lens. A forensic analysis of your budget? A microscope may be best.

Another aspect of scope is having good peripheral vision. In this case we are referring to the capacity to let things that are far afield catch your attention, especially in uncertain and future-looking situations. Futurists and marketers often have this skill.

Jean Paul, the world-renowned marketer, was sent to Carol for coaching and said, "I know why I'm here. I'm too sensitive. We have to work on getting my skin thicker."

"No, we don't!" Carol replied, stunning him. "Your sensitivity may not serve you well with criticism, but it's your superpower. You have so many antennae that pick up tiny signals of where the world is heading, and you see it before anyone else does. You can't let that go."

His Vantage Point shifted quickly. "I get it, I have to manage my antennae. When someone criticizes me, a thousand of them start activating, and I should cut that down to maybe ten."

You need to be able to widen or narrow your focus at will. When assessing a goal or a course of action, ask yourself, "If I looked at this with the widest possible view, what would I see?" And then, "If I narrowed down, what would that add?"

The right level, neither too high up nor too close to the ground

Related to how much of the horizon you need to see is where you should be on the vertical axis. To read the business challenge you face, will a five-foot, five-thousand-foot, or fifty-thousand-foot view be the best Vantage Point? You should be able to zoom in or zoom out when assessing a challenge and deciding which Vantage Point is best.[1] You may be more comfortable with one over the other. For example, one physician we worked with managed a large group of clinics and was most comfortable zooming in, as when she was with patients. But that view was too low to help her manage a much bigger scope. This became an external challenge for her, to learn to be able to shift Vantage Points depending on the task, despite one being more comfortable than another.

Use these four parameters to pressure-test the validity of your Vantage Point. Each offers a way to help you step back and assess how well you are surveying the landscape around you, how well you are seeing your internal landscape, and how well you are relating to others. They can reveal flaws in the ways you are choosing to see situations, and others.

How to Check If Your Vantage Point Is Off

Your Vantage Point informs how to meet all the three-dimensional aspects of leadership and what options you have generated and chosen. How can you take stock of your choices?

First, reflect on when you've done well. When in the past have you seen things clearly, with the right resolution, breadth, and depth? Have you noticed times when you may have seen things more quickly and accurately than others? Of course, we all must get it wrong some of the time. Hopefully, you don't keep making the same mistakes; it's better to make new ones.

When you apply a Vantage Point to internal, external, or interpersonal priorities, ask yourself:

- Are you exaggerating the demands on your leadership?

- Are you minimizing or discounting a challenge or opportunity?

- Have you just gotten it wrong?

- You may be correct, but on reflection, are your goals or options not viable?

For each of these questions, probe deeper with the set of questions in table 9-1. Name the demand on your leadership or the goal you think you should achieve, then ask yourself:

TABLE 9-1

Questions to ask about the demands on your leadership

Am I exaggerating the demands on my leadership?	Am I minimizing or discounting a challenge or opportunity?
Is this as important as I believe? What feedback about this have I heard from others? Do they agree? What might be driving my sense of urgency?	Are the stakes higher than I have recognized, or have I set my sights too low? If others are alarmed, do I have a blind spot or deaf ear to the urgency? Is something distracting me from seeing the importance of this challenge? Is what I need to accomplish more complex than I think?
Have I just gotten it wrong? Have I missed the point because I took someone's advice over my own signals or ignored theirs? Did I lose perspective and get hijacked by something that felt urgent but isn't? Could someone have accidentally or deliberately misled me? Was I pulled into a fight or challenge that isn't mine to win or lose?	Are my goals or options viable, or have I set my sights on the impossible? Am I overly eager or optimistic or rushed? Are the resources I expect and need really available when I need them? Was the data supporting my choice sound? Can I narrow the goal, scale it back, or divide it into manageable phases?

These questions apply equally to internal goals. For example, if you've been told you need to work on your mindset, confidence, gravitas, or emotion regulation, use the same questions to develop a solid Vantage Point so that you work on the right issue at the right time for the right reasons. Similarly, for interpersonal leadership goals, if you've gotten suggestions to pay more attention to your peer relationships, or if you've received comments like "We don't see you developing your team," run through these questions as well. And, as always, call on the Five Cs to keep yourself grounded and steady whenever you need them. To help yourself improve, have a ten-out-of-ten conversation with the people who gave you feedback. If that's not possible, do the exercise as best you can by yourself.

Getting Stuck in a Stance Can Tilt Your Vantage Point

Of course, your Vantage Point is related to your stance; your default stance affects how you see your world. We suggest that you take a second look and discipline yourself to check your view using the Four Stances. Even if you like your Vantage Point, pressure-test it, asking yourself, "OK, I'm leaning with here. What would it look like if I were leaning back?" And so forth.

If Amanda had known this exercise, she might have realized that her default stance, lean in, pulled her to the big acquisition strategy, and that her optimism—her rose-colored glasses—didn't help her check herself on this stance and Vantage Point. Getting her to lean back was key to her Vantage Point correction.

Each stance sharpens your visual acuity in some ways and dulls it in others. Those with strong default stances find it hard to break out of a tendency to see the world as aligning with that stance. Imagine two leaders: One agrees it is better to be feared than loved and leans in, and the other believes the opposite and leans with. Even if they have the same exact goal, the leaders will see it from very different Vantage Points, meaning they're going to focus on different data sets when thinking about their goals, their development, their styles of leading, and what options to choose. If these two were to make mistakes, we could probably guess what they would be. The lean-in leader will be overly aggressive, possibly burn out the team, and take on too much change. The lean-with leader might struggle to make progress when seeking consensus, while dealing with a dysfunctional team they haven't been able to align.

TABLE 9-2

Vantage Points and stances, strengths and weaknesses

Stance	Vantage Point +	Vantage Point −
Lean in	Quick to see opportunities and threats and prepared to act	Overindexes you to accept more risk than might be wise
Lean back	Helps to see the big picture and use data to inform that view	Leads to overvalidating reality and revisiting decisions because data is available to do that
Lean with	Helps to tap into other perspectives and widen your view by having "other eyes" on your challenges	Leads to overconsulting and potential consensus building when consensus won't work
Don't lean	Helps to be open to what's "out there" through intuition and pattern recognition	Leads to carelessness and an overreliance on hard-to-evaluate notions like instinct

Try the following thought experiment: Think of a significant challenge you are facing. Now, visualize four people who operate from each of the Four Stances. Imagine what advice each one might give you. Table 9-2 shows how the stances relate to different Vantage Points. Your job is to take a solid look into each stance and see how it can inform and validate, or invalidate, your view. Hopefully, when you make a mistake, it will be a new one you can learn from.

Get beyond the Limits of Your Knowledge

Beyond the stances, here is another way to validate your Vantage Point. There are four categories of knowledge, of what we can know.[2] These are: 1) What do I know I know; 2) What do I know I do not know; 3) What do I (in fact) know but don't know I know it; and 4) What do I not know that I don't know.

The first two may seem self-evident, but think through them with regard to your leadership challenge. The third category is a bit trickier, so read it carefully. There's simply no easier way to phrase it:

What do I not know that I know?

The fourth is the most dangerous and hardest of all, but we will help you with this, too:

What do I not know that I don't know?

These are not riddles. There are answers to each category, and when you start filling them in, it really helps inform your Vantage Point. We'll take a quick look at each.

What I know I know

You are comfortable with your knowledge of the situation. However, still ask yourself whether you are overconfident and overestimating the accuracy of your knowledge, or whether you are not comfortable because you underestimate yourself.[3] Be clear on the limits of your information and expertise.

What I know that I don't know

You are informed and self-aware enough to know where your expertise or knowledge base ends. You can then decide if the challenge will need you to have more complete knowledge, and if so, to search for the resources you need to complete the picture. What can get in the way and erode the quality of your Vantage Point is if hubris or ego makes you feel that, if you don't know something, it's not important—or that if you feel you *should* know something, you should hide the fact that you don't. You need to develop the self-awareness (internal challenge) and courage to own your incomplete knowledge and work to remedy it. Learning to lean with will help you feel more comfortable seeking answers to what you know you don't know.

What I don't know that I know

You aren't immediately able to access information or wisdom that is untapped inside you. Often, we don't slow down enough to connect the dots or allow what we know to surface. You may assume the limits of what you know are accurate, but there is usually more to access. If you slow down or switch contexts, new thoughts can surface, activating what had been "preconscious." Not leaning or leaning back are two ways to access knowledge you don't know you possess. Close your eyes a moment and ask yourself, "What do I know about (this person, challenge, etc.) that I don't realize I know?" and see what surfaces.

Good conversations and provocative questions can help create that "aha!" moment, when what you didn't know you knew surfaces. It can be startling when someone asks, "If you knew the answer, what would it be?" and a sudden insight pops up.[4]

This happened with Amanda. Her company was profitable, and the next phase of work was upgrading her executive committee. She had clarity on all of them, except one. "I don't feel I can fully trust Bradley to deliver," she said to Carol.

"On a scale of one to ten, looking at his performance, how well has he delivered this year?" Carol asked, trying to get Amanda to articulate her concerns.

"I'm coming in at a two."

This was lower than expected and not in alignment with much of what Amanda had shared in the past. Carol wondered if some recent event was coloring her Vantage Point. "Does that feel like a fair assessment, or are you feeling cranky about him for some reason?"

"You're right. Hmmm, OK. Actually, it is more like a five. Yes, a five, I think."

"What could you do to be more certain about your rating?"

"I don't know."

Carol then asked a question she frequently uses to help someone expand their Vantage Point. Normally, she asks the leader to ask the question of themself; now, she used it to help Amanda crystalize her thoughts. "What percentage of his being a five is due to him, or to team dynamics, or to the overall organization?"

"Honestly? Now that you ask, I think it's 70 percent him, 10 percent the team, and 20 percent could stem from organizational issues." Carol wanted Amanda to realize she already knew the answer, even if she didn't know she knew. Often in this case, it's a matter of asking the right question.

Amanda sighed. "OK, OK, I know, I'm just putting this off. He's got to go. I've been giving feedback and coaching; I got him an external coach last year, and nothing is shifting. I need a ten, or even a nine. It's just that there are so many changes I need to make. First, get my COO transitioned, then there are four other major moves to put in play. Then I can worry about how to help Bradley leave and be happy about it." And that's what happened. Amanda helped Bradley get a job offer that maximized his talents.

What I don't know I don't know

To overlook this question is dangerous and can put your project or even your career in peril. But it sounds impossible to manage: How do you take into consideration something you don't know? How do you get a Vantage Point on something that might not exist? Simple. Ask many people many questions. Look beyond your organization and start scanning everything around you, every conversation, movie, article, or book. There are reliable ways to shrink this space. Your greatest threat here is having a fixed mindset and being overconfident that you always know the score. The key is to be humble about the idea that is unexpected, and to become a magnet for the unknown things that can emerge and completely change your priorities and exponentially expand your Vantage Point. You need to be prepared for that. And the agility work we've been doing to access all of this in real time will help.

Beware of Blind Spots, Being Blindsided, and Being Blind

These are different categories to help you explore what you don't know. We begin on a smaller scale and increase from there. These are very real threats to your Vantage Point. But you can prepare to deal with these even if you're, by definition, not seeing what you need to see.

Blind spots

You have a general idea of what is happening, but parts are missing.[5] It may be a flaw in your strategy, and you are not seeing the bigger systemic or strategic picture. To counter this, maintain a broad network of advisers you respect and be vigilant to subtle cues. Maybe you're sensing that people don't understand your point of view when you explain some external priority. If so, ask yourself what you're missing, rather than what they're missing. Take any critical comments seriously. Find someone who actively disagrees with your Vantage Point to see if their perspective can expand your horizon or uncover what's hidden in your blind spot. Don't overlook education, mentors, and reading as tools to fight blind spots.

Blind spots are often behavioral. Remember Marcus, the hotshot on the fast track to CEO, who had no idea that being dismissive and not listening could cost him the position? What his behavior was doing to his team was a blind spot, so it wasn't in his Vantage Point. The course correction here is to take any 360-degree feedback, development conversations, or relevant information to heart. We like to have people follow the "stereo rule"—if you've heard similar feedback from two or more people, and you don't agree with them or you think their data is wrong, it is far more likely they have identified something you don't see. Don't find reasons to argue against it. They're not wrong—you're just not seeing what they do. This could be your blind spot. Go to a different stance and work on the Five Cs to become more calm, clear, curious, compassionate, and courageous, so you can settle your ego or anxiety and take in the information. Being overly confident or defensive will keep that blind spot firmly in place.

Being blindsided

This form of you don't know what you don't know is when you are confidently looking out from your Vantage Point, only to find you've completely missed seeing what you most needed. Often this can be painful and surprising. One of our executives spent a year developing a new technology. Two hours before the press conference to announce this amazing new product launch, an industry giant announced essentially the same product. Could he have known?[6] Did he ignore cues? Or was he the victim of business espionage and blithely unaware?

You can also be blindsided on a personal level. If you are someone who leans with and is trusting, you may not pick up on cues that someone wants you out of your job so that they can take it for themselves. (We see this more than you may think.) Or, you may miss that someone dislikes you so much that they are undermining your efforts. One of our leaders was blindsided by a direct report who was being lovely to her face while backstabbing her constantly when he got the chance. She ignored those who were warning her, and even defended his criticisms as accurate. It turned into an eighteen-month tribulation before he resigned.

To avoid being blindsided, pay attention to cues, keep your ear to the ground, and ask questions. Speak with people outside your circle. A stray remark could spark an idea that illuminates what you have not seen from your Vantage Point. Being able to step into other stances helps so much here. Often, we are blindsided because we just don't want to believe someone or something is working against us. Our default stance and our inner strengths may reinforce our optimism or desire to lean with. The ability to see a situation from a different Vantage Point could prevent being blindsided.

Being blind

There are many things that are invisible to you that you need to see. Our Vantage Point can be obscured by beliefs so deeply ingrained that we don't know we have them. It's like the proverbial question: How does a fish know it's wet? It doesn't. We can be so immersed in our culture and beliefs we are utterly unaware of their presence and blind to the impact they have on ourselves and others. The greatest of these are our *unconscious biases*, our *cognitive style*, and *our emotional profile*.[7] These are largely beyond the purview of this book, but we need to at least name them. As Confucius tells us, naming things is the beginning of wisdom.

Three of the most common *unconscious biases* are:

Similarity/affinity bias, when we value people who are like us, are drawn to those who are familiar, and exclude those who feel different or "other."[8] It's not hard to see how that will affect your Vantage Point.

Affirmation/confirmation bias, when we favor information that aligns with what we already believe and discount information that doesn't. For example, you felt so great about a job applicant that you didn't heed the warnings others shared with you. As a result we can be inappropriately confident in our point of view.[9]

Attribution bias is how we piece together our world; it's our assumption of links between cause and effect.[10] Did you win an award because you are outstanding or lucky? These are the stories we tell ourselves, and tend to automatically believe them. We connect the dots and create a picture even if the dots don't actually connect that way. You may think the boss who rushes past without saying hello is a dismissive jerk. Then again, maybe he's on his way to pick up a sick child.

These unknown and unconscious processes can lead to the most dangerous mistakes, those you have no idea you might be making. The biases that lead us to exclude people or undervalue their talent are the most pernicious and damaging. Yet they can be illuminated. As you explore the invisible forces impacting your Vantage Point, make sure you also talk to others and make a commitment to be educated. It can take a village to see clearly, past our blinders.

While biases are about what we think, *cognitive style* is about *how* we think.[11]

Have you examined how you process information? It impacts you far more than you know. Appreciating and harnessing diversity of thought can vastly increase your capacity to see the whole picture more accurately.

Cognitive style and the Four Stances overlap but are not equivalent. For example, when two people work to validate a Vantage Point, they may not realize how differently they approach it even if they have the same default stance. We differ in our clarity, precision, default width, and altitude. Like the proverbial three blind men and the elephant, we can see very different things in the same situation. This can lead to necessary differences of opinion but also to avoidable conflict.

Some ways we differ on how we process information include: being precise versus impressionistic, being drawn to ideas/concepts versus practical applications, and thinking fast or slow.[12] Fast thinkers draw on pattern recognition and intuition; they can see things instantly and often be right. Slow thinking is analytical, logical, and effortful. All differences can be complementary or divisive. If we are not blind to them, we can harness these differences and reach convergence of thought at the right time.

Your *emotional profile* can affect your ability to have a clear Vantage Point.[13]

Have you thought about how emotions are, in a way, actually data? Emotional intelligence is the ability to recognize what emotions you are experiencing, understand how they impact you, and learn to regulate them.[14] If you can do these things, they add an invaluable layer to your capacity to assess the accuracy of your Vantage Point and the subsequent choices you make. At times they sway you from having a clear view; at others, they can be the only ways to reach clarity. When one of our leaders worked hard to overcome what she had labeled her "irrational" reactions to a new hire, she and her team suffered as a result, because her instinct turned out to be correct. Another common error is to judge the intensity of how others feel by your own measuring stick. Some people heat up and cool down quickly; others heat up slowly and can't cool down even when they want to. Each of us has triggers that hijack our capacity to have an accurate Vantage Point. Returning to an awareness of your three-dimensional demands, being able to observe from all Four Stances and pulling on the Five Cs is critical. Doing so will help you have a clear Vantage Point with the right resolution, scope, and altitude. It will help you locate where you are with regard to what you know and what you do not.

• • •

Amanda narrowly avoided an ill-advised major acquisition by checking her Vantage Point. She used some of the techniques above after falling prey to some of the blind spots and biases we listed.

We were impressed by her willingness to reexamine her options based on her new Vantage Point. We also knew the kind of inner strength she would need to face down the board when she pivoted to this less spectacular, albeit wiser, approach of smaller acquisitions.

We don't know what would have happened if Amanda hadn't changed her Vantage Point, but there was a significant chance it would have been a company-killer—a situation high-stakes enough that finding another Vantage Point seemed crucial to us. The pressure she was under had locked her into a lean-in stance. The only way forward seemed to be that big acquisition. The intensity of the high stakes momentarily clouded her judgment, so she couldn't see clearly or broadly. All she could initially see from her Vantage Point was one way out of this short-term pressure. Even if she hadn't taken a new tack, Amanda needed to see that other ways out existed.

We use Amanda's story precisely because of the super-high stakes involved. Having the wrong Vantage Point, or having blind spots in yours, can carry dire consequences. It's crucial to work hard to see your Vantage Point clearly and keep reevaluating it lest it undermine your leadership.

Summary

Validating your Vantage Point is necessary. We can all be overconfident about our point of view.

- Assess the accuracy of your Vantage Point with respect to:

  - Clarity

  - The right resolution

- – The right scope

- – The right level

- Go through the Vantage Point checklist in table 9-1 to identify where you might be off target.

  - – Are you over- or underestimating opportunities or challenges?

  - – Are you coming up with unrealistic options?

  - – Are you just missing the point?

- Look at your goal from the perspective of someone in each of the Four Stances.

- When you are exploring a challenge, consider each of the four categories of information that inform your Vantage Point:

  - – What you know you know

  - – What you know you don't know

  - – What you don't know you know

  - – What you don't know you don't know

- Pay special attention to the things you don't know you don't know.

- Explore which biases might blind you to an accurate view of others, including:

  - – Similarity/affinity bias

  - – Affirmation/confirmation bias

  - – Attribution bias

- Examine your cognitive style to understand how it impacts your decision-making.

- Take note of your emotional profile as a factor in how comfortable you are assessing the accuracy of your Vantage Point.

MOVE

**Engage
and
Effect
Change**

10

Communicate Your Intent

Conductors must give unmistakable and suggestive signals
to the orchestra—not choreography to the audience.

—George Szell

After an international career in business followed by time in the German public sector, Aria had joined a Geneva-based nongovernmental organization (NGO) devoted to mitigating climate change. Despite Geneva's conservative nature, the institution made a big bet on Aria, the first nonbinary executive at the organization, based on their amazing track record. (Aria's pronouns are they/them.) The board brought them in as executive director (ED) following the previous ED's retirement. Board members loved Aria's charisma and vision to expand and diversify the organization's mission.

But eighteen months in, Aria's change agenda had gained little traction. Funding levels had stagnated, and no new programming had been implemented. Aria brought David in for coaching in the middle of year two.

They agreed to an immediate 360-degree assessment to get perspective on their situation. First, David would talk to the chair. He started this conversation, as he often does, by asking about Aria's strengths. After a long silence, the chair tersely replied, "I'm hard-pressed to think of any."

David was nonplussed but gathered himself and asked the chair to say more.

She continued her unsparing assessment. "Aria has a vision that they have been utterly unable to implement. When they arrived, I told them, 'Drive it like you stole it.' That's an overstatement, but it showed how much we wanted change."

"What happened?" As David probed into the chair's thinking, he saw her begin to shift her stance.

"The board insisted on a long transition from the old ED while he was still here, and he marginalized Aria. He wasn't comfortable with them, excluding Aria from key decisions. Many senior people felt they could just push back at will or ignore the new ED."

"What did you do about it?"

"We didn't intervene," the chair admitted, "so the resulting train wreck is partially on the board."

But the chair wasn't going to let Aria off the hook. "I have coached Aria endlessly to get their team aligned and to make some big resource asks from us in order to implement their growth strategy. They have done nothing. Now some team members are approaching board members to tell us how ineffective Aria is. At the next board session, in two weeks, I need to raise the possibility of replacing them. If I don't move now, it makes me look weak."

David realized how high-stakes the situation was. He became even more concerned for Aria's future. He asked, "Have you been explicit that their time might be up?"

"Uh, no," the chair replied. "It seems obvious to me."

David thought that it was probably pointless to challenge the chair's casual remark. Instead, he asked, "Would anything change your mind about Aria?"

She replied, "Sure. If, overnight, they magically became the leader we thought we hired."

Sending Leadership Signals to Amplify Your Impact

In their first few sessions with David, Aria had identified the most important three-dimensional priorities (M), considered various options to achieve them (O), and validated their Vantage Point (V) to the extent possible prior to the 360-degree assessment. So far so good, but as the two of them talked, it became clear that Aria was stuck on how to engage and effect change in external priorities at scale (E).

To effect change, they needed to send some clear leadership signals—using words and actions as a leader that would galvanize the other leaders. Otherwise, they would remain in serious trouble.

The first signal: Articulating your Leader's Intent

Many leaders charge ahead to meet their external priorities, and when (or if) they look back, they find they have no followers. Don't let this happen to you. It's easy to give your team too little guidance by delegating everything to them or deciding to stay at the one-hundred-thousand-foot level. In those cases, your people spend their time trying to guess at what you actually want and need, or fight with each other because they have no common goal that they all buy into. At the other extreme, you can give too much direction, micromanaging or second-guessing your team, underutilizing their skills, and in some cases tempting them to delegate up to you because they have given up on having any autonomy in their job.

You need to find the right balance between giving too little and too much direction. We call this the Leader's Intent, and it is an art form. The concept is derived from commander's intent, a military leadership framework taught to us by Chuck Jacoby, a four-star US general whose last role before retirement was leading Northern Command.[1] We've modified his work for nonmilitary applications.

Your Leader's Intent is designed to align your people around the destination you're all heading toward. Getting this right can be the key to your entire career; certainly, it will serve your organization well if you get it right.

With the Leader's Intent you name your highest-stakes external priorities, prescribe guidance at a high level based on what an acceptable range of options might be to achieve them, note constraints on resources and behaviors, and finally visualize for others what winning looks like. In other words, you're publicly signaling your M and O to your team and organization. The signals you send can range in intensity and can be mapped to the Four Stances. Giving very clear directives that need to be followed to the letter is a leaning-in signal. Gathering input from the team is a leaning-with signal, and so on.

But you cannot stop here. After aligning with your team on your Leader's Intent, executing those priorities requires you to seek signals from your team and from the rest of the organization, so you can monitor what's working and how the situation may be evolving. Based on their signals, you update your evaluation of M, O, and V, and then refine your Leader's Intent and the signals you transmit back as you continue to engage and effect change—the E in MOVE. Engaging and executing is doing the thing, but it's also feeding the continuous process of knowing what to do and how to do it.

Your Leader's Intent is the first signal you can send to effect change at a large scale. This is not a solo act. In highly uncertain environments and with newer teams, you will want to cocreate the mission, getting a wide range of inputs and getting others' buy-in at an earlier stage. This is often an iterative process, and every leader is "incomplete."[2] Even if you already have a well-defined point of view on the mission, invite your team to pressure-test it with you.

Developing the options to achieve your Leader's Intent is also collaborative. For most external priorities, it is important not to be overly prescriptive about methods. Provide high-level guidance about options based on input from your direct team, insights drawn from others with diverse experiences inside and outside your organization, and data. Then step aside to let your team and organization use their skills and ingenuity to find the best way forward.

More buttoned-down and prescriptive intents are appropriate in only a few scenarios. These may include, for example, environments where there is only one correct way to proceed, such as in highly regulated sectors where health and safety are paramount.

The Leader's Intent concept is empowering because it recognizes that for most complex missions, it is neither possible nor ideal to prescribe a command-and-control approach. Conditions change on the ground all the time, in surprising ways, and everyone is operating without complete or even reliable information. Thus it's better to make the most of your people's skills, experience, and assessment of real-time conditions. You can set high-level boundary conditions for how they operate, but how they engage and effect change is up to them.[3]

Leader's Intent can also be used throughout the organization, so everyone has the ability to know what is inside the leader's head. This is done by cascading your intent to the next level of leaders, who come up with their own Leader's Intent for their teams, following the spirit of your intent. As the intent flows down and sideways, it reaches all the way to the edge of the organization, and people in the field apply the intent to the local conditions they experience. Whether or not you are present, your signal is generating the right behavior. These principles also apply to "flat" relationships, where people need to understand where you are coming from with your intent in order to codesign it and align it with their own.

So, your Leader's Intent includes:

- What and where: What do we need to do, and where is our destination? That is, what's a ten out of ten for the most important external priority for you, the team, and the organization?

- Why it matters: Why are we going there? How does the priority relate to the organization's purpose, how does it create strategic value overall, and how does it benefit individuals in the organization?

- How: How will we get there? That is, how do we outline at a high level which options could be acceptable?

- Constraints: What limitations do we need to operate within? This could include, for example, tasks that need to be performed, available resources, time, ethical behavior, and legal and regulatory compliance.

- Signposts: How will we know we are winning along the way, in terms of important markers or milestones that we can name?

The answers here need to be specific and tangible. Here is an example we developed with one of our leaders who was responsible for the organic products division of his food and beverage company:

- What and where: We will improve our NPS (Net Promoter Score) from seventy to eighty-five in the next three years while maintaining our margins.

- Why it matters: This is the most important driver to help achieve our long-term goals of becoming one of the world's best-loved brands and providing more healthy food to the planet. Higher NPS will allow us to reach more people, increase our market share, and increase pricing, which will drive value creation for our brand. A more powerful endorsement by our customers will increase employee engagement and create the opportunity for higher compensation.

- **How:** We need to acquire new talent in marketing, tie our division's brand promise more closely to health, accelerate new product development, and transform our quality assurance processes.

- **Constraints:** While we invest to increase NPS, we must maintain annual earnings growth of at least 8 percent.

- **Signposts:** Rebrand our division within nine months, launch our new killer product to coincide with the rebranding, obtain endorsements from consumer ratings groups and prominent wellness brands within eighteen months, cut product defects by 50 percent by the end of year two, and be ranked in the world's top thirty organic food brands as rated by consumer surveys by the end of year three. These initiatives are expected to translate into a seventy-five NPS in year one, an eighty in year two, and an eighty-five in year three.

Notice that the example is explicit about "where" the team needs to go and "what" needs to happen, but gives a lot of latitude in terms of "how" to proceed.

Your Leader's Intent should be shared with the entire team together, and then also one-on-one with each member of the team, because it will be interpreted by each team member from their own Vantage Point. But they need to see it from *your* Vantage Point before they can cascade their own version of it to their reports. Again, this is equally true with colleagues and when communicating upward. Using the food and beverage example, the head of customer experience will have a point of view on how they can best contribute to increase NPS, which is different from how the CTO or the head of product can contribute. All those perspectives are important and can be leveraged so long as the various ideas mesh with your intent.

• • •

Aria's instincts told them that the NGO could do more. The high-level expression of their Leader's Intent was, "We need to widen our programming to the countries we serve and expand our geographic reach through growing and diversifying our funding sources."

The board instinctively got it and was supportive. But the team wasn't having it—the intent was too open-ended, and people were happy enough doing what they were doing.

David asked Aria how they had tried to get the team on board.

"I once heard that for people to 'get' a new idea, they have to hear it eight times. So, I told them over and over. I even said things like, 'Consider this the fifth time that I am telling you.' Eventually I gave up."

Notice how little collaboration is there. Aria handed down their intent the day after the transition with the previous ED was complete, as if it was a given. The team had no opportunity to explore and refine it together, despite how broad-based the change to the organization's mission would be.

We've all been in Aria's shoes, but ouch! It wasn't that the team didn't get it—Aria wasn't getting it. Being handed a "what" with no input and a Leader's Intent that was not specific enough about where, how, and why didn't help the team understand how they would do this expansion. Why should this team care when they were already having widespread impact and were proud of their work? What's more, since Aria didn't give them priorities or signposts, it was hard to see how the team would get to this faraway goal with no path or stops along the way before them. The team couldn't do anything with this plan.

After reflecting on how their Leader's Intent could have been approached differently, Aria wished it were possible to turn back time. Fortunately, the board remained supportive of the new high-level direction. If Aria could somehow make it through the next board meeting, Aria knew they would approach the team to get their support through more of an invitation and less of an ultimatum.

Stay Engaged beyond Leader's Intent: Continue to Send Signals

Once you craft your Leader's Intent and get the team aligned, you need to continue to engage, sending more signals that support the successful execution of your priorities. Some signals are strong and unambiguous, like giving an order or making a decision. When you make a massive capital investment decision, that's a strong signal. Other signals are weak, tentative, or implicit, which isn't necessarily bad. Don't confuse weak with negative or not useful. Weak signals are necessary and often effective. They can take the form of an exploratory discussion on an issue, asking open-ended questions, or phasing in an initiative in several stages.

In general, you'll send stronger signals when you're more confident that:

- The path you prioritized in the Options Generator will achieve your top external priorities.

- You have enough personal leadership range available right now, or can work on increasing your range in time to pull it off.

- Your team and organization are prepared and willing to receive your signals.

For less clear situations, your signals should be weaker. Think of them as viable signals that are just strong enough to be received by others and that you can learn from. The key here is calibration. You're engaging and effecting change by taking the first steps to activate an option you identified. Don't send too strong a signal if you're not confident in your options, time, or team preparedness. But don't be too timid if you feel good about the options and your personal leadership range.

Next, gather feedback to see if the signal received was the same as the signal sent. We call two-way check-ins with your team and other stakeholders "confirmation cycles." The confirmation cycles should happen at a higher frequency in higher-stakes situations and more uncertain operating environments, to keep you tightly involved with your team and peers and ensure that you stay aligned. One of the executives we coached had a particularly vigorous debate with his team on how best to respond to a competitor's change in pricing strategy. As they concluded the discussion, they all agreed that they had a clear path forward. Our executive wasn't so sure, and before ending the meeting he asked each team member, "What was your understanding of what we agreed on?" Each person read back to him a different impression of the decision. Situations like this happen all the time—you believe the decision is straightforward and everyone gets it, but they don't. You can never overdo a confirmation cycle.

Based on what you learn after taking new actions, you can develop an iterative process to modify your signal strength. As you go, you will update your understanding of M, O, and V, which will lead to refining your signals to better effect change.

For example, you may decide that you are aiming at the wrong target, like Matt did in the introduction and chapter 1. He thought his priority was to show off his detailed knowledge to the board, when it should have been instilling confidence in them and showing his character as a leader. Or your option may not be as viable as you initially thought. Or feedback may show that you have misread your Vantage Point.

Getting your signal strength right is sometimes easy, sometimes hard. Take Samantha, who was recruited from the autonomous vehicle division of a tech company to accelerate the digitization of a UK manufacturing business. The digitization project was in its earliest stages and was a tricky project. Since her work would interact with every business unit and every function in the company, alignment was a major challenge in this high-stakes digital transformation.

Samantha arrived, assessed the situation, and within a few months made a series of bold recommendations. They were promptly rejected by the rest of the leadership team.

This put Samantha into a fighting posture. She dug in, telling David, "I'm not just right. I'm damn right! What is the matter with them?"

David knew Samantha from her previous job, and knew all had not been rosy in the autonomous vehicle project she had managed there as well. "Remember when that was underperforming expectations?"

"Sure I do," she said. "We had kept our budget for sensors low to keep costs controlled, until we realized sensors were the key to optimizing the data that helped the vehicles navigate more effectively, and for longer. After we massively increased the budget for sensors, vehicle navigation improved and the project got back on track."

David turned her expertise into a metaphor to help her see what was happening. "Is it possible you are acting like a self-driving vehicle without enough sensors on your front bumper?" he asked. "You're crashing into a lot of people. How about adding sensors by asking them some questions before telling them the answers?" Samantha cracked up laughing, but the point hit home.

If she was going to effect change, she couldn't push such strong signals out of the gate. She needed to create weaker signals and attune to how they were being received.

When Samantha next met with her team, she adopted a more open and curious mindset. She asked where they saw opportunities. She took their feedback and iterated her point of view on what needed to happen.

It turned out that not all her signals were wrong; they were just poorly sent. The right signal delivered too strongly, or too weakly, will often get rejected. Samantha learned that the long-tenured team had turned down her ideas partly because they felt she didn't yet know enough about the company. After they got to know her better, they loosened up, even admitting they may have had a "not invented here" attitude toward her. They made it clear that they were open to change but wanted to do it in partnership, taking Samantha's fresh pair of eyes and intriguing ideas and helping her shape them.

• • •

At the other extreme was Aria, the executive director at the NGO. After being rebuffed on the brutally strong signals—saying things eight times in an effort to get people to buy in—they had swung to the other extreme, sending signals that were weak and ineffectual. "I run into a dead end everywhere I go," they said, exasperated. "I've resorted to working directly with skip-level junior people who will follow my lead."

Things were not looking good for Aria. Their support had eroded, and while the CFO and head of fundraising supported them (with reservations), the powerful Chief Program Officer was dead set against Aria staying. When David spoke with him, the CPO was toxic in his comments "I'm not taking any guidance from them, nor will I collaborate with them under any circumstances. I've told the board it's me or Aria, not both."

David called an emergency session with Aria to convey the bleak assessment from the 360. "You need to make some dramatic changes," he said, "or you have no more runway."

The direct, unequivocal delivery of the message shocked Aria, but they knew taking it in was necessary. Aria slumped back in their chair and quietly replied, "I guess I knew it was bad." After taking a moment to recover, they said, "All right. I own this. Help me fix it." Tough messages can land well when people know it's driven by your commitment and deep respect for what they can offer the world.

We revisited Aria's M, O, and V together to see how they may have changed based on the results of the 360-degree report. To summarize, they shifted external priorities rapidly, away from day-to-day leadership to a two-stage external goal: survive the next board meeting and then get some immediate traction on the vision. For options, they had overindexed on leaning back, delegating so much to the Chief Program Officer that they were left exposed and vulnerable to being undermined. And from Aria's updated Vantage Point, it was clear that bold action was the name of the game or their time was up—Aria wouldn't get the chance to effect the change that was clearly possible.

David knew Aria's fractured relationship with the Chief Program Officer had to be addressed. They needed to know the intensity of the danger. He asked how the relationship was going.

"He's completely unresponsive. I finally sat down in his office to have a chat. He said there's nothing to talk about, and basically dismissed me. What do I do now?"

"He's your most important team member, and if I am clear from our previous conversations, he stands in the way of everything you try to do, right?"

"Yes."

"And while you have tried to improve the relationship, you have tolerated his behavior for almost two years now?"

"Yes."

"Do you think there is any way to improve the effectiveness of your relationship with him?"

"No."

"Do you believe in your strategy?"

"One hundred percent."

"OK then. What is the fastest way to get traction in your job right now?"

"Terminate him, I think. He's standing in the way of any and all progress." Aria knew it wasn't that simple. "But what would the team say? He's been around so long and has a lot of supporters. Besides, it's not in my nature to rock the boat that much, and I'm inherently a kind person."

David had seen this before. He had to help Aria find a way to lean in effectively and he pressed on just how high-stakes this moment was. "You only have a few weeks to turn this around. I know you are kind—it shines through in all of our conversations. And it's not a decision you would take on personal grounds. Parting company can be done with compassion. Does that change your thinking?"

"I guess it's him or me at this point, and I believe in my vision more than I believe in what he brings to the organization. He needs to go, I need to be more explicit with the board about how I will turn things around, and I need to better connect with my team."

Aria had gotten backed into a corner but was finally ready to send the right, strong leadership signal to their team and the board. It was high risk, but together with a few additional moves, it could help Aria to stay in the game.

Finally, Aria was engaged and effecting change.

Summary

- Engage (E) pulls together everything from M, O, and V to leverage your impact as a leader of leaders so you can MOVE.

- You amplify your impact as a leader by sending leadership signals.

- The first type of signal is your Leader's Intent, which is often formed in collaboration with your team and expresses several things:

  - What do we need to accomplish, and where is our destination? (This draws from your external priorities.)

  - Why are we going there?

  - How will we get there? What are our high-level options for the mission (from O)?

  - What limitations do we have in terms of resources or behaviors, and what signposts will tell us along the way that we are winning (from V)?

- Subsequently, gather feedback to see if the signal received was the same as the signal sent, and iteratively refine your guidance based on what you learn. Use a series of two-way check-ins with your team and other stakeholders, known as "confirmation cycles."

- You can learn to control the strength of your signals to match a situation. Strong signals work best in highly certain situations to keep everyone aligned and moving forward. Weak signals are better in uncertain situations to continue to gather information and adjust the plan as necessary. Using the wrong signal can disrupt your message, so work on making sure you're not too strong or too weak with your signals.

11

Boost Your Signals

There is surely nothing quite so useless as doing with great efficiency what should not be done at all.

—Peter Drucker

T o optimize your leadership, you must focus on sending only the signals that help effect the change you want. To avoid sending the wrong signals, we need to borrow one more principle from General Chuck Jacoby: concentrate on doing what only you can do, and leave the rest to others when you can.[1] That seems simple enough, but we've seen with many of our clients just how hard it is to send only high-quality signals. It requires great discipline.

Improve Signal Quality by Focusing on What Only You Can Do

It makes sense that a general would use this approach. The military term "general" derives from the word "generalist." When you become senior enough in rank, the scope and scale of your role mean you can't specialize. There will be many things you don't and can't know. This can be a daunting truth to accept. Many leaders arriving at the generalist level struggle to accept it. One way they deal with it is to focus on the things they know and love and to delegate everything else. Some try to compensate for their lack of knowledge by micromanaging and second-guessing their team. Some throw the proverbial spaghetti at the wall—spraying out a lot of words and orders to appear decisive until they see what sticks.

All of these approaches are understandable, but none leads to an optimal outcome.

The best leaders start with articulating their Leader's Intent and then identify and focus on sending the highest-quality signals related to the decisions that are reserved for them alone. In General Jacoby's final post, leading Northern Command, there were very few things that only he could do, few decisions or actions that rested solely on him. His first priority was to articulate his Leader's Intent. Beyond that, only a couple of issues were "reserved" for him at the highest conceivable level of impact and risk, including the authority to shoot down incoming intercontinental ballistic missiles in the event of an attack on North America. Most other issues were reserved for others.

When he was pressed to make other types of decisions, Jacoby would often ask two questions. First, "Is this within my intent?" and if so, "Is it legal, ethical, and moral?" If the answer to both questions was "yes," his reply was usually, "Then do it." Notice how he can confidently give away the authority—by combining the right level of guidance through his Leader's Intent with optimal delegation. This can cut through a lot of complexity and fog.

You can apply this approach to improving the quality of your signals, too. Think about which decisions rest solely with you. These are called "reserved decisions," and for many leaders they might include approval of strategy, plans, and budgets; hiring, firing and promoting; compensation and codes of conduct; and balancing workload against resources.[2] If you mapped out your time, how much is devoted to these types of reserved decisions and how much is for things that could conceivably be delegated?

Some context is needed before you start making a list of reserved versus nonreserved decisions. First, don't sit back and wait for people to surprise you with a request for approval on a reserved decision. Instead, you should be participating from start to finish for all reserved decisions, using confirmation cycles like we described in the previous chapter to provide and receive input and to give guidance at key junctures. Second, you need to have reporting and compliance policies in place so that you can effectively monitor everything that is within your sphere of responsibility and be confident things are on track, even if many parts can be delegated. Third, you need to be able to assess the competence of your team members, even if you are not an expert in each of their roles. One way to do this is to selectively conduct deep dives in different areas. You are look-

ing for assurance that what you delegate is being implemented appropriately by alert, knowledgeable, and capable leaders. As one CEO told Carol,
"I don't believe in micromanagement, but I do believe in micro-
observation." Another leader said, "Dashboards might be all green on a
Friday and then turn all red by the following Monday. Know when to
question the green!"

By following the "do what only you can do" ethos, you'll be best positioned to effect change through high-quality signals. You'll neither micro-
manage nor disconnect from any key issue. If you have weak team
members or skill gaps, if the team is not working well together, or if the
culture isn't right, that becomes the top external priority to address. It
will require some tough conversations and decisions. You'll need a lean-in
stance. Selecting and building a strong team with complementary skills
and diverse experiences and setting the tone for a healthy culture are definitely things that only you can do. In our experience, it's also what many
leaders take too long to do, which they later come to regret.

Veering off track from what only you can do can be easy, so you need
to stay mindfully alert. Let's say you have been promoted to lead your
division and you were previously chief revenue officer. How tempting is it
to spend your time diving into sales issues you understand best? How *com-
forting* would it be to retreat there? That focus comes at the expense of
the rest of the business. Sending effective signals means being highly selective about which meetings you decide to call or attend. How about when
the chief marketing officer leaves and you decide to "double hat" for a
while to learn their job because you aren't a marketing expert? Don't do
it. One of the worst examples of breaking the "do what only you can do"
rule we've witnessed was with a first-time CEO who prided himself on
his decisiveness. When directly approached by individuals in his organization, he would make off-the-cuff decisions all the time, not involving
the right team members up front. He found himself having to reverse himself time and time again—his signals were rarely clear or right.

• • •

Back to Aria, the executive director of the NGO. Firing the Chief Program Officer was something only Aria could do, but so far they hadn't
done it. And they had given up on their Leader's Intent by not hiring a
single new leader to build new capabilities on the team, fearing the disruption and the fight with the cost-conscious board it would most likely

cause. But if Aria wanted to deliver on the strategy, these things had to be done. These were the high-quality signals that could save their job.

After a lengthy meeting with David to plan the turnaround, Aria gained confidence. "It's now or never to send some strong signals," they said. "I am going to sever the Chief Program Officer, reorganize to eliminate that job, and have his team report directly to me so that I have more of a direct connection with key leaders. And I need to start retained searches for at least four additional officers who will join my new senior leadership team."

Strong signals indeed. At last, Aria was rising to the occasion, but David sensed that getting even more space to think was necessary. "How do you plan to show up at the board meeting?" he asked. He was happy to hear the response.

"First, I need to take accountability for the past two years. I will ask for one more year. Next, I'm going to give more detail to my growth plan and get them to approve my reorganization and talent acquisition strategy. I recognize that the growth plan won't be ready to be presented as a strong signal until I have my new team in place, get their input, and drive alignment on the plan. I will preview all these recommendations with key board members before the meeting and ask for their support."

The board was shocked and pleased with Aria's newfound boldness and decisiveness. The last thing they wanted was to deal with the uncertainty and dislocation of an external search for a new executive director. Despite prejudice and resistance, Aria remained a continuous learner and cleared the bar to be granted another year.

Aria's grin told the story. "I'm in the game again!"

It was a turning point, for sure, but there was a lot of work ahead to build trust, execute on rebuilding the team with great care to recruit the right people, and make progress on the strategy. Eighteen months later, Aria had effected real change, focusing on the things that only they could do as executive director. The team was in place, the leadership had the trust of the organization, and the NGO had a record year for funding and programming. Aria felt at last that they belonged.

Scaling the Other Two Dimensions of Leadership

So far, we've looked at executing on external priorities, the first dimension of leadership, through Leader's Intent and other leadership signals. We must also address internal and interpersonal priorities. If the highest-quality signals to effect change at scale emerge from Leader's Intent and "do what only you can do" on external priorities, with internal priorities the directive is to answer "Who do you want your team and organization to be?" with clarity. Answers to both questions translate into culture at the team and organizational levels, and reinforce your ability as a leader to effect change at scale and have a lasting impact even beyond your tenure.

Shape culture through a special type of signal

Who you are and the choices you make have the power to influence how each person in the organization behaves, what they believe about the Three Dimensions of Leadership, and what stances might be optimal. The survey of one thousand CEOs concluded that in terms of effecting change, it starts with the CEO.[3] We agree, but we also believe it starts with any leader. You can be a role model for the culture you want to create. Do this by sending leadership signals to reinforce or change the culture that others can repeat. Who you are is what you do.[4] The way you address goals and people becomes a template for what choices others make.

Because a full treatment of culture is beyond our scope here, we use the shorthand definition of "how things are done around here."[5] Some cultures prioritize results over all else. Others value innovation and collaboration. And so on. Behaviors that are aligned with culture are embraced and rewarded, and those that go against culture are discouraged by colleagues, either explicitly through a sanction or by implicit disapproval and marginalization.

Role modeling the culture you want is a powerful way to send leadership signals about desired behavior. Sometimes very small signals that you send are quickly picked up on by others and replicated, gaining enough momentum to take off across the organization. These small signals end up having a disproportionately positive impact. We've referred to the power of what you "emanate" as a leader and to how your behavior and mindsets are absorbed by others. Attitudes, mindsets, and emotions are contagious.[6] What do you want others to catch from you?

Take this on and try different ways of role modeling cultural norms, testing and learning as you go, to find those that have the largest possible amplification effect.

One of the leaders Carol worked with was chief creative officer (CCO) at an advertising agency. The agency was part of a holding company that provided global marketing solutions and that was organized into many entities, including advertising, digital marketing, communications, and media. The holding company also had a CCO for the overall group to encourage collaboration in pursuing client business opportunities and sharing creative insights. But the various entities in the ground had deeply embedded cultures and saw each other as enemies rather than allies, creating unbreachable siloes. They continued to resist working together and constantly pushed back on the group CCO.

One day our leader was stuck. He had a crucial pitch coming up, but he and his team had run out of ideas and he desperately needed a breakthrough solution. "I need to shift how I'm seeing myself," he told Carol. "I don't want to be someone who is afraid of being vulnerable. If I'm hoping to transcend the silo mentality around here and start new ways to collaborate, I need to take the first step."

He reached out to his counterpart in the group's specialty digital agency, whom he thought could help. The two had seen each other at large meetings but hadn't gotten to know each other, let alone exchange ideas. To their mutual surprise, the meeting gave our executive the breakthrough he was looking for. After negotiating some basic rules of engagement with the help of the group CCO and some advice from Carol, he was more than happy to team up with the specialty agency, and the joint pitch ended up winning the new business. That broke the impasse at the group level and became the root of a new collaborative approach across the organization. What patterns of behavior do you want others to replicate? Which could be the most powerful signals for you to send? These have the power to ripple throughout the organization and begin to shift the culture.

Send signals that reinforce psychological safety

You must send consistent signals that tell people it is safe to speak their minds with you and with each other. In the airline industry, when people hold back information out of fear, the results are devastating. It shouldn't be different at any other venture. Speaking up without fear is a precondition to successfully effecting change at scale. Amy Edmondson of Harvard Business School pioneered the concept of psychological safety: a shared belief by a group that it is safe for members to take moderate degrees of interpersonal risk by offering unhedged perspectives or insights or by calling reality how you see it.[7] It is a form of trust among a group. In safe environments, individuals feel they can bring their full range of skills, experiences, and insights to a team environment without fear of negative consequences in self-image, status within the team, compensation, or career prospects. Amy measures the level of psychological safety in a group by scoring people on a series of scenarios, including "when someone makes a mistake, it is often held against him or her" and "it's easy to discuss difficult issues and problems."[8]

Fostering psychological safety and inclusion is crucial. When people are not afraid to engage, they are more likely to tell you and each other the truth about what they are seeing or feeling. Better ideas and decisions will surface and execution will improve. More importantly, being able to engage without fear is a core requirement for people to be able to truly feel included and part of the heart of the organization. Without this, the health of the organization is compromised.

If you are to engage and effect change, you, the leader, need to constantly signal that you are committed to creating a safe and inclusive environment. You can't limit this simply to your team and the part of the organization that you are responsible for. For example, you can't leave out your peers and even your boss.

It takes a lot of attention to build a psychologically safe and inclusive environment because it can be so fragile. Small moments of unsafe behavior have an outsize impact. For example, we did an exercise to anonymously measure psychological safety in real time with one wonderful leader and his top management team. We had a great, positive discussion. Then at the end of the workshop we asked each member of the team to anonymously rank the usefulness of the day from one to ten, with ten being most useful. Eleven of the twelve team members rated the day a ten, and one rated it an eight. The leader looked at the results on the screen and said "OK, who's the eight?" Silence. "No, I really want to get your perspective, it's OK to say!" Silence.

It's one thing to profess a commitment to the concept of psychological safety, which in his case was genuine. It's another thing to consciously integrate it into your behavior as a leader. Our leader immediately saw what he did, apologized to the team, and strove to do better next time.

● ● ●

Once you start transmitting the right signals, you should focus on the quality of those signals. High-quality signals are about things only you can do. They help shape culture across an entire organization, and, crucially, they foster psychological safety. If you find yourself doing this well, you're effecting change. Next, it's time to take on the biggest challenges yet.

Summary

- To engage and effect change at scale, focus on doing what only you can do. Send the highest-quality signals by not getting distracted by issues that can best be attended to by others.

- Remember, in very big roles it's not your job to be the specialist; you are the generalist. Draw on the second dimension of leadership to embrace the concept that others know more than you.

- Be mindfully alert to those decisions that are reserved for you and those that are not.

- Have good structures in place to support this effort: use confirmation cycles for these decisions, have reporting and compliance in place, and make sure your team is capable.

- Find your ideal balance and avoid micromanaging, but also do not disconnect.

- Scale internal and interpersonal priorities to see how you can apply them to the overall organization.

  - Embody and model the kind of culture you want to have through behaviors that can be noticed and easily replicated by others. These can ripple throughout the organization.

  - Always model psychological safety as a fundamental building block of culture.

MOVE

in a
Big
New
Role

12

Change Your Vantage Point

It's like being a fighter pilot and having a lot of experience in the simulator, but regardless, when you go up there and get in your first dogfight, it's different.

—Trip Miller

Congratulations! You've achieved your dream and gotten that incredible job. You are going to breathe the rarefied air at or near the top. This is a new beginning and a wonderful opportunity to make even more of a positive impact on your employees, customers, and external stakeholders, and possibly the world. Your access to resources, information, and people has expanded, as has your ability to make decisions on important issues and to drive change.

Of course, the challenges expand as well.

In fact, one of the highest-stakes, highest-risk situations a leader will face is the big new role. It's high-stakes because of the increased demands on you. It's high risk because everything is new to you—the priorities, the people, and often the whole organization. There's more uncertainty than ever, which results in more unexpected developments and unintended consequences, both good and bad.

You're bound to have moments when, as Trip Miller says, you realize all the training and imagining you did to anticipate what this would be like still don't prepare you for the real thing. Mike Tyson said it more rudely: "Everyone has a plan until they get punched in the mouth."

Fortunately, we can help you deal with your new role, applying MOVE specifically to this particular high-stakes scenario. This is a rich ground for storytelling because of the wide range of issues a new leader can face, so we will be sharing many illustrations of executives we have advised.

The Key Is Your Vantage Point

In a big new role, turbulence is inevitable. When it hits, if you're not prepared, you could be tossed and tumbled upside down. To prevent this, we'll apply MOVE with a specific strategy, first by adjusting your Vantage Point. Once you are grounded in your new Vantage Point, you can apply the rest of the MOVE framework.

It's so important to get your Vantage Point right that the rest of this chapter is going to focus on just that. The next chapter will apply the rest of MOVE to your big new role.

Adjust to your new Vantage Point

In chapter 9 we described a ten-out-of-ten Vantage Point. It includes:

> Clear vision: Recognizing how your wishes, fears, and conscious and unconscious processing distort reality

> The right resolution: Knowing whether you need a sharp view with all the data, or if a fuzzier view will do

> The right scope: Understanding when you need a wide scope to put things in perspective or a narrow scope for a laser focus

> The right level: Figuring out when you need to take a tactical, shorter-term view versus a strategic, longer-term view

There are some special aspects to a big new role that map to the ten-out-of-ten outcome. To wit:

> Clear vision: You have a whole new set of relationships with your boss(es) or board, peers, and team, some of whom may be former peers. From your new position, you need to see each of these key players clearly for who they are now. You can't be clouded by your hopes and wishes for friends or subconscious bias toward, say, your former department.

The right resolution: You have a new mandate to fulfill, which may or may not turn out to be what you thought it was. Evaluating from here may require not a laser focus but a fuzzier view because you're taking in a broader landscape.

The right scope: You must recognize that you need to lead in a different way because your role is bigger and broader, and, in the words of Marshall Goldsmith, "What got you here won't get you there."[1] Your scope will be wider.

The right level: You can see the world differently from your higher elevation, and you should make the most of that by seeing further ahead and more broadly to spot new strategic opportunities and threats. The view here is less tactical, more strategic. That is, you're flying higher.

We will help you familiarize yourself with each of these Vantage Point shifts that are unique to a big new role.

Recognize the Need to Scale Your Leadership

All these attributes add up to the fact you are now operating on a grander scale. And leadership approaches that worked at small(er) scales may not work so well here. This is best illustrated by what we call the *subject matter expert trap*, a trap Leo fell into.

Leo is a brilliant scientist with an incredible memory. He was known to be able to keep track of his three hundred scientists on twenty research teams, and even help them understand their own science better and synthesize the various streams of research between teams. His inspirational style led to engagement scores in the nineties with scientists. His ability to show how everyone's work served the organization's mission—to save lives and help the underserved—seemed nearly magical.

When another division leader suddenly left the company, Leo was inserted as interim division head. It was a scramble: twenty-five more teams, three hundred more people, and two weeks to decide which projects to keep and which to cut.

"Oh my God, Carol, what am I going to do now? I don't know their science, and the parade of projects is starting tomorrow!" Leo said.

"Knowing you, you have a plan, right? What is it?"

He closed his eyes and confessed. "I've secretly hired three scientists to go over each project to assess their flaws. They'll tell me their assessments, and when I weigh in no one will know I'm not the expert."

Carol managed her sinking sensation. Leo's brilliance was in being open and authentic. This was the opposite and could be disastrous for his leadership. She simply asked, "You're comfortable with that?"

"What else can I do? They won't respect me or follow me otherwise."

"That is a pretty big assumption. Any chance it's wrong?"

Carol shared that with this new role, Leo's external priority wasn't to personally assess the quality of the science of the dozens of lab projects and hundreds of scientists. It was to step up and to lead at scale. He was at his best when he was transparent. Who knew what side effects his secret plan would create? Like many, Leo had to overcome his fear that without being able to rely on his special expertise, he had no value. He needed to step into a new Vantage Point so that he could be the one responsible for creating a positive environment to foster great discoveries and collaboration. For the first time in his career, he didn't need to be on top of all the science.

Once he understood, his face lit up. "It's a huge burden off my back!" Leo successfully made the transition to a larger-scale role. He now spends 80 percent of his time supporting thriving communities of experts. Twenty percent is reserved for his own lab, where he can lead the science as well as the people. As he learned to lead through others and overcome his need to be the subject matter expert, he then learned to rise above his science siloes and become a true enterprise leader seeing across the entire organization and beyond. And his new position became permanent.

Use Your New Vantage Point to See More and Farther

In this big new role, you're afforded the luxury of a grand Vantage Point, capable of taking in the bigger, broader picture and thinking in longer time frames. This is when to leverage systems thinking to sharpen your worldview and strategic perspective. You should be assessing longer-term macro trends, opportunities, and obstacles and identifying potential risks that can arise from external forces. Inside your organization, use your broader visibility to spot trends in performance, engagement, and culture.

How well you can see depends on strategic insight, which resides in some combination of you, your team, your broader organization, and outside advisers, as well as in how much you decide to invest in others' insights. What you need to see depends on the business context. If your environment is reasonably predictable and the strategy is well defined, execution may be the most important. If your environment is highly disrupted or if your business model is in flux, then a high-powered strategy may be in order. Use your broad Vantage Point to assess whether you need to be more of a long-term strategist, a strong tactical operator, or an artful blend of both.

• • •

Jake was the long-serving COO of a US food company in the Midwest when he got a sudden field promotion to CEO. The company was about to embark on a major international expansion plan, primarily through acquisitions. Jake immediately embraced a new external priority that required him to shift his Vantage Point to a higher altitude and longer-term focus from what he was used to, which was mastering the daily details across the organization.

A bit like Leo, Jake kept letting himself get drawn back into the details because that was his comfort zone. He did not realize how dangerous it was to get distracted from longer-term thinking—potentially scuttling the expansion plan if he wasn't on top of it. David and Carol coached him to recognize that he could still sample day-to-day operating issues, selectively "trusting but verifying" by deeply probing crucial areas, while spending an increasing amount of time on strategy.

"Got it! I love using binoculars for that long view. But I better keep the microscope on my desk," Jake said. And he did, finding he could balance the long view with the details.

See People Clearly

It's harder than you think to master this part of your Vantage Point when starting the big new role. If you have moved to a new organization, then nearly every relationship will be new. But even if you have moved up inside your own business line or function, you still need to update your Vantage Point. Old friends are now reports; some who used to be senior to you are now your peers. The relationship dynamic has irrevocably changed, and you must change how you interact with people because of that. There are sacrifices to moving up in an organization, and you must make them.

Take a look up. There's always someone above you, maybe even a constellation of people. You have a new boss or a set of them—a board of directors, a CEO, a member of the executive committee—or you may have dual reporting lines. Get to know your new boss(es) to understand what they care about and what they expect from you.

Now look sideways. With each step upward, peer relationships become more valuable; the larger and more complex your role becomes, the more interdependencies you have with your colleagues. How you collaborate becomes even more crucial. Most who enter the big new role don't realize that they'll be judged on how effectively they connect with peers. Research indicates the quality of these relationships, even more than those with your boss or your direct reports, predicts who is likely to succeed or fail.[2] And while there are clear guidelines on the interpersonal dimension of leadership with one's boss and direct reports, it's less clear with lateral relationships. Spend time cultivating these. Be mindfully alert to the cues you're getting from peers. Don't overdo it, but don't overlook what you sense. Some peers will partner with you generously. Others may just pretend, or even be directly menacing, and interactions with them should never happen from a place of vulnerability.

Now look below to your team. Having an accurate read of their capabilities, potential, and character is a prerequisite for your success in the new role. In chapter 9 we described the many ways we can misperceive others based on our biases, emotional tendencies, worldviews, decision frameworks, and personality factors. In the early days of a new role, personality factors can have an outsize impact on how you see others and how they see you, which can eclipse work and life experience, capabilities, character, and potential. It is crucial to raise your awareness of these factors as you begin a new role. Your tendency will be to make snap decisions about how good an individual is based on how they show up to you in your first few interactions. This can lead to you not only overestimating or underestimating their capabilities but also misreading whether they are friend or foe.

• • •

James was recruited to be chief revenue officer of a fast-growing manufacturer. He was under tremendous pressure to turn on all the taps to deliver record sales right away. But his number two team member was driving him crazy.

"My hair is on fire, but Kristi doesn't have a care in the world despite her team not bringing in a new global client in months," he said, rolling his eyes. "Generally, she avoids me, but when I seek her out to talk, she laughs it off, saying that everything is under control. I don't feel heard. Beyond that, I can't even understand what her plan is. She talks in sentence fragments and mostly name-drops."

Something sounded off to David. "Have you spoken with anyone who has known her for a long time?"

"Yes, no one else on the sales force gets her. Her clients swear by her, although they can't really put their finger on what she does other than saying, 'She's great.' The CEO loves her too."

James's frustration grew, but six weeks later Kristi delivered the largest sale in the company's history. At the next quarterly business review, the CEO chuckled and said, "Yeah, Kristi only hunts for trophies. You can't count on her in any single quarter, but you better know you can count on her overall."

Misreading people can be particularly acute when you are under stress—like James was to deliver results immediately. Kristi's behavior certainly wasn't collaborative, but James could have spent more time exploring with her and others about what her superpowers were and how she had landed big clients in the past. Rushing to judgment will lead you to skip over data and make rash assessments based on wishful thinking. This is the time to keep yourself centered and practice the Five Cs. Find which one will help you the quickest.

• • •

Alejandro was an heir to a European conglomerate, and he and his brother were in competition for the CEO succession. Alejandro was handed a ragtag set of businesses to knit together and grow, while his brother got a high-performing business to run.

Alejandro was panicking. Carlos, the most senior leader on his team, was bad-mouthing him inside and outside the organization as an untalented "entrepren-heir." Carlos resisted Alejandro's every move, emboldened by his relationship with the patriarch CEO, built through decades of making money for the family.

But Carlos made a fatal error, crossing the line with the patriarch during a heated meeting. That opened an opportunity for Alejandro to fire Carlos. He found someone in his network whom he thought had great experience and who was known and trusted by his father. But the results of a confidential check on the candidate's track record were disastrous: six negative references, two neutral, and one positive.

Alejandro didn't listen to the feedback. "I think the karma here is so special," he said of the poorly rated candidate. "He likes me, knows my dad, and was best man at the wedding of Carlos's number two, so he will be great in retaining talent when I fire Carlos."

Alejandro was on the verge of making a career-ending move because he was stuck in the wrong Vantage Point—one with a blind spot created by his laser focus on replacing Carlos.

"It seems to me that you're going to do this no matter what, aren't you?" David asked.

Alejandro smiled wryly. "It's that obvious?"

"Yes, it is. I'm here for you whatever you decide. But let's imagine what life will be like a year from now. Never mind the quality of the working relationship. Given your business strategy, what skills does this new person need to execute?"

Sometimes the best interventions don't land. This one didn't. "I know where you are going with this. But I'm telling you, it's karma. I've made up my mind."

Alejandro is now reporting to his brother, the new CEO, and David is coaching him on how to stay resilient under stress.

We all can make snap judgments. Be aware of a tendency to judge capability or character, good or bad, on the basis of only a few data points. Consciously hold yourself back and expand your set of criteria beyond your reaction to their personality. Remember to include experience, skills, and potential to grow to get a broader and more fully informed perspective. No matter your personal reaction, ask yourself, What have they done that I respect or that has added value to the team?

Validate Your Mandate

Often, mandates for new jobs turn out to be "as advertised," but you can't count on it. Sometimes you get to your big new role and find out your Vantage Point on your mandate isn't what you thought or hoped it would be. The reality could almost be the opposite of what you were led, or allowed yourself, to believe. If you don't check your Vantage Point, you can lead yourself astray. Fortunately, there are some options you can consider before you take the job to reduce the risk of misreading the mandate.

Bertrand had been a New York–based CEO of a midsize media company for ten years, but he was feeling bored and unfulfilled. He had always played it safe, going for incremental initiatives because he felt a tremendous obligation to protect the livelihood of thousands of employees. While the company consistently grew revenue and earnings, it was losing ground to its bolder competitors. Bertrand engaged us to help him explore what was most important to him at this point in his life. After a few sessions it became clear to him that he wanted to embark on a new adventure "anywhere outside of media" and to become more of a risk-taker at work. At a social gathering, Bertrand met a board member of a well-known arts nonprofit, who casually mentioned that the board was looking for a new executive director to grow the organization. Bertrand told him he would be open to a discussion about the role.

Things moved fast from there, and after only a few interviews, Bertrand was offered the job. We advised him to slow things down because he hadn't done much due diligence, but on impulse he accepted the job.

It turns out the board was delighted to find Bertrand after a long, unsuccessful external search process. When he started his new adventure, he discovered the organization was not positioned to grow; it was actually on the verge of losing major donors. The executive team was in disarray, and the entire governance and operating model was in need of major transformation. The worst part was Bertrand *could have* known had he slowed down to validate his Vantage Point. He ruefully said, "I thought I would be spending a lot of my time with fascinating emerging artists and learning content, but instead I'm mired in a big mess."

Bertrand's case happens all the time, where the promise of new opportunities can often override reason. There are other ways to misread your mandate. How about when you are given a license to "change the DNA" and transform a business and its culture? Sometimes the well-intended people who gave you that mandate will stop you in your tracks, ensnared by the very DNA they said they wanted to change.

More often than you might expect, when you are invited in to be a change agent you wind up experiencing organ rejection. These mandates frequently do not really have the support that you've been assured of. Sometimes bosses and boards are in love with the idea of change, but when they see what it entails, they decide not to go there after all.

• • •

Andrea was recruited to head the transformation office of a Canadian industrial products company, with a mandate to take out 25 percent of the cost base. The CEO assured her that he would back her.

She had a playbook on how to lead a transformation from previous experience, and closely collaborated with her new peers to scope areas of opportunity. But when she presented her brilliant plan to the executive committee, the team erupted with objections. Flustered, the CEO grasped for a way out, stumbling through questions and comments about stranded costs and imaginary savings. Andrea had been meticulous in building the case, and frustrated, she shot back at the CEO: "Stranded costs are your job to deal with, not mine." A week later, we were sad but not surprised to hear that Andrea had moved on from the company "for personal reasons."

It might seem like Andrea couldn't have prepared for such a mandate flip. She had the Vantage Point the organization was promising. But usually, we find, there are signs and clues to whether the people giving the mandate have validated *their* Vantage Point. Understand that you can never do too much due diligence prior to getting into such a situation. For example, if you have access to your predecessor, spend time to get perspective on their experience in the role, including the quality of their interaction with key stakeholders. Talk to other leaders in the company to get their take on your mandate. Then come up with a draft high-level plan of what you want to get done in the first ninety days, and test it with your new boss or the board (or even test it before you take the big new role) to see how they react.

Listen closely to what company leaders say about your plans. If you mostly hear "Yes, that works for us, absolutely," then that's a promising sign—although no guarantee of what will happen once you take the job. But if you hear "Well, that would really depend on a lot of things," followed by lengthy hedging statements, then that is a red flag. Clarify expectations before taking the role. When you do arrive, pay attention to behaviors more than words. Vantage Points are validated best when they are validated by brain, heart, *and* gut.

Summary

Validate your new Vantage Point. When you step into a big new role, your first task is to be aware that your Vantage Point must change. Step back and take another look at your priorities, operating environment, and new relationships. Expand your Vantage Point to see more and see further.

- **Get the right clarity in your Vantage Point.** Your relationships and interpersonal challenges, the third dimension of leadership, shift significantly with a new role. Even well-established connections are impacted by new dynamics, and you need to test your assumptions. Look up, sideways, and below to start to understand all of the new players in your role. Learn as much as you can about your new boss(es). Former peers and friends may now report to you, and you must adjust how you interact to get the right Vantage Point. Cultivate relationships with new peers, too. This is the hardest to do but also the most important; good peer relationships are the strongest predictor of success in a big new role. Get to know your direct reports. Don't let wishful thinking, or your fears, cloud your capacity to assess others.

- **Get the right resolution in your Vantage Point.** One of the most important reality checks is whether the mandate you believe you have been given is actually true. Do as much due diligence as you can before you take the job. Once you are in your new role, if you sense something is off, look more closely. Don't be afraid to probe and test the limits of your mandate and to see if it is changing.

- **Get the right scope in your Vantage Point.** You are operating at a bigger scale and scope than ever before, which will require you to lead in a different way. This is less about doing the work yourself and more than ever about orchestrating the right conditions for others to be at their best.

- **Get the right level in your Vantage Point.** Now that you are higher up in the organization, you can see the bigger picture and the horizon is further out. Use this Vantage Point to think more strategically and less tactically, doing more long-term planning, and connecting beyond the organization. Sharpen your strategic perspective by looking at longer-term trends and using systems thinking to identify and assess new opportunities and threats.

13

Do What Only You Can Do

A journey of a thousand miles begins with a single step.

—**Lao Tzu**

We saw in the previous chapter the importance of validating your Vantage Point (V) right away in a big new role. So, the MOVE sequence shifts with a big new job to be MOvE. With the proper Vantage Point you can now pivot to creating Mindful Alertness in your new job.

Be Mindfully Alert to New External Priorities, and Find Options to Meet Them (M+O)

A new job creates new external priorities. You can use classic approaches to accelerated integration as a preliminary expression of the new priorities.[1] Typically these focus on the first ninety days to address any issues such as the key elements of accelerated integration, which are:[2]

- Bonding with your team
- Accurately reading the organizational culture
- Understanding the expectations and motivations of all your stakeholders
- Driving quick wins
- Beginning to work on longer-term strategy

We believe getting those priorities right in your first three months is necessary but not sufficient for your success. Because everything is so new, new demands will pop up without warning—you must be prepared to face the unexpected. Also, while you're focused on those first few months, from the very beginning you should have a much longer time horizon in mind about your success—say, three years. At this level, that's a strategic necessity.

Sudden shifts demand you stay mindfully alert

Not only can your external priorities change in a moment, but because everything is new, it is more likely that as you learn about your position, you may suddenly detect a new set of demands that supersede the original ones. This can happen even if you come in with a very clear Vantage Point.

Take Rick, for example. With his excellent pedigree in sales and marketing, he was the perfect CEO choice for an insurtech company. It had just gone through series C funding, and the leadership team was on a sprint to an IPO off the back of their groundbreaking new product.

Day one was flawless, at least sartorially, with Rick in a Zegna Techmerino navy blue blazer. He called a meeting of his fledgling sales team and gave them an inspiring speech. Together, he said, they were going to take the company from 100,000 customers to one million in less than three years. The team was revved up and with him all the way.

Rick excitedly told David, "I have so got this! It's everything I dreamed of. A killer product, a dream team at the top, and the founder couldn't be a better partner. All I see are green lights all the way."

David was worried that Rick might not be probing deeply or widely enough. He suggested that Rick meet some skip-level team members in addition to his direct reports, but Rick rejected the idea. "There's a mountain of work to do in sales and marketing, so I'm pretty much focused on that team. It's where I can really add value. I'm working hand in hand with the CFO, and we have a strong COO, so I can rely on him for a lot of the day-to-day."

Two months later, Rick finally visited the call center. He was horrified by what he heard. Many customers were outraged, complaining of bait-and-switch tactics for the new product, something that hadn't shown up in the metrics presented to the senior leadership team. Rick immediately put his team to work, searching for the root causes of the problem. They found product design flaws and sales incentives that actually discouraged the sales force from checking if the product was suitable for their customers.

So much for scalability as Rick's external priority. A surprise crisis was now his top challenge. Rick found himself accompanying the founder and general counsel to a meeting with regulators to lay out what had happened and present a plan to fix it. The coaching shifted from how best to scale the business to how to execute in a crisis.

Had Rick been more mindfully alert, he may have caught this before it became a problem. But he had locked in his external priorities and wasn't checking himself.

Leaders in big new jobs *must* expect these kinds of surprises and therefore balance speed and the accuracy of their external priorities. Do your homework before you come up with your priorities, but don't lock them in stone. As with design thinking, come up with a prototype priority and then try it out, while staying open to data and experiences that confirm or refute that priority.[3]

Be prepared to scale back or shift in order to deliver

Taking on a big new role often leads people to want to prove themselves by setting the bar for goals, and for themselves, too high. This is a time to stay mindfully alert. Overambition is common and blinds new leaders to both the resources that will constrain them and the fact that people's appetites for change can also constrain them.

A bitter family battle had led to the sudden expulsion of the CEO of a European aerospace manufacturer. After an emergency board meeting, Arjun got the nod to lead the company. He went from leading a team of twenty to being responsible for several thousand.

His appointment surprised everyone, including himself. Arjun had joined the executive committee less than a year earlier, and he hadn't been on anyone's formal list of CEO succession candidates.

At his first meeting with David, Arjun showed the kind of wild spirit and lateral thinking that could help him rocket to success as CEO. "Let's face it," he declared, "we have been myopic in the past and very, very conservative. For the past three years I have been burning to try big new things."

"Well, the chair put you in the job for a reason. What do you have in mind?"

Arjun articulated a set of options that were breathtaking: a game-changing potential merger, product innovation, robotics initiatives—the list went on.

Arjun's passion flowed, but David had seen this many times. He wondered how much Arjun had thought through his ideas and how much he was driven by an impulse to prove himself, as he was the proverbial kid in a candy store. Had he considered how much his team could realistically take on?

David led him through a series of questions to get him to see this. "Seems like you have a good perspective on the various possibilities. What additional upsides or downsides should you take into account for each of these major initiatives? What do you think your team's capacity for new initiatives and change is? And how are you thinking about prioritizing and sequencing the list?"

From that conversation, Arjun decided it would be best to dial back on some goals and push harder on others. He also played with different combinations of initiatives. After a few conversations, Arjun could see the chess board a few moves out.

Pay attention to long-term priorities and options for achieving them

Leaders in new jobs must think in terms of the first few months but also farther out, say, three years. Be deliberate in imagining what a ten-out-of-ten outcome would look like for your external priorities in three years. Then work backward to what a ten would look like in two years, one year, six months, and today, to figure out what intermediate priorities are required to succeed over the long haul. No doubt your view of longer-term success will change over time as you learn new things and conditions evolve, but this is a good strategic discipline to cultivate right from the start.

Now that you are paying attention to your longer-term external priorities, you need to generate options to meet them. Stepping into a new role comes with increased uncertainty, so you will need to generate even more options than usual. The good news is that because you have been promoted, you probably have more resources to do this.

As an example, what if you were to generate options for achieving a ten-out-of-ten for ambitious financial or talent goals? Scan through the (partial) list of possibilities in the box below, which complement the external Options Generator in chapter 6.

Options to Reach Financial and Talent Goals

- New talent to upgrade or extend your team's capabilities

- New product development

- New applications of technology

- Geographic expansion

- New pricing strategies

- Better customer segmentation

- New customer experiences

- New channels

- Innovation initiatives

- Ventures into new business models

- Mergers and acquisitions

- Strategic partnerships

Ask yourself, What different mixes and sequences of the above options could get you to your ten-out-of-ten outcome in three years?

Be Mindfully Alert to New Internal and Interpersonal Priorities, and Find Options to Meet Them (M+O)

Your big new role may require you to withstand pressures—and require a level of stamina that would previously have crushed you. One CEO, dropped into a turnaround situation, said, "It's like there are two guns pointed at my head. Do one thing, the first one fires. Do another, and the second one fires. All my available choices have huge drawbacks."

Prepare for bookings on your calendar to skyrocket. Expect to be on call 24-7. People will talk at you as they push their agendas and ideas, tell you what *you* need to do, and expect you to make instant decisions. Time spent with you bestows bragging rights, and you'll endure endless "casual" conversations with not-so-hidden agendas. As one new *Fortune* 30 CEO told us, "Everyone thinks they own me!"

And in a way they do. The higher you go, the more you are stepping into a new identity where you now represent your entire organization. Others see you less as a person and more as an "enterprise entity" who stands for and speaks for the whole organization. You also need to watch every word you say or write and how you behave, both because a stray remark could impact your stock price and because your personal reputation now has an impact on your organization's reputation. This level of pressure and presence will feel new, exhausting, scary, and possibly lonely.

Stress is higher, but there are options to manage it

Fortunately, there are good options to deal with each of the challenges that require you to develop your inner strengths and identify new internal priorities.

You have wellness options to adjust to your big new job. High performance is supported by a high level of holistic health, including sleep and recovery, nutrition, physical activity, mental energy, and personal motivation. We help the leaders we work with assess their overall wellness and come up with new options for self-care.

Some stress is driven by environmental factors, but a lot is needlessly self-inflicted. Many of the executives we work with suffer in a new job because they are impatient with themselves. Many get caught up in constantly trying to rate their performance, which creates artificial highs and lows in mood and energy. Don't try to keep a running assessment of the value of your actions. Yes, every day counts toward cumulative accomplishments in your job, but use some self-compassion to stop yourself from overindexing on the short term.

Building your capacity for patience is an important internal goal in the new job. In most positions, it takes a full year to see all the aspects that are involved in a job and to begin to build strong relationships. Only then can you really start taking stock of whether it's right for you and how well you have done.

Identify with the organization, not just the areas you lead

Another internal priority when you have been promoted is to rise above the silo challenge. Your job may very well require you to shift your identity to encompass the entire organization, not just the part that you are directly responsible for. To be most effective, senior leaders must see themselves as an embodiment of their organizations, and others must see that as well. If you ever operated with a siloed mindset, now is the time to adopt an enterprise identity to act in the best possible interest of the overall organization.

Doing this is more natural for CEOs than for others who may have been incentivized largely on the performance of their teams or silo. Teaming up with peers requires you to transcend your personal agenda and point of view. For example, it can be jarring to lend resources to help a peer achieve an important milestone for the company while your individual achievement lags. As you step up, it feels like a sacrifice, but shifting your balance to enterprise leadership creates more value for the organization. Ask yourself, are you willing to suboptimize your area in favor of another for the greater good?

On the plus side, having an enterprise mindset offers you a chance to have a broader impact as you take on more accountability. One of our scientist leaders has saved millions of lives through her institute's research. At public events she is swarmed by people. As an introvert, she often feels tapped out with no more to give, but she keeps soldiering on.

"One day it flipped," she said. "I realized I was a conduit for hope through my institute, and I didn't need willpower to dredge something up. I do have hope and I could let it flow through me. That moment changed how I saw myself—by representing science. It's bigger than I am, and I stopped feeling drained."

It's more important than ever to live a life beyond reproach

You are now so influential that your personal reputation affects your organization's reputation, so there is a heightened internal priority to self-regulate. Be deliberate about everything you say and do, and live in congruence with your personal values. At no time in your career is your personal brand more scrutinized than when you step into that new role. Your success can bring out the best or worst in others. Gossip, speculation, and wagers about you will run rampant.

With the growth of social media, whistleblowers, and investigative journalism, life is so transparent that you need to be ever mindful of your public behaviors and digital footprint.

Suzette was a high-ranking member of the Cour de Cassation, the supreme court of France. She was front-page news for her adroit handling of difficult issues. One jealous colleague with a history of indiscretion had been passed over in favor of Suzette and had just thrown a rock at her glass house. Suzette met with Carol for an emergency session because her colleague had released a video to the media. Suzette slid her phone across the desk to show Carol. It was bad.

Seeking a carefree, observation-free vacation, Suzette had jetted to the United States to celebrate Mardi Gras. The three-second video of her already had three hundred thousand views. The fact that every woman with her was doing the same thing didn't matter. The neon-green headline read, *"La vérité nue est révélée!"* That is, "The bare truth is revealed!"

Suzette looked physically hurt, like she'd been sucker punched. To her credit, she said, "I need a plan." She hammered it out, was deadly strategic, proactive, and not defensive, and she survived the damage.

Retaliation wasn't even a temptation. "I handed her that opportunity on a silver platter," Suzette said about her colleague. "She's revealed her character. I won't forget that, and I will never compromise myself again." Suzette learned the hard way. It's better to think about your reputation before the fact rather than after. But if not, taking immediate responsibility can save the day.

New jobs bring a host of new relationships

In the previous chapter we saw the importance of clearly viewing who all these new people are in your new job. It is equally important to invest in building relationships with them and to do this as skillfully as possible. Think about what an ideal relationship, a ten out of ten, would be with your boss, each of your peers, and each of your direct reports. Considerations include:

- How open, direct, and frequent you want your communication to be with each other

- How well you would like them to know you and to understand and care about what you think and feel

- How much you want to get to know them

- How you want them to view you

- What impact you want to have on them

Start this exercise with your new boss in mind. Some of the usual flashpoints in "managing up" occur because the new leader gets out of step with their boss, either underinvolving them or being overly solicitous.[4]

Anu was named CEO of a public industrial products company. The board paired her with an executive chair whom they believed could be a supportive guide.

From the get-go, Anu did nothing to build the relationship with her chair. She didn't keep him up to date and wouldn't return his calls. "It's my company. I know what I'm doing. He's a distraction," she told David. Her overconfidence was palpable, but she was adamant. "I'm sick of his 'suggestions.' Come on, they're orders. I'm seeing him later today and telling him it's either me or him." She was ready to lean in, big time; but she needed to be able to generate and be open to a different option.

After a long discussion on the merits and dangers of her stance, David finally said, "Anu, Marshall Goldsmith has a saying: 'CEO good. Chairman better.' I say, 'Executive chairman best.' You take him on and you're dead."

Anu cooled down a bit and acknowledged some of the wisdom in the executive chairman's advice and questions. Likewise, after meeting with David, the executive chairman realized that he needed to let Anu have more room to lead. It put the relationship on a better track.

*   *   *

Martin had the opposite problem of Anu, seeking *too much* guidance. He had just been promoted to head up the largest business unit of his travel and leisure company and called the CEO daily about all manner of decisions. Frustrated, the CEO met with us. "I tell Martin he's got the best job in the world. He's the boss. All he has to do is think about the second- and third-order consequences, and then act. Then he can go home and sleep at night. What's the matter with him?"

The matter was Martin didn't recognize that his new boss had more of a lean-back style. His boss embraced the "do what only you can do" approach, and Martin was bringing up problems his boss felt Martin should solve himself. We worked with Martin to help him see his new reality and to come up with new options for decision-making, including finding other sounding boards and reserving only the most uncertain, highest-impact decisions for discussions with his boss.

Eye-rolling from peers is dangerous; strong relationships are a springboard

Seb was poached from a tech company to be chief digital officer of a retail company desperate to shift to e-commerce. His reports loved him; his boss wanted him to be his successor and gave him carte blanche to hit the numbers. But still . . .

"I'm worried," Seb told Carol. "My boss wants me to light a fire under my peers and challenge them. But I'm catching looks." He was smart to worry. His boss had been passed over for an even higher role for being too aggressive. It seemed the boss was now getting Seb to be the aggressor for him. "I can see it coming—I get him the numbers, he moves up, and then I am the one passed over for not being collaborative."

When Carol asked Seb's peers about him, one powerful player said, "If Seb becomes my boss, I'll quit." Others were on the fence, but it was clear if he kept up his aggressive behavior, he'd be passed over like his boss was. He changed course, shifting his interpersonal goals and his stance from lean in to lean with. He worked with two peers to come up with a collaborative plan to hit the numbers. It worked, and soon Seb was promoted to his boss's old job. Those peers were now reporting to him and all but one (the contender for the role) said Seb was the first choice. Seb's contender, Dick, was far more senior and had expected the job. Hearing the news, he wept. Seb needed to lean with his team even more now. He sped to Dick's office. "I won't be in this job long, and you are my natural successor," he said. "Let's pump up your compensation, agree on priorities regularly, and stay in close touch. Call when you need to and I'll do the same."

Stunned by the unexpected support, Dick wept again, this time from gratitude and respect.

How others might see you and what to do about it

The higher up you go, the greater the distortion in how people perceive you, because the distance grows between you and others who are deep in the organization. People are definitely not mind readers about who you are, what you care about, and what your intentions are as a leader. Even if you are a naturally good-hearted leader, that doesn't mean others will automatically see you as the caring, appreciative person you believe yourself to be, or that they understand what your underlying motivations are.

You can never underestimate the impact of your power when you are someone's boss. Others experience you as being more powerful than you experience yourself. We call this the gorilla effect, after a joke Carol heard from her best friend as a child. "A thousand-pound gorilla walks into a really crowded bar. Where does it sit?" The friend giggled when Carol had no idea what the answer could be. "Anywhere it wants!" she announced triumphantly.

When you control or impact someone's access to resources, compensation, promotion, or anything else, you are the gorilla. And no matter how much you or others imagine otherwise, you are never not the gorilla. You throw out your arms, and bodies go flying. You can manage it well and even harness it, but you can't forget it.

• • •

David worked with John, a senior executive at a global media company. John was generally a constructive and supportive leader, but occasionally lashed out at team members in front of their peers when he felt they had failed him. One peer said, "John is 99 percent like Luke Skywalker and 1 percent like Darth Vader. If he wants to become great, he needs to take out 99 percent of the 1 percent that is his dark side." Once he received that feedback, John decided it was important to work harder on his self-regulation. Developing this second dimension of leadership can make all the difference to your stakeholders.

When you hit the top, people look at you but may only see a cardboard cutout figure of what a CEO, SVP, or VP HR role means to them. Some will idealize you and put you on a pedestal; others may devalue you and try to throw you off it. This can shift from meeting to meeting. It can give you emotional whiplash until you realize a significant portion of this isn't personal. Practicing any of the Five Cs can help you stay on an even keel.

People will have exaggerated opinions about you and act in accordance with these distorted beliefs. It's painful when people block or bait you or throw up distractions. It's even worse when you are betrayed by people who portray themselves as fans but sow the opposite message to the organization or even to the board.

Whether you're thrown down or lifted up, create that space between whatever stimulus comes your way and give yourself options for how you respond. Name what is happening, steady yourself, and pause long enough to come up with an effective response. If you're hurt or angry, work on not being triggered into a rash action. When you're adored, manage your ego, because hubris leads to overconfidence, and overconfidence is deadly.[5] It predicts business failures more than insecurity.

Anna was taking over merchandising at a firm, replacing a much-loved executive, Janice. Excited to start, Anna dove into the data only to be met with, "That's not how Janice did it."

As an experienced leader, Anna was not defensive. Instead, she used her analytical strengths in a new way. She stepped back and asked extensive questions about Janice's methods. In her coaching we encouraged her to go further—to understand how her employees saw her, what they needed from her. Anna decided to start from the ground up to get to know the wider organizations, and vice versa. She began a series of "let's get to know Anna" forums, where people could ask her any question they wanted. She also spent a week working in a store while wearing a trainee name tag, which showed her sincerity about better understanding the experiences of her employees. Her capacity to lean with proved to be crucial. Her flexibility, humility, and good humor while engaging at ground level helped people see the real Anna. She was able to overcome the "she's not Janice" attitude and truly claim her place in the big new job. Choosing to lean with paved the way for the shift for people to see who she really was.

• • •

Investing time and effort so people can get to know you reduces the reality distortion field but doesn't eliminate it. Some uncertainty about intent and meaning is inherent in every interpersonal interaction. Keep in mind that people often connect the dots using their fears or wishes. Or, equally important, communications can fall between the cracks given the high-pressure, whip-fast life of a senior executive. We had one client whose CMO was shocked to discover that his boss had interviewed a high-profile chief experience officer (CXO) without even checking in to tell him. The grapevine had it that the CMO would report to this new CXO. "It felt devaluing," he told Carol, "after all I've done for this company? To not even be told? It's humiliating." It felt bad enough that he called the CEO. Though he sounded calm, he was very distressed and knew he'd consider leaving if he had to report to this new person.

The CEO was equally startled by the call. "No!" she said, "That's not it at all. Yes, I should have slowed down and talked with you, but the opportunity popped up out of the blue and there was no time. But you have it all wrong, the CXO would report to you, not the other way around!"

This is why confirmation cycles, as discussed in chapter 11, will be crucial to building stronger alignment between you and your people, especially if you or they are new to the organization.

It is lonely at the top; finding someone who is happy for your happiness is rare

At higher elevations there are fewer people you can turn to who will not have a personal agenda when you have a sensitive issue to deal with. If you have been in the organization a while, you can mitigate this by relying on that small group of people whom you have known and trusted enough to tell you the truth as they see it.

But what about when you just want to celebrate a personal win, or let your guard down, or laugh with someone? It turns out this space is hard to find because most people don't have the capacity for what Buddhists call "spontaneous joy," or the ability to experience happiness or enthusiasm for another's success. But it's crucial to do so. Marriage research has shown, for example, that as damaging as it is for a partner to not get support during a difficult time, it's *more* damaging when partners don't celebrate successes together.[6]

Likewise, leaders in new jobs need to find people to celebrate with. It could be a coach. One newly minted *Fortune* 30 CEO showed up for a coaching session with us with the brightest eyes and an infectious grin. "My first earnings call went great! A key investor said I had the Midas touch," he exclaimed. "So glad to talk, I can't brag about this to anyone else!" Another CEO started our session by informing us that eighty thousand of his people would vote on a possible strike in the next hour. He refused to reschedule the session and talked for more than the hour. "This was great," he said at the end. "I feel rejuvenated, I can do this now. You're the only ones I can laugh with."

Because it's so lonely at the top, find a friend, coach, or a trusted adviser to share your journey and lighten your load to help you sustain high performance.

How to Engage and Effect Change in Your New Role (E)

Here are some practical things to do as a leader early on in your new role that will pay off.

Don't just broadcast: Make communication a two-way street

In a new job, outlining your Leader's Intent and gaining alignment on it is key, as we discussed in chapter 10. To have a good two-way discussion on Leader's Intent, you will need to work hard to make sure psychological safety is sufficiently high so that people share what they really think. This may require you to signal over and over again your genuine willingness to have a dialogue before your team takes you up on the offer.

One way to accelerate great two-way communication is to take the opportunity in your first meeting with your direct reports to ask them about their day-to-day challenges, their hopes, and their fears. One powerful question to ask is, "What energizes you the most at work?"

Experiment with the "grant three wishes" approach, which we borrowed from a fast-track executive in industrial products who was routinely promoted every eighteen months. He would ask, "What are two to three things that I can realistically do right now to make your life better? I promise to make them happen." Your team is unlikely to expect this. They will be grateful for the offer and even more loyal to you when you deliver.

All of this will build goodwill and pave the way for some early wins when you engage.

Stop doing stuff others can do

Make sure those early wins you go for count as much as possible by winning at something only you can do, rather than a bunch of tactical wins your team is capable of.

Your team may not have the right talent and governance model in place to allow you to concentrate on the kinds of "reserved" decisions that we identified in chapter 11. If that is the case, fixing that is the first thing that only you can do. We urge you to get on with it and score that early win.

Jiro was promoted to lead Japan and Korea for his educational services company. A humble and frugal leader, he was determined from day one in his big new job to eliminate what he felt was wasteful spending, which he found personally offensive. Jiro immediately tightened up requirements for flying business class, lowered client entertainment budgets, and made black car expenses nonreimbursable.

We asked him about these moves. "How important was it to you, on a scale of one to ten, to tackle this right out of the gate?"

"To me, it's an eight or a nine. I think the spending is egregious and it's something I can act on early to show my leadership."

He admitted several other people could do this—the COO, the CFO, and others—but thought it would be a stronger message coming from the regional CEO. Jiro also readily admitted it wasn't an important move to the company, just something he was focused on and saw as an easy early win. He even noted that the things only he could do, aligning his team to accelerate growth and increasing margins, were just harder.

The temptation to go after early wins that are easier is real, but if they're something other people can do, don't engage. It's not just going to be yourself you're battling here, either. Sometimes your team will pressure you by trying to "delegate up" and get you to do things for them. Actively manage these situations by weighing in only when someone else can't make the decision.

Not caving to what's familiar and easy is one of the hardest aspects of a big new job, but you must develop the self-discipline to engage on only the things that only you can do.

You don't always have to break the tie

One thing you'll learn that only you can do in your new job is be the ultimate decision-maker on a divisive issue. Just because you have the power to decide on something, and it is within the scope of something that only you can do, doesn't mean you always have to do it. There can be consequences if you are regularly overriding team members, even if you ensure their voices are heard. The best course of action may be to table the decision and to try to gain consensus down the road. Or you may simply conclude that you are going to close the books on the decision, because the rancor that a decision would create is not worth it to you or the organization.

Delay people decisions at your peril

Building your team will be a primary responsibility in the new job. In our experience, being attentive to and action-oriented about this is crucial. As one of our leaders joked, "The last time I waffled on people, I got flattened like a pancake in my job."

This doesn't mean you decide people's futures for the sake of deciding. Nor does it mean panicking and reflexively acting on someone's career because you feel extraordinary pressure to make a move. It does mean moving quickly on those people decisions that matter most, and pacing them so that the team can absorb the changes without missing a beat.

In chapter 11 we equipped you with some pointers on how to evaluate your team members in terms of their leadership capabilities and potential. In some cases, the decision to keep someone or let them go is clear-cut, but often it's not. When it's not, you should be clear in your own mind about what minimum acceptable performance looks like and communicate that to the individual, along with development advice if appropriate, to give them a chance to work up to the level you need.

When Michelle was promoted to run a division of her industrial products company, she inherited a CFO, Jeff, who had been put into the role a month earlier as a stretch assignment. Everybody loved Jeff. He was smart and collaborative and had strong technical skills.

But in Jeff's first full quarter, his division missed its internal forecasts by a mile. Turned out there was a serious flaw in Jeff's forecast model. Michele was surprised but didn't take immediate action because everyone said, "Jeff's so good, this is out of character."

It wasn't. Jeff soon threw two promising staffers under the bus, and they left. When it came time to kick off a new three-year strategic plan, Jeff said, "I got it," but he didn't. Despite Jeff's popularity, Michelle pushed hard for a new CFO and prevailed.

The "halo effect" had protected Jeff.[7] His charisma and competence in some areas pulled people to see him as better than he was. Not moving fast enough on people issues is one of the rookie mistakes that can kill a new leader. Fortunately, Michelle moved just in time. If Jeff had stayed and bungled the three-year strategic plan, Michelle likely wouldn't have survived it.

Summary

In a big new role, your external, internal, and interpersonal priorities and options (M and O) will change. You'll experience new ones and need new strategies to generate them before you engage to effect change at scale (E). Here's what to know:

- Classic accelerated integration programs that focus on the first few months in a big new role can help you get started, but you also need to develop longer-term plans (three years out) and generate many options for getting a ten-out-of-ten outcome on your three-year outlook. Work your way back from there to look at two-year and one-year outcomes as well. You should be thinking ahead more than you used to.

- Expect the following new dynamics in a big new job:

  - External priorities will shift suddenly, even when you have a solid Vantage Point. Be prepared to shift with them.

  - You will want to do too much too fast. Check your ambition, match your goals to your resources, and be aware of people's ability and desire to take on the amount of change you're introducing.

  - Your internal demands will increase, especially on your health. Focus on sleep, nutrition, exercise, counseling, and other physical and mental self-care to ensure you have the stamina to meet the demands of the job.

- Be mindfully alert that you are now an "enterprise entity" as well as a person. This means that:

  - You must identify with the whole organization, not just the parts you're comfortable or familiar with.

  - You have new relationships with former peers who may now report to you, former bosses who may be peers, and new bosses whom you may not know. Get to know them all, and adjust your behavior to the relationship. Take special care with peer relationships, which will be most crucial to your success.

  - You live in a glass house and must behave in a way that is beyond reproach. What you say and what you do will be scrutinized and used.

  - The higher up you go, the greater the distortion in how people perceive you; they see you as more powerful than you see yourself. People will fill in their uncertainty about situations with their fears and wishes, whether that's your intent or not. Invest in letting people get to know you as much as you can to break down these misconceptions.

- It will be lonelier in the big new job. Find someone you can share private moments, wins, and laughs with. Sharing successes is crucial.

- When engaging in your new job, make sure you:

  - Signal your Leader's Intent and then have a two-way discussion about it; don't just broadcast it.

  - Do what only you can do as a leader, and don't overexercise your decision authority.

  - Don't delay on making people decisions. One of the top regrets of new senior leaders is that they moved too slowly on getting the right team in place.

MOVE

to
Drive
10x
Change

14

Shoot for the Moon

Shoot for the moon. Even if you miss, you'll land among the stars.

—Norman Vincent Peale

Cheryl's team was exhausted from a year-plus of unprecedented crisis management, but things were easing up and they were now grappling with their new three-year stretch goals at the consumer packaged goods company. What they didn't know was that CEO Cheryl was on the verge of internally announcing Sky, a bold initiative to become the leader in their market within seven to ten years.

Would they rise to this new challenge, or resist it? And even if they all bought in, could they execute?

• • •

Up to now when talking about your goals as a leader, we have focused on specifying what a ten out of ten looks like—the best-case scenario for any given real-time challenge.

This chapter and the next focus on what a *100 out of 10* would look like, or what we call 10x performance on your biggest plans. One of the things that only leaders can do is set the level of long-term ambition for their team and organization. We hope that you are drawn to the idea of setting supremely high goals. Even if you are not, there is an extrinsic driver: Some of your competitors will be trying to achieve 10x results to outperform you. You better get there before they do.

You can use MOVE to craft and execute on long-term 10x goals while simultaneously dealing with the turbulence of your highest-stakes day-to-day and medium-term leadership priorities. When we say aim for 10x, we don't mean it as a literal multiplier or some real metric, at least not in all cases. Just think of it as your most ambitious, transformational external goal that you believe you can motivate others to work toward.

If you are in a startup already growing at 200 percent a year, 10x to you may be to come up with a brand-new offering to create a new market for you and the world. If you are in a fast-growth sector in an established company, it could mean tripling in size in five years. If you are in a large mature business battling to capture a single basis point of additional market share, your 10x may mean a small increase in your Net Promoter Score, which could translate into billions more in earnings.

Usually, 10x tends to be big and long term—three years, five years, or longer. If you can look out ten years or more, your 10x ambition is limited only by your imagination. We therefore encourage you to come up with very big 10x goals for the long term. And remember, 10x goals don't replace all the others you face that aren't as big or ambitious. You still have to achieve all your other external goals day-to-day.

Achieving 10x Goals with MOVE

You apply MOVE in much the same way with 10x priorities as you do with any others. So here we'll just highlight what you'll additionally need to consider when thinking bigger and longer term. This chapter covers how to come up with 10x Three-Dimensional priorities and a set of high-level options to achieve them. You will need to be committed to being even more mindfully alert than before. The next chapter covers validating your Vantage Point, setting your 10x Leader's Intent, and sending out additional leadership signals to take the first steps toward proving the viability of your 10x options.

M: To achieve 10x goals you need to be 10x mindfully alert

Most of us are not naturally equipped to think in 10x terms because we are consumed by the day-to-day. Push yourself to take a longer-term view than is typical for you. Then start dreaming big: name the best and worst possible outcomes for your most important long-term goal. This is based on what you currently know, what we called imaginable unknowns in chapter 3.

Before Cheryl had fully conceived of the Sky initiative, she started by extrapolating what would happen if her company would be able to continue to make inroads on market share for several years in a row.

The key to 10x is to expand this type of thinking to explore a set of currently unimaginable unknowns. Don't worry if this sounds odd! In the early 2020s, geopolitical developments upended the world in ways that many believed were unimaginable just months earlier. But the following exercise could have helped people and organizations to develop some prescient contingency plans. You do this by tapping into the most creative thinking available inside and outside your organization, including:

- Crowdsourcing input from your team, your organization, and customers, partners, and other stakeholders

- Exposing yourself to massively different environments and contexts to look for insights in other industries and geographies

- Soliciting the insights that the best strategic consultants, scientists, academics, futurists, government leaders, activists, and others have to offer

For example, one global technology group we work with has an annual meeting where they invite the best science fiction writers and futurists to explore possibilities together.

Once you have done this exercise, try to describe the "what, who, when, where, and why" version of the best possible outcome for that goal, like we outlined in chapter 3.

It's natural that what you fill in on that worksheet from chapter 3 will be vaguer, fuzzier, more directional, and higher level than is typical with other external demands, because there is so much uncertainty about ambitious long-term goals. Framing 10x priorities requires a deft hand at sensing your team and organization's appetite and capacity for uncertainty and the ultra-high performance it can lead to.

Cheryl and her team had already been proactive in ramping up their official three-year targets for growth and profitability, which the board had approved. As a reminder from chapter 3, they specified their new external priorities as follows:

What: Double annual growth in revenue and profitability compared to prepandemic plan

Who: Leadership team

When: Over a three-year time horizon

Where: Companywide, with higher growth targets in international markets than in the United States

Why: Take full advantage of favorable changes in our competitive operating environment

This was a good expression of medium-term stretch priorities. But now Cheryl was thinking about 10x goals. "Thinking in three-year time frames is good, but in this context, not enough. We have to go big. I want to push us to be an unbeatable force in the marketplace. We anticipate some of our competitors will experience further deterioration that we can take advantage of. My team has also been looking at how we can create more sustainable products and newer technologies that might help us leapfrog our competitors."

David applauded her foresight and ambition. "I love this—can you frame the ambition?"

She replied, "I don't have all the answers and I need help detailing the vision, so I want to keep it high level and inspirational for now. It's too early to form my Leader's Intent. I'm just going to call it Sky. My aim is to get the company to a point where we are universally acknowledged to be far ahead of our closest competitor."

David advised that she must carefully consider her next step given how stretched the team was, but Cheryl seemed unconcerned. "I expect they will be like me—raring to go."

He wasn't sure but wanted to support her. "Maybe. You've had months to think about this and to emotionally prepare yourself, but they haven't. Look, I sense they are solidly with you on the three-year goals. At the same time, they're exhausted, and aside from you and your head of strategy, there's no one on the team with proven long-term thinking. You need to be careful about what you add to their plates now and how you do it."

David suggested a soft launch of the idea as a hedge. Cheryl liked that. "I'll get a group together for an offsite on our long-term future. We'll call it Blue Sky and you can facilitate it. If it works, we drop the 'Blue' and launch Sky off the back of that."

* * *

Setting 10x external priorities has implications for your internal and interpersonal priorities. When one dimension of your leadership ramps up, the others must as well.

Internal priorities: When thinking 10x, internal demands are all about taking a hard look at your personal risk appetite, because the bigger the external goals, of course, the higher the risk of failure. If you have a high appetite for risk as part of your inner game, and tend to lean in to challenges, then setting big goals probably won't require you to summon a special quotient of courage. For many leaders, however, 10x goals are beyond their risk appetite; that means they require bravery, which can be achieved by working on your internal game.

Also, recognize that things will go wrong, always, when pursuing 10x goals, which means you will be dealing with setbacks and the accompanying feelings of stress and failure. Under great stress, it is hard to maintain emotional self-regulation, and it can also be tempting to betray your values by cutting ethical corners, falling into "the ends justify the means" thinking, or avoiding accountability by pointing fingers at others. Maintaining your balance and integrity in times of stress is crucial.

You may also need to guard your integrity when things succeed beyond all expectations. Then it can be tempting to cross the line by applying the same "winner takes all" approach to a trusted partner that you might with a more transactional counterparty or enemy.

Interpersonal priorities: Another common issue with external priorities is being overly ambitious relative to available resources and others' willingness to change. You will need to be especially agile with using the Four Stances, as we outlined in chapter 5. Attaining 10x goals requires 10x levels of trust and commitment. Some people will thrive when you lean in and challenge, others need more space to think or be, and others need caring to thrive. As a leader you need to understand what people need in order to buy into your 10x priorities, be supported, support one another, and create the synergies for success.

● ● ●

David asked Cheryl how she was thinking about her internal and interpersonal priorities.

"I'm not taking this lightly," she responded. "I'm staking my reputation on Sky, and I've had to conjure up a lot of bravery to get myself in the right frame of mind to contemplate announcing it. Delivering it will involve wins and losses, so I will also need to continue to draw on my determination. For me, that translates into committing myself in advance to never getting rattled and to learning from whatever happens. There's another aspect to bravery here, too: I can be overly loyal. You know half my team is already in stretch roles, and statistically some of them will just not be able to rise to 10x challenges. I know I'm going to be torn between loyalty and striving for peak performance and will have to make some tough choices."

"Based on how you handled the crisis, it's clear to me that you have the capacity to always be mindfully alert of your inner state, and you'll need that for Sky," David replied. "It's good that you called out the values conflict around loyalty and how it could hold you back from leaning in. Let's note that for now and unpack it later."

O: Generating options requires a group effort

Many of your challenges have you generating your own options. But 10x challenges are unlikely to pan out if you're trying to do that here. With something so big and ambitious, you're going to need people with other expertise, creative and innovative people, and much more to come up with options that make sense. Ensure that you, your team, and your organization are equipped to be creative and innovative *together*.

• • •

Before the Blue Sky offsite, Cheryl asked David to assess the company's capacity to innovate, through a survey and many executive interviews.[1] He looked at cultural factors such as purpose and shared values, which affected their will to innovate as a company, and he took into account capability factors such as the ability to have robust dialogue about new ideas and skill in experimentation, which affected the "way" they innovated.

Results were mixed: while culture for innovation was strong, the company's execution capabilities were weak.

Together, Cheryl, her team, and David identified three root causes for the weakness. Creativity was low because the best ideas were not making it to the senior leadership team—as the leaders' emphasis on executing against plan encouraged one-way, top-down decision-making. Also, top leaders prioritized being nice as part of their culture, and they associated constructive debate about different ideas as not being nice. Finally, although some experimentation was going on, a lot of it was haphazard, a vestige of the organization's old propensity to "fire, ready, aim."

Cheryl would not have come to these conclusions on her own. She needed broad-based input from her organization and the active engagement of her team to conduct the assessment and to craft effective recommendations. Together she and her team were able to commit to improve their ability to create innovative growth options by:

- Moderating their top-down decision-making approach to ensure that ideas could surface and be entertained from anywhere in the organization

- Creating conditions for discussion forums to provide enough psychological safety to support rigorous debate about options

- Putting clearer prioritization criteria in place

Although the process of growing innovation capacity in an organization may require a significant investment of time and resources, it doesn't always have to. We often find that a few relatively small actions, like those Cheryl and her team took, can have an outsize impact on the organization's ability to innovate.

Options to achieve external priorities

We help our clients come up with options to achieve 10x external priorities by showing them how to infuse whatever creative capacity they have with an exponential mindset: thinking that is both creative and focused on radical, not incremental, change.[2]

First, you identify and explore potential applications to your business model of new technologies that are already disruptive and exponential—things like augmented reality/virtual reality, artificial intelligence, gene editing, blockchain, robotics, quantum computing, and space exploration.

Then you complement this effort by nudging leaders to create a range of future scenarios for geopolitical, macroeconomic, and other long-term societal trends to see how these might translate into disruptive opportunities or threats that could affect the achievement of your 10x goals. One of the leaders we worked with regularly projects trends across multiple generations to reinforce an exponential mindset in his organization. The goal of all this is to get ahead of emerging trends and to come up with possibilities that are otherwise unimaginable to you, rather than catching up by reacting to trends and forces that are already emergent.

Our process goes like this: Bring a group of dreamers together from various parts of your organization and across multiple levels of seniority.[3] Start with a ten-year time horizon. Take any or all exponential forces you identify, and see how they might be used as options to achieve your

10x goals. The group is likely to find this process enormously engaging and produce powerful results, as was true when we pulled on the collective intelligence and ambition of Cheryl's leaders.

• • •

Cheryl hosted the Blue Sky offsite with her team and thirty high-potential executives. She purposely did not name her 10x goal, wanting to ease them into the idea by seeing for themselves that they could come up with radical growth options for the company and then work together to help her frame the initiative. She started the meeting by leaning with to be encouraging and supportive, understanding that psychological safety increases creativity. "One failure that is not acceptable in our organization is a failure of imagination. I know that for most of us it's a new mental muscle, so let's work on it together," she said.

David facilitated so that Cheryl could step back to let the group find its footing. They started by widening the group's peripheral vision, detailing promising new technologies and future trends accompanied by many exciting possibilities. This was followed by warm-up questions designed to help the group stretch its thinking. The group reflected in pairs on the following questions, and then there was a short plenary discussion before moving on to the next question.

- What about the future most excites you? Most terrifies you?

- What are the biggest problems that you and your customers face? What value would be created by solving these?

- The cost of digital biology is plummeting, opening up new frontiers for genetic modification. What implications could this have, good and bad, for society and for the company?

The discussion brought out the group's exponential thinking. Next, everyone was asked to focus on generating options that could deliver large amounts of future value creation for the company. These could be new ideas generated there at the offsite, or they could be existing seed ideas in the three-year plan that they "10xed" by making them bigger and more ambitious.

It worked well. The group was inspired once it saw how to use technologies and trends to develop long-term options for future growth, in line with Cheryl's ten-year time horizon. After that, the five most important value drivers were selected using voting rounds, and small groups mapped each onto options for new products and services, customer experiences, and business models.

At the end of the day, each small group pitched its ideas. The positive energy in the room was palpable as they narrowed the ideas down to a top five, several of which had the potential to generate billions of dollars, at least in theory. They were surprised at how far they had come from what had seemed an insurmountable ask at the beginning of the day.

Cheryl had smartly chosen a don't-lean approach during the session to allow the group to create its own momentum and enthusiasm. As she concluded the day, she leaned in by saying, "I'm delighted with this group and proud of all of you. And there's more to come. We now need to take these long-term ideas and figure out how to take some first steps to test them out in the next couple of months—really start to effect change. Today I'm announcing the official start to Project Sky: to be number one in our space and untouchable."

The concept was launched. Now, Cheryl needed to develop her Leader's Intent.

Options to achieve internal and interpersonal priorities

Your 10x plans hit many challenges, and when they do, you will need to draw on the second and third dimensions of leadership. You can find options to increase bravery, improve your capacity to handle setbacks, maintain integrity, and cultivate interpersonal agility by looking at each quality you need to work on through the Four Stances and applying the Five Cs. Cheryl needed these options right out of the gate.

• • •

Within a month of announcing her 10x initiative, Cheryl hit her first major obstacle: a surprise regulatory ruling required the company to discontinue sales of its most successful product and take on a mass recall. It was all-hands-on-deck, and no time for Sky.

Cheryl says that when she first got news of the recall, "I was unhinged for a moment. My reflex was to panic. I couldn't believe our bad luck to have this happen right after everything we had been through. Within seconds, I switched to rage. How could I have been blindsided? What had my team failed to do? Seconds later, I caught myself and asked what my role was in all this."

"You righted yourself incredibly fast," David said. "What allowed you to do that?"

It was how she had consciously named her internal priorities and generated options to deal with them. "I spent the previous three months grounding myself in the big picture and looking out long term at the possibilities. That was my way of creating a viable option for me to be brave enough to pursue Sky. When I took a moment to breathe, I asked myself how this setback affected my bigger vision, and it didn't. It was a major pothole, for sure, but just a pothole."

"That's a great perspective," David commented. "How did that change your behavior?"

"I realized that I needed to let go of emotion and get on with connecting the dots. What did that new development just show us? It exposed some of our weaknesses—I am so loyal to my team, but based on this test, I'm going to need to set an even higher bar." Her diligent practice of the Five Cs had paid off.

Fortunately, the company had a contingency plan in place for such a development, so they were not caught flat-footed. Dealing with yet another crisis, Cheryl leaned in with her team until they fleshed out their plans for the recall, and then concentrated on leaning with. They worked it out, but Cheryl still winces at the memory. "The recall cost us two quarters of growth and took a huge additional toll on the whole organization when fixing our quality problem. It also put me in the penalty box for a while with the board and shareholders. But eventually we got back to a position where we could refocus on Sky."

Summary

- The ambition of 10x leadership is aspirational. It involves focusing on what a 100 out of 10 (rather than a 10 out of 10) would look like for the success of your biggest, most ambitious long-term external goals.

- How to set 10x external priorities:

  - Take your external priority and look at the best possible long-term outcome.

  - Then expand your vision to come up with an even better outcome, something that is currently unimaginable to you, by tapping into new thinking from others.

  - Pick your 10x goal.

- How to set 10x internal and interpersonal priorities:

  - Recognize your 10x goal will require new internal priorities for yourself, such as working on your bravery, emotional self-regulation, and temptations to stray from integrity when things go wrong.

  - Continue to cultivate agility in the Four Stances as an interpersonal goal, since you will need your whole team's buy-in and best effort to achieve 10x goals.

- Generating options is a team effort:

  - You first need to create the conditions for your team and organization to be creative and innovative by assessing your organization's capacity to innovate and tuning the most important drivers of innovation as appropriate. Concentrate initially on a small number of changes that can create disproportionately positive results.

  - Accompany your leaders on an exponential thinking exercise, translating possibilities into opportunities for new products and services, customer experiences, or business models.

15

Scale New Heights

Keep your eyes on the stars, but your feet on the ground.

—Theodore Roosevelt

I n the previous chapter we addressed how to come up with 10x priorities in three dimensions (M) and high-level options (O). Now we will deal with validating your Vantage Point (V) and effecting change at scale (E). Vantage Point is tricky in a 10x world because what you see can be deceptive. Very small developments can compound over a long time and could massively influence how realistic your priorities are and how effective your options might be. The need to be clear, with the right resolution, scope, and altitude, becomes markedly more important when working with 10x challenges. And while effecting change to achieve long-term goals involves first painting the big picture with your Leader's Intent, it often means taking small steps in the beginning to experiment, test, and learn to prove the viability of your priorities and options.

V: Validate Your 10x Vantage Point

Assessing your Vantage Point will make or break your 10x efforts. Hyper-vigilance about small developments is key, because over such long time frames, small changes can amplify or scuttle your options to achieve your 10x goals. New developments are continuously emerging in the operating environment around technology, competitors, macroeconomic shifts, and many more areas. Tracking a moving target requires constantly learning new things and collecting data as you implement your business strategy.

As the leader of a 10x priority, you need to actively look for what you don't know you don't know. Any new intelligence you detect could compound over time, resulting in anything from an infinitesimal to a massive change in the expected outcome of your external priorities, as well as in your upside and downside risk profile. Because of this, you need to be extraordinarily alert to detect and assess positive surprises as well as negative surprises.[1]

Even if you are diligent in detecting changes in your environment over time, you may not have gotten your Vantage Point correct. In fact, your Vantage Point can only cover a portion of the big picture that makes up 10x goals. There is simply too much uncertainty and imperfect information around 10x goals. You may think you've expanded your Vantage Point as far as it will go, but you always need to think about opening it even further, relentlessly looking for a bigger-picture perspective that you haven't yet seen—a global maximum. That expanded vantage point could prompt you to adjust your goals and options.

As an example, say that you have set your sights on climbing a high peak. Maybe you live in Sonoma County, California, where the highest point is North Peak, at around thirteen hundred meters in elevation. If you've lived in the area your whole life, that's as high as you know you can go. It's as high as you've seen. But if you expand your Vantage Point, you'll find out that there are thousands more peaks beyond what you can see that are higher than thirteen hundred meters. And if you really go global in your Vantage Point, you'll see that there are more than one hundred peaks that are higher than seven thousand meters—10x challenges compared with North Peak.

Driving toward a global maximum is particularly risky, of course. All of the mechanisms for gaining a good vantage on your progress with 10x initiatives, and continuously monitoring how your resources stand up to the priorities, must be rigorously applied if you decide to go for a maximum. How can you do this? Make it a group effort by seeking out many different points of view inside and outside your organization. This gives you the chance to test whether there might be something better beyond your horizon.

Be careful not to overload your team. If you don't have a good Vantage Point on whether you are appropriately balancing your priorities with the supply of talent and resources, you may try to press forward with options that are not viable.

• • •

Cheryl, our consumer products CEO, wanted to challenge and expand her current Vantage Point on Sky, the breakout initiative we introduced in the previous chapter. The exponential thinking workshop had really sparked her imagination. One of the five big ideas that was generated at the off-site was to create a branded media division that could offer a unique customer experience in stores and a digital experience in the metaverse. Cheryl took that idea and, with a small group from the initial Blue Sky gathering and a few outside resources, used it as the central idea of a mind map. They first built out the media company concept, and then looked at implications of the mind map (second-order consequences of the media company). This included the possible creation of company-branded characters. The next step was to consider the "implications of the implications" (third-order consequences), such as the possible demand for toys and clothing based on the new characters. The exercise generated many additional ideas around the edges of the mind map that could form additional options for her 10x goal. This was a practical way for Cheryl to keep expanding her Vantage Point.

Less encouragingly, though, Cheryl's Vantage Point had become clouded when it came to monitoring the load on her team. Because she was confident and clear in her assessments of the innovations the company should invest in, buffered by a strong track record of making great calls, she could be impulsive and overlook the interpersonal aspect of her leadership.

So it didn't go over well when she unilaterally changed the priority order of the seed ideas agreed to at the Blue Sky meeting, and then added some new priorities to the pile to boot. Several team members told David they were distressed when they learned Cheryl had taken one of these new priorities to the board without a team discussion. This added even more to their already long list of priorities.

When David shared the team's feedback with Cheryl, she wasn't in a good frame of mind to receive it. She was letting her instinct to lean in cloud her judgment, and she got defensive. "Things move fast. From my Vantage Point, I frankly think the team just doesn't have my vision," she told David. "Also, I keep repeating that they need to keep up by delegating better and making sure their bench is top-notch. Can you tell me who is most uncomfortable? I don't do well with one-off anecdotes. They should just talk to me."

Cheryl was momentarily not living up to her internal goals of being emotionally regulated and open to feedback, and she needed a reminder.

"You know that's not how it works," David replied. "I don't sense ill will in the team. They are genuinely concerned and pushed to their limits. Why don't I do a full sounding of the team? It would be good data for you and would update your Vantage Point."

In this case Cheryl was so focused on the external challenges before her that she lost track of her internal and interpersonal priorities. If she had been mindfully alert to all three dimensions, she could have seen where things might be going wrong with her team. Her inner alert system didn't catch her attention. Engaging in the Five Cs can help at times like these, when urgency and ambition distract you. Knowing these tendencies in herself is part of why Cheryl knew she needed regular Vantage Point corrections, and why she had David on call.

The "180-degree" review of how her team was experiencing her was a breakthrough. The team was unanimous that they had run out of capacity and were at a breaking point, as were their own teams below them. They also wanted more of a voice in qualifying and selecting ideas that would go forward as top priorities. Cheryl could not dodge that feedback, and she reluctantly updated her Vantage Point based on it.

E: Engage and Effect 10x Change

As discussed in chapter 10, engaging and effecting change start with articulating your Leader's Intent. This is a powerful way to send clear leadership signals about your 10x goal.

With 10x challenges, calibrating the signal is even more keenly important. You need to craft your signal to inspire your organization and carefully avoid scaring people or turning them off. One of our executives had a vision for his company to serve 10 million customers, but for three years the organization had languished with just 250,000 customers. The sales force loved the 10x vision, but the executive team rejected it because it was not time-bound and it gave no meaningful guidance to get them out of their current situation. There were no milestones along the way that would let them know they were winning. The CFO crudely explained the leadership team's attitude: "If you set the treat too high, the dogs won't jump." Our executive needed to reframe his Leader's Intent to better engage his team in the near term.

Fortunately, Cheryl had just the right touch: she brought her people along by first helping them see the possibilities, then announced her 10x goal of becoming the undisputed leader in their market, and then leveraged her team to help her articulate a fuller statement of Leader's Intent.

Engaging and effecting change for 10x priorities is a long game, and the exact path to success is highly uncertain. While they may be based on blue-sky thinking, 10x goals need to have some foundation in reality. Once you have stated your Leader's Intent, your next leadership signal is to identify the very first steps you can take to prove out the viability of your options, attaching clear milestones to those steps so that you are clear on what success looks like. From there you will move in increments that your people will see it as both possible and promising to increase their level of confidence in the selected options. The magnitude of those increments will vary depending on:

- Your conviction

- Your organization's current appetite to take on risky initiatives

- How far your existing resources can stretch to accommodate new things in addition to day-to-day responsibilities

- What new talent you believe you need to achieve goals

- Your confidence that you can unlock additional resources needed once you show initial progress on your 10x priorities

If your initial steps fail, come up with an alternative experiment. Effecting change to achieve 10x goals will require safety nets. One CEO we work with said, "Once we are in a business, we need to execute flawlessly to maintain our very thin margins. But when we are exploring new businesses or new products, we have a high tolerance for experimentation. We are confident that our overall portfolio of experiments and new initiatives will deliver, but there are inevitably losses as well as wins."

Then all along the journey to your 10x goal, lean in to ensure demands are carefully balanced with the available supply of time and resources, so your team doesn't burn out. As a rule of thumb, running at 99 percent capacity creates a huge level of strain and leaves no slack to deal with an unexpected crisis. Running at 95 percent supports more of a sense of sustainability and mastery. Your job is to find that 4 percent difference for you and your team by being realistic about your collective capacity, checking in regularly with your team, being open to their feedback, and prioritizing accordingly.

In the 10x Vantage Point discussion, we identified the importance of detecting and assessing changes in the external operating environment. That job continues here during engagement. Invest in intelligence-gathering capability; scour communication flows inside your organization to detect new developments in your operating environment or to pull new data and insights from day-to-day activity. This may involve seeding some activities like research to collect more data and market intelligence, teaming up with new types of partners, or improving the flow of communication inside your organization to transmit new data and learnings as they arise. Assess these new developments through scenarios to anticipate how they might play out and affect your strategy, priorities, or implementation model. Then respond by adjusting your leadership signals as needed to activate an existing contingency plan or implement a new one.

Cheryl Effects Change in Her Personal Leadership

Cheryl called a meeting with her team to have a candid discussion about the feedback she had received on switching up priorities. She opened by saying she accepted the feedback and was ready to address it with them. This was exactly the right thing to do, because although the team had come a long way on psychological safety, they were still more likely to have conversations with her about her leadership on a one-on-one basis rather than in a team setting. Her comment smoothed the way for them to have a discussion as a team.

They agreed on two important course corrections. Responding to the feedback that the team was at a breaking point in capacity, Cheryl acknowledged having a blind spot. After a group discussion, she committed to not add new priorities without deprioritizing some others, and to fully involve the team in those deliberations.

But her team also wanted to make the most of Cheryl's talent for spotting great opportunities, and they suggested that Cheryl take ten minutes at their weekly Monday morning meetings to talk about what she was seeing in the marketplace and what ideas she was mulling over. She would assign a "degree of conviction" to each idea. Everyone knew that once Cheryl had conviction around an idea, she would use her tremendous results orientation to drive it through, so they had to make the most of the window of time before that happened to provide their input in a productive way.

They then moved on to the need to create a better environment for innovation. Based on the results of the creativity and innovation diagnostic, they decided to send three major signals to the organization: flipping decision-making from top-down to more bottom-up where possible; driving more internal debate about new ideas; and starting to change their reflexes from "fire, ready, aim" to "ready, aim, fire."

Each member of Cheryl's team also developed their own Leader's Intent with their teams, based on their understanding of the new direction. This was crucial to support more decentralized decision-making and to cascade Cheryl's signals down through the organization.

Encouraging productive conflict to pressure-test new ideas was more difficult given the culture. Leaders in the organization tended to be long tenured and reluctant to potentially destabilize relationships for any reason. The top team decided that for their next key decision, they would designate some members to take what they called a "gold" perspective and argue the merits of a decision, and the rest to take a "red" perspective to challenge that decision. For the next decision after that, gold members would become red and vice versa. Leaders became increasingly comfortable with the structure because it created new norms for leadership behavior in which pointing out problems was not antithetical to culture.

To counter their reflex to move overly fast off the mark, the top team built in short questions to ask before they made any key decisions at the senior leadership level: "What problem are we solving for here?" and "How does this support our customers, employees, value creation, and brand?" These simple but powerful questions instilled a new operating rhythm for the team and helped them all create space between the bias for action and the decision to move. The group engaged regularly on practicing the Five Cs on themselves and with one another to make this aspiration a reality.

All these initiatives not only helped drive more creative long-term thinking but also improved the team's ability to execute short-term and medium-term priorities and helped them get through their regulatory setback.

The Team Engages to Jump-Start Sky

After the regulatory setback was dealt with, Cheryl's team was enthusiastic about making a launch pad for Sky from the five ideas they came up with at the exponential thinking offsite. Cheryl leaned in to do what only she could do by accepting her team's recommendation to set up an incubator to launch more experiments and to create a small fund to seed investments with external startups. She also asked her head of strategy to stand up five working teams corresponding to the five exponential ideas they had generated.

Then Cheryl leaned back to delegate. She let the head of strategy mandate that each team focus only on the next thirty days, with a few bite-size goals: do desk research to further qualify the ideas, reframe them as appropriate, and then come up with a small initiative designed to explore the viability of the idea. If the initiatives were promising, they would build on them to further advance the case for the exponential idea. If the initiatives failed, they would craft a different initiative to test and learn in the following thirty-day period.

At the same time, the head of strategy developed a charter for the seed fund and started to scan the environment for potential startups that could advance the Sky initiatives. He also decided that based on the volatility of the operating environment, the company needed to step up its ability to detect, assess, and respond and set up a small risk intelligence unit reporting to him.[2]

Sky is still playing out, and as you would expect with bold and uncertain priorities, it often feels like two steps forward and one step back. But Cheryl and her team are building a solid foundation to make Sky a 10x success.

Summary

Your 10x challenges are the highest of high-stakes leadership situations. They require a different level of vigilance and agility from leaders. You must:

- Continuously expand your Vantage Point beyond what you see now, always looking for what you don't know you don't know.

- Build capacity to detect and assess small changes in the environment that could have big long-term implications for your 10x goal.

- Keep searching for a global maximum for your 10x goal, rather than a local maximum, by exploring ideas and data that are well outside your normal frame of reference.

- Always be attuned to balancing the demands on your organization with the available capacity.

- Practice the Five Cs to keep yourself and the team on an even keel.

• Cocreate a statement of Leader's Intent with your team based on the results of your innovation initiatives and the ideas generated through exponential thinking.

• Send additional leadership signals that name the very first steps to be taken to begin proving the viability of your options, attaching clear milestones to those steps to be clear on what success looks like.

• Iterate based on the results of your first steps toward your 10x goal.

16

MOVE Strategically

Absorb what is useful, discard what is not, add what is uniquely your own.

—Bruce Lee

W hen we advise and coach leaders, we usually have the freedom to iterate through the full MOVE model. However, we may not go in order. The acronym is handy, but don't be limited by it. You can home in on parts of the model. Especially if you need just-in-time, real-time intervention, you can learn to scan through the model in seconds and see what aspect jumps out at you. For more involved work you can also apply M, O, V, and E in different sequences.

Take a situation you face and do a light run-through of the model. Think of it as a checklist—here's what to ask:

- How mindfully alert do you think you are, and are you clear on your external, internal, and interpersonal leadership priorities?

- Do you feel that you have several options you can call on to achieve your priorities, and won't just depend on your default approach?

- Where might your Vantage Point be distorted or where might you have blind spots?

- Are you clear on your Leader's Intent and the other leadership signals you need to send to engage and effect change?

Sometimes, one of these just won't check out, and that's a good place to start working. You can do this in ten seconds, ten minutes, or you can take as long as the complexity of the situation requires.

Managing Hypergrowth in White Space

Here's an example of a 10x challenge that was solved by focusing mostly on E—how best to engage and effect change.

We were in Tokyo when we both got texts from a Bay Area startup in artificial intelligence. In just two years the billionaire founder had grown the company from two employees to more than one thousand, with offices in California, New York, and London.

Notice we said we got "texts," plural. That's because the founder was building the organization with a "teal culture," a new and nearly unprecedented model of management with no hierarchy or designated decision-makers. Employees were meant to self-manage. So instead of our normal CEO leader, we had to deal with a kind of "hydra" leader—in this case a multiheaded being that emerged from the teal culture.[1] Sure enough, the same request was texted to us from two different individuals. Within the hour, another six people texted us.

Carol had been working with a group of fifty people, called G50, in the company who were nominated by their colleagues to find a way to lead the business together. She had taken small groups of them through a series of workshops to enhance trust and understanding within the larger group. Tricky stuff, but Carol had made real progress. They were thirsty to connect with one another, but they still didn't know how to effect change at the larger group level.

The texts were an SOS. They asked if we could get to San Francisco in forty-eight hours to provide emergency help in facilitating a meeting of the G50. They'd been preparing to hold an offsite for months to agree on a purpose, mission, and vision; a strategy; a governance model; and an operating model. But suddenly they realized they weren't prepared.

We were initially incredulous as we read the scope. But a call with some of the team members made us realize how serious they were. The group had been trying, and failing, for months to get alignment on their direction. Tempers had flared to the point where some of their best talent was prepared to abandon the company.

We believed that this company had the potential to enjoy spectacular success and have a positive impact on the world. At the same time, it could also crash. We decided to take on this high-risk project and do what we could to help them tilt the odds in their favor. David changed his flight to stop off in San Francisco. Carol was already booked with another leadership team in Singapore but helped David plan out an approach.

We felt that the group was mindful and quite clear on its three-dimensional priorities: they needed to define the operating model for the group, grow their individual capacity to understand and trust one another, and be agile across the Four Stances to help make and implement the best decisions together. In their workshops with Carol and conversations with David, we knew they had already sketched out various options for purpose, strategy, governance, and operating models. They'd updated their Vantage Point, recognizing the precariousness of fifty well-intentioned but independent voices trying to make a collective decision.

However, what they didn't have was agreement on the best next steps from the options. We felt, even before David arrived at their site, that what they most needed was to get unstuck—to engage and effect change as a group.

For the G50 It's All about E: Engaging and Effecting Change

The fifty employees were angry, frustrated, and even despairing. Each one felt they had veto power, and it seemed that no one could agree on anything. Compounding the tension, the company was live streaming the meeting worldwide to employees; part of the radical approach to a teal culture was to be fully transparent with colleagues.

The colleagues weren't impressed. The chat overflowed with comments like "Once again you completely missed the point," "Wrong, wrong, wrong!" "This group has no guts," "Why won't you tell the truth about what's really happening in this company?" and "Who is this guy David and why do we need him?"

After arriving, David knew he first had to pull on empathy with the G50 and to lean with to get started. Here's how he opened: "I can only imagine how much frustration you are feeling and how much you want to make progress. I know that you're all equals here, and I need you to delegate the facilitation for today to me. Do I have your permission?" There were lots of nods and a few eyerolls, but no one rejected the request.

David then helicoptered out to see if there were any first principles that could be used as common ground to engage the mob. "We all know our destination—a fully articulated purpose statement straight through to a governance model. Let's unpack it into two parts: what we know right now, and what a good first step might be toward our destination."

No pushback. So far, so good, David thought. "Let's start by individually reflecting on what you think you know for sure about opportunities in this space, then what you are highly confident about, and after that, two or three big hypotheses that you would like to test out."

David split them into eight groups to exchange their views, which they then played back in plenary. Because the space the company was playing in was brand new, very few things were felt to be known with certainty. Remarkably, there was quite a bit of consensus around areas of high confidence. Beyond that, they were all over the map on hypotheses they wanted to test.

"For the themes where we have high confidence, what would we need to believe for these to be confirmed?" David asked. Again, quite a bit of consensus.

That was enough to get some traction. "OK, I know that this company is big on design thinking—putting yourself in your customers' shoes, then experimenting with different things that could help them. How can we use that here?"

One member of the group called out, "What you are saying is we need to experiment based on what we know right now?"

"Exactly. It's anyone's guess about how this white space will unfold. Why don't we put a stake in the ground based on what we know right now, try some stuff, and then iterate forward when we get new data and insights?" Without being explicit about it, David was asking the group to come up with some early leadership signals. This was a first step to crafting a collective Leader's Intent—the first and most important signal when engaging and effecting change.

Many participants started to lean forward, intrigued. Another one said, "This is some kind of meta-application of design thinking, right? It's about thinking about how we think about the market?"

David replied, "That's a great way to put it. How do we specify version 1.0 of our purpose based on what we know right now, then connect it to a strategy, an operating model, and a governance model? You know about minimum viable prototypes, right?"

Right.

"OK, then let's do minimum viable purpose, strategy, and governance. What are the most basic things we can identify, starting with purpose and then going straight through to strategy and into the governance model? Let's also make sure that each part connects in an internally consistent way. Then we'll start to implement that version 1.0 while also gathering data to confirm or refute what we need to believe about areas we are confident about, and launch new experiments to test promising hypotheses for parts of the space we know less well."

A wave of enthusiasm and relief swept through the room, and the chat turned hopeful. A few group members said, "I think we have a way forward." One asked, "On a scale of one to ten, who is a nine or a ten for trying this?" Most hands went up. "Seven or eight?" More hands. "Six or below?" A few hands. "Anyone seriously opposed to trying this out or have a better way?" Silence.

Soundings from the room indicated that it would take ninety days to develop a draft charter for the company using this model.

There was one more intervention for David to make. "You've all been great, and today we had a breakthrough. But ninety days? Come on! This space may be upside down in that length of time. You move at warp speed, so do your competitors. We need to get ahead of the curve. How about detailing version 1.0 in thirty days?"

Startled, one of the participants who had been quiet up to then said, "Absolutely right! I'll see you and raise you. Version 1.0 in three weeks." That sparked a wave of support from the whole team, and after planning some next steps we adjourned for a group dinner.

The group of fifty widely credits that offsite for being the turning point for when they started to collectively engage and effect change. Two years later, the company owns its space, has just completed version 1.6 of its minimum viable strategy, and is preparing for version 2.0.

Working on More Interpersonal Options to Help Drive a Turnaround

Sometimes, generating options is the big challenge, and it often comes from when interpersonal priorities are unclear or you're not meeting those challenges.

K. L. was founder and CEO of a business process outsourcing company, which he had taken public several years earlier. It grew steadily, until a year ago when everything seemed to go wrong all at once. Customer acquisition stalled, retention sharply declined due to the poor implementation of a new technology platform, and sales force turnover spiked. Turning this performance around was a classic high-stakes MOVE challenge.

We knew we shouldn't implement the full MOVE approach to start, because there was an overwhelming pain point putting a stopper on all progress. K. L. felt his team was letting him down, and he couldn't stand it. He had recruited a team of all-star senior leaders from companies ten times the size of his. He felt he should now be able to not lean and let the team steer the turnaround.

This was a poor move. K. L. had recruited some of these all-stars from combative business cultures, where their skill sets were attuned to driving mid- to high-single-digit growth in $50 billion businesses. None had much experience taking on a declining $5 billion top line, turning it around, and then tripling it. As soon as K. L. decided against leaning in or leaning with, several of the new all-stars imported their old cultures into their new roles. It led to a predictable fight for dominance. Conditions at the executive committee (exco) were deteriorating. In some cases, team members' dynamic verged on open warfare.

K. L. invited us to sit in on an exco meeting, where he torched his team for not performing. Team members blamed each other and pointed fingers in every direction. Tensions peaked when the CFO accused the COO of lying to him, threw his iPad on the floor, and stormed out of the room. In a remarkable and remarkably ineffective display of not leaning, K. L.'s default style took over. It was stunning to watch. He acted as if nothing had happened and continued with the meeting.

Centering the Leader to Better Engage His Team

We decamped to K. L.'s office, where he ricocheted into leaning in, with a vengeance. He was livid. "I wish they would all just go away so I can start over again. I don't want to deal with them. I've earned the right to not have to deal with ***holes."

We glanced at each other. Although we really wanted to ask him what he thought his role was in the company's underperformance, we knew he first needed to calm down. At moments like this, humor can disarm. To do that, Carol playfully offered him a new Vantage Point, saying "OK, let's assume you get rid of all the current ***holes. Aren't you just going to come up with a new definition of ***hole for the next group and just do it all over again?"

K. L. blinked and then barked a short, sharp laugh. "Yeah, I see your point. But they keep laying turds at my feet, expecting me to deal with them. That's not on me, it's on them."

Not so. We knew this was primarily about K. L.'s lack of options for his interpersonal priorities. He had chosen his option: don't lean, to the point of aggressive passivity, dotted with the occasional aggressive lean in, mostly to excoriate the team. These were all-stars, he thought; the company should run itself. He assumed his not-leaning stance was right and anything that was wrong with the company was unrelated to his interpersonal leadership. Team members were yelling at each other and throwing iPads, and still he generated no options to change his leadership. He just kept unskillfully and relentlessly staying in his don't-lean stance.

We needed to get K. L. into a more effective set of stances with his team. He had to learn to lean in more effectively and to lean with.

David countered K. L.'s buck-passing by reorienting him to the Three Dimensions of Leadership. "Let's triage what you have going on with the team."

K. L. said, "OK, I'm calm now." Notably, the interpersonal options were his blind spot. Even in his current state, K. L. could recognize his internal priority in this moment, and he was surprisingly open to being challenged.

To fix his interpersonal options, we reevaluated his top external priorities. There were five. He said he would hand two over to the team, but admitted he'd need to give them more guidance on two more, and the fifth—an issue with an institutional shareholder—he'd have to take on himself. He had new options now other than "let them figure it out."

Next, we needed to work with the team. K. L. gladly agreed to it, convinced that once we had worked with individual team members, we would see that they were the problem, not him!

The Turnaround Team Works on Interpersonal Relationships

We worked with the group to find new options to improve their relationships with one another. We asked them to identify what a ten out of ten would look like for their work together. They made the wise suggestion that it would include presuming everyone was competent and had good intentions and everyone would listen, be open, and share perspectives productively. Of these, the first two—competence and good intentions—were flagged as both the most important and the ones where they needed the most work.

It emerged from these sessions that the team was allergic to Randy, the CFO, whom they felt was arbitrary and dismissive. As the session unfolded, Randy volunteered, "I'm sorry I sound dismissive. I sometimes don't know how to articulate what I'm having difficulty with." The team immediately started to attack him until Carol intervened. "Wait, everybody stop. What did Randy just say?" The team couldn't recall, so Carol asked Randy to repeat it. He did. At their lack of response she commented, "He said, 'I don't know how to articulate what I'm having difficulty with.' Well? What should you say next?"

After a moment of baffled silence, one team member leaned toward Randy and asked, "Can you tell us more?" One look at Randy's face and the tension in the room evaporated. It was an important marker, because for the first time a team member had started to change their relationship to Randy, shifting from disdainful leaning in to leaning with, seeing him as a partner.

Randy's skin tone went from flushed to something healthier, and the tension left his nonverbal expressions. He engaged. (We rarely get real-time pivotal shifts like that as advisers, but it's wonderful when we do.) That moment kicked off some positive change for the team, and Randy went from being the most skeptical of team coaching to its strongest proponent. We continued to work on new options for working together, focused on better leaning in and more leaning with. We also facilitated more sessions with K. L. and the team, focused on working toward a more effective two-way relationship between leader and team by using a broader range of interpersonal options.

These interventions were enough for the company to halt its decline and eventually resume its growth trajectory. K. L. kept all of his team members in place.

Mateus the Maverick: Using MOVE in a Different Sequence of Steps

You may notice that while these examples focus on one particular part of MOVE, the whole framework is present, if not focused on it. K. L. revisited his M (his external priorities) briefly in order to generate new interpersonal options. David had the G50 at the artificial intelligence company resurface their options before engaging and effecting change.

This is one of the great beauties of MOVE—you can revisit any of the steps any time and lightly sample them, almost as a check on yourself. You may find when you do this that some high-stakes situations go through the entire framework in a completely different order. Here's a case of that, where the client ended up using MO(v)E quite naturally.

Our client's CHRO briefed us. "Mateus created a multibillion-dollar digital business from scratch when he was at headquarters in São Paulo. We moved him to head the US division to get more international exposure, and now he's our number one internal succession candidate to be global CEO. The problem is how mercurial he is. He can be very, very harsh in some cases. Then in others he just withdraws and disengages completely. We're afraid we might have a sociopath on our hands. This is a high-stakes situation, and we need the two of you on it." Both of us were stunned and intrigued.

"Let's be clear," Carol said. "If he *is* a sociopath, we will be coaching you, not him!"

Mateus as the legendary innovator in Latin America was known to be unforgiving and overly demanding, and it could get extreme. One colleague said, "He's like a fury—like magma is roiling inside of him. Someone has to open him up and have him face it." Another direct report said, "He's the most brutal person I've ever met. He ruins people, and some were so stressed they had to be hospitalized." Another said simply: "He smashes people with his words."

With us, that didn't happen. Though there were times he'd say something so baffling or shocking one or the other of us was temporarily rendered speechless.

Anyway, that was the Latin American innovator Mateus. The "US" division leader Mateus was shockingly different. His US COO said, "He is the best leader I've ever worked for. He is always kind and inspiring. The problem is that although he's a fantastic strategist and comes up with breakout ideas, he is completely hands-off after that. He throws out an idea, makes a proclamation, then heads to his office, leaving us to figure out what in the world it is we are actually supposed to do."

Though these two perspectives seemed hard to square, we managed to square them. After we explored Mateus's underlying drivers, it was clear he was no sociopath. Situational context drove his leadership approaches, and both approaches were actually consistent with his identity.

Our first meeting with Mateus was in a nondescript glass-walled office. After sipping from his water bottle, he said, "I got an email from the chair, and I don't know what you are being asked to do with me. The concern is my behavior? Fine. If they don't need me, fire me now. No worries."

We told him that they didn't want to fire him. They wanted him to become an even better leader.

"Leadership?" he repeated, looking blank. "I'm here to accomplish our mission. That's it. I care about society as a whole, not individuals." There was a long pause. "I know I'm immature. I never think about myself. All I want to do is immerse myself in the business, think about innovation and how I can make a long-term contribution to society. When I'm asked what my secret to success is, how I achieved things, I don't know what the answer is. I don't think about it, I just do it."

Mateus wasn't seeing that success alone was no longer enough at his level. A new external priority was to scale his leadership so others could step into his shoes. He had to teach them his world so they could share his Vantage Point. To do that, he had to first be able to see things from their perspective, not just his own. At this point, at his level in the organization, if he were to become the global CEO, to care about society as a whole was dependent on caring about individuals. He could no longer separate these things.

During the two-hour meeting, we noted an interesting quirk. While Mateus drank from his water bottle, there were no glasses in the room, and despite the room being quite hot, we were never offered anything ourselves. It seemed a perfect example of what could be a pattern. He was doing his job and was utterly unaware of anyone's needs other than his own. This aligned with the external priority he'd had as long as he could remember: set the goal, get it done no matter what it takes, repeat. Nothing else at work mattered or even appeared on his mind's radar screen.

After the meeting we headed to dinner, at his invitation. We piled into his aging Toyota Prius and swung by his house to drop something off on our way. He was proud of his old car and small house and shared how he gave his homemaker wife a modest weekly budget to keep expenses down. By the end of dinner, we understood why he did these things, and why he could so confidently proclaim in our meeting that he'd be fine if he were fired. He would never allow himself to be dependent on anyone.

At dinner, a different side of Mateus emerged. He was engaging, caring, and curious, interested in our opinions and our lives. Our conversation became more personal as the evening went on. He asked about our child-hoods; as we shared honestly about our lives, soon he did as well.

"I saw a bad world growing up, and this has made me want to help this one. My brother and father went in a more criminal direction. As a child I was sent away to work in a gravel pit, basically forced labor. It was terrible, but it made me innovate. I had to find a way to produce as much as the men, who were twice my size, and I did! Finally, I realized I could just walk out the door. Somehow, I made it to college, found computers, and never looked back. I may be tough on people, but I get just as angry at myself. I hate losing. I throw golf clubs when I make a bad shot." That explained the twisted iron David saw in Mateus's car.

Mateus had grown up and become a successful executive without depending on anyone else. His behavior toward others could be unacceptable, but it didn't come from core meanness. If his people couldn't get on with the task at hand, he would erupt if he thought they were not giving their all, or he would completely withdraw when asked for guidance because he didn't know how to give it.

We were determined to do our best to help.

Pushing Mateus to Expand His Vantage Point

The next day, Mateus was 100 percent clear on how he saw his priorities. "I am all about 10x. To lead this company to success, I have to come up with the best ideas. Breakthrough thinking is 95 percent of the challenge. The rest? Leadership, management, none of it matters." He lived in complete alignment with this vision and spent over twenty hours a week looking twenty years into the future.

You can't develop someone to go where they don't want to go, so we simply asked him to tell us more about his top current external priority and to frame it with the what, who, when, where, and why questions of M.

He happily spelled out his thoughts.

> What: Assess the impact of artificial intelligence on current and potential markets for the company, and possible implications for my workforce. Spend the maximum amount of time exploring this and the minimum amount of time in management and administration.

> Who: I am the one to figure it out because I am the only one with the track record and capacity to do so. I need to be my most strategic self.

When: I want to have a strong point of view on possible break-through ideas within six months.

Where: I'm going to start with the US business, but I expect that my ideas will influence the company globally.

Why: This is the single most important issue that will determine the company's future.

"That's pretty clear," David said. "How confident are you that you have the correct priority?"

"I'm absolutely certain."

David replied, "How many companies that are true innovators also capture the most value from their innovations?"

Mateus answered in a way we would get to know well. First, he acknowledged his pleasure at the inquiry. "Good question!" Second, he leaned back and stared at the ceiling, as if he were trying to bore a hole through it with his eyes. A minute or two seems like a long time in that context. He was thinking through his answer, beginning to end. Third, having already mentally leaped through a few hypotheses about the question, or even about the purpose of the question, he snapped back to us, often to counter with his own question. This time he asked, "What else are you trying to make me think about?"

David continued, "I'm wondering about innovative companies that disrupt and then die out or flatline."

"Many companies don't capture value from their innovations," Mateus agreed. And with his unusual combination of confidence and unconscious arrogance, he added, "But the obstacles are easy to overcome if you are competent."

David kept advancing his effort to make Mateus aware that his nonstop lean-back and don't-lean stances had disconnected him from his team and threatened to prevent his company from capturing value from its innovations. We'd seen his US team trying to manage hypergrowth without his guidance. They desperately needed a leader to help them talk to one another and find a way to fly in formation. If he could see this, Mateus would shift his Vantage Point, which would cause a serious rethinking of top priorities.

But we had to move very slowly and deliberately with someone like Mateus. "I'm curious, what role do you think leadership plays in situations like that? And how's it going with your team? Are you happy with the progress?"

"I know I just said obstacles are easy to overcome, but that applies to me, not necessarily to my team," he said. "I got to build my own team here. They are good, very smart, and I hired them because of their independence. But now each department is trying to manage itself, creating silos, and it's keeping them from getting things done. Back home I seemed to always inherit people who were waiting for me to tell them what to do. I hated it." He leaned back and bored another hole in the ceiling.

Mateus Reframes His Top Priorities and Finds New Options

"Yes," he said after another long pause. "I get it. My team can't deliver on their own, and I need to be able to delegate with confidence, or we will fail. My number two is always asking me how I do what I do, and I can't explain it. I guess I need to face facts and do something about it."

Mateus was beginning to get it: from his new, broader Vantage Point he could see that his top priorities must include building a bridge from his mind to the team, while also spending as much time as he could on the future vision for the company.

Since he'd never seen any value in the interpersonal dimension of leadership, Mateus had defaulted to either a don't-lean or a lean-back stance with his teams. Now we were asking him to build a bridge between his mind and the team, but he didn't know how to start. We asked him to talk to his US team about his philosophy of winning, which turned out to be a way of leaning in with them as their teacher.

He described to us what he shared with them. "I believe that in innovation many small successes lead to a big win, so I go for the small but great successes." He told them he surmised that they took on too much, kept swinging for the fences, and didn't play as a team. "That's why you were always failing." The team was startled that he had not shared this with them earlier, but were grateful that he was beginning to engage.

Progress in connecting with his team was slow. It was difficult for Mateus, but he leaned into teaching them and breaking down his thinking into small enough pieces that the team understood him better. He began to consciously challenge his default position of I *shouldn't have to change, they should*.

It also became clear to us that he really did care about individuals, despite his earlier claims to the contrary. He understood that developing people is necessary, even though he didn't particularly like doing it.

Sometime later, Mateus had taken on a high-profile enterprisewide project that included senior leaders from HQ in Latin America. "Well," he said on our Zoom call while looking up and wincing. "I just had a three-hour meeting, and I was good? Maybe good? Until the end."

Carol asked what happened.

"I believe in total freedom and total responsibility: do whatever you like as long as it creates value for the company, and make sure you deliver what you say you will. In this case they failed. I yelled at them and said: That was important for the company! You failed! You should leave this company, and in fact you should just die!"

There were a few seconds of astonished silence. Coaches aren't surprised by much, but this one put us off balance. All Carol could think to ask was, "What was that like?"

"It was fun!" he said.

David was speechless; fortunately, Carol was not. She tried to probe to understand this vexing and disturbing aggression. Unless Mateus had a good explanation for his statement, it verged on sociopathy. "What made it fun?" she asked.

"Everyone was laughing!" This time Carol was speechless, and David stepped in.

"People laugh for different reasons. It could be that they were scared."

We should have been used to this by now, but were still taken aback when his eyes shot to the ceiling. He was silent and motionless for minutes. We texted each other, "Is the screen frozen?!" We waited. He then put his head in his hands and exclaimed, "I am so stupid!"

We waited for more.

"I thought yelling at them makes them better. That's how I got better. They are different, but I keep on yelling. You made me think more about why I yell at home but not here. It reminds me of my favorite authors from my country. When he wrote in English, he said it created a space for him between his thoughts and his words, and he wrote much differently than when he wrote books in Portuguese. I think some of that is happening when I work with HQ compared to when I work in the United States."

Carol leaned in, hard. She knew that to get Mateus to create an alternative he might try, it had to be equally intense, just the opposite. "How about this? Instead of saying, 'This was important, you failed, you should leave the company or die,' do the opposite. Say, 'Hey! This was important to our company, I believe you can make it, but if you fail, get up. No matter what, I'll have your back.'" While she didn't spell it out, she wanted to harness his intensity but point it in a different direction. To do this it had to catch his attention, then he could create a space between the stimulus and the response, and to change to a lean-with stance, versus the highly aggressive lean-in or relentless don't-lean set of choices that had been his default.

Yet again, his gaze shot to the ceiling. More silence. Then he snapped his focus back to us.

"OK, fine. I'm going to stay exactly the same with 50 percent of my people. I'll try that have-your-back thing with the other 50 percent, and I'll see who delivers. You know I like to test and learn when I innovate."

That was as good as we'd get. He now had a plan to use this new option and send some different leadership signals to engage and effect change as a leader. We agreed, said good-bye, and wondered what we would hear next.

Three weeks later we got a text from Mateus, who was on a rare holiday.

"I tried that have-your-back thing!!! it worked!!! had no idea!!!"

Only then did we realize. He'd essentially been a slave, escaped a terrible life, and fought his way up, never having experienced positive power. Finally, he had. And he liked it. It was an epiphany for Mateus, and we were told later by the board chair that, from that moment, he never again returned to his dark side.

Two years later Mateus was named global CEO. We texted our congratulations to him, and he immediately replied, "Thank you. But it's just a title change :) I will just push harder to accomplish our mission with my team, that's it."

You can see here that instead of going through MOVE step by step and in sequence, we picked and chose different parts to deal with, depending on what we thought were the most pressing matters to attend to. You can do the same: MOVE is flexible, and you can do light or heavy applications of some or all components in whatever sequence you feel would be most helpful.

Summary

- For most leadership situations, we recommend going through the full MOVE model. Even when your challenge is urgent, it makes sense to quickly scan the entire model.

- For some situations you can draw on just a subset of the MOVE model.

  - Start by seeing if one or more elements relate to a big gap you need to reflect on, and then double down on these.

- You can also use the elements of MOVE in any sequence you want to tailor to your situation.

CONCLUSION

Be Extraordinary

Let us reflect on what is truly of value in life, what gives meaning
to our lives, and set our priorities on the basis of that.

—His Holiness the Dalai Lama

What does it take to be truly extraordinary? Not just a leader who
gets results and has good followership. One who changes the conversation, raises heads, and leaves a legacy.

Great leaders can rise to the occasion when it's needed in high-stakes,
high-risk situations. They *create a space* between stimulus and response
and exploit that space—whether it's seconds, hours, or longer—to make
wise choices.

The most extraordinary leaders *live in that space.*

Imagine a leader who operates at the highest levels of the Three
Dimensions of Leadership—the external, the internal, and the interpersonal. They fully embody all Four Stances and feel freedom to choose
any number of options for any given goal or interaction. They live in a
centered place, embodying the Five Cs. Everything they choose to do or
say is driven from a deep connection to their core being and their purpose in life and has led to an upward spiral in their career. They've
achieved total self-responsibility and total self-awareness. They are their
own version of ten-out-of-ten in all of these areas.

We know that achieving *all of that* all of the time is impossible. Nev-
ertheless, we should all aspire to be that leader. It's the 10x version of who
you want to be. It involves continuously setting high personal standards
for yourself and then living in full coherence with them by being a real-
time leader, all the time.

Take the Measure of Your Leadership and Your Life

Read any research or listen to how extraordinary leaders are described, and you'll notice that what emerges most often is not their achievements.[1] What you'll read are words like integrity, self-awareness, courage, humility, respect, kindness, openness, curiosity, and gratitude.[2] Notice that these are all part of the second dimension of leadership: your internal priorities.

When you judge your leadership, and your life, is this where you focus? As Thoreau said, you do not want to get to the end of your life and realize you never lived. What does living mean for you? Would it be measured by only the first dimension of leadership, your achievements with external challenges? In a world of Three-Dimensional Leadership, it can't be. Living must include being in alignment with your deepest internal qualities, your strengths, and your values, which in turn drive the caliber of your interpersonal relationships.

So extraordinary leaders are extraordinary humans.

To deliberately become an extraordinary human is to flip the script from what most leaders think it is. Most leaders focus first and foremost on the external dimension of leadership. For us, the leaders who are extraordinary humans focus first on internal and interpersonal priorities.

Let's be clear: being an extraordinary human is not in opposition to being a great business leader. It does not have to mean being saintlike, or taking your eyes off your external priorities. It does mean being authentic and connected to your sense of why you are on this planet, particularly when you are under stress. In fact, far from being in opposition, becoming an extraordinary human increases the chances of meeting your external priorities and feeling good about how you've done it. It makes you an extraordinary leader.

Posing a Radical Challenge: Become Even Greater Than You Imagine

Think back to chapter 4—name who you want to be. What were your best qualities you identified, and what did you want to work on as a leader? For example, perhaps you are generous, fair, and have good judgment, and you want to work on speaking up more.

Now think of stepping into these qualities at a new level well beyond a ten out of ten, more than you ever thought you could. You can bring 10x growth to develop yourself as a person. One of our leaders worked in an organization that prides itself on decency. He worked relentlessly on becoming the best person and leader he could be. Even he was surprised when a new hard-edged board member said to him, "I thought I understood what decency meant. Now that I've seen you in action, I know what it really means."

Being extraordinary also means you hold yourself to the highest standards and own up to falling short. One of the leaders we worked with valued humility deeply and lived up to it daily. But when one of his peers acted against his values, he became steaming mad. He felt this guy was the opposite of humble; he craved being the center of attention, broadcasted his successes, took all the credit and none of the blame. "I was so angry," our leader said after the incident. "I see now that was driven by my own ego. I thought his behavior was a personal affront to me. I now realize that if I were truly living all my values and being truly humble, he would have no effect on me, and I could more effectively deal with him for the benefit of all." He found a whole new level of humility to aspire to.

What is your 10x version of your internal priorities? It's about taking your personal growth and existing strengths to a new level, while always making sure you also have a few qualities that you are working on, to cultivate a continuous personal development plan.

The Most Important Vantage Point: What Matters Most in Life?

Extraordinary leaders are clear on the contribution they want to make in their lives. Meaning is what matters most to you, and purpose is how you act to fulfill it. Looking at everything you say and do through the Vantage Point of your purpose will drive what you actually say and do, as both a leader and a person.

Many leaders who have been firefighting for years and are at the top of their game are disoriented when they "graduate" from their CEO or other top-of-the-house role. People they thought were friends may not return calls, and when they enter a room they are no longer the most important person in it. Being extraordinary means transcending your role, pulling on your values and purpose, and stepping up rather than back or out when no longer defined by career success. How can you have an even greater impact on the world around you? It's been a privilege for us to work with elite athletes and top leaders who have a sense of what really matters to them. When it's time for them to leave their current occupation behind, they see it as stepping up, not dropping out. It doesn't happen without effort.

The most successful at this begin the active transition up to two years before the moment comes, when they're still at the top of their game. Start noticing what truly energizes you now, so that when the time comes to leave your leadership role, you are ready to step up, not out.

Your deepest purpose, one that transcends stages of life and careers, is not something you discover.[3] It is something you uncover. Start by asking yourself what you loved doing as a child.[4] Was it:

- Being curious about different ideas, experiences, and people?

- Taking things apart to figure out how they worked?

- Helping others?

- Picking big new challenges and going through every wall to achieve them?

Then, draw from your internal strengths and values for guidance about what matters most to you. Finally, think about the hardest times you have had in your life and what you learned from them. Talk to your trusted friends and colleagues about what they see in you that represents your purpose.

Pulling all these things together, try to come up with a single phrase that represents your purpose. If you find it a bit scary but you feel invigorated when you write it, you'll know you're on the right track. It's quite likely that the more you reflect on your purpose, the more you will iterate on it and refine it. You've arrived when you look at it, and on a scale of 1 to 10 you are excited at a 12. Then you can use it as a new Vantage Point by asking yourself whether this is any new opportunity that comes along or what you pursue lines up with your purpose or not.

Here's a great example from a superstar professional athlete. He worked with us to look ahead and see how he could continue to be fulfilled once his athletic career inevitably ends.

Kit is one of the highest-paid NFL receivers in history, with multiple unofficial world records beyond football. People jokingly say that his fingers are made of glue. With two to three years left on his contract, he began diving into deep purpose work with us to prepare for life after football. He answered our first question, "What did you love doing as a child?" with no awareness of the brilliance of his answer. "I was a nature boy growing up. I caught fish, frogs, tadpoles, turtles, crawfish, crabs. Anything that could be caught, I caught it. I felt free in those moments. Fully immersed in the challenge."

We looked at each other and grinned. Kit was stunned when we replied, "Hello? You loved *catching* things? Now, what is it you do for a living?" He quickly got it and began his personal journey to find the thrill of spotting and catching new opportunities as an investor, entrepreneur, and philanthropist. We were delighted for Kit as he began to help others catch opportunities as well.

Knowing your purpose rounds out your internal priorities for extraordinary leaders. It will certainly affect *how* you act on your external priorities. It will definitely inform how you respond to difficult situations.

Your purpose also affects *what* external priorities you choose to pursue in the context of your current career. For example, you may choose a different job or industry, or be even more selective about the type of business your organization will or won't take on the type of customers it serves, and how your business affects the long-term viability of the planet.

Reach for Extraordinary

Becoming the extraordinary leader that we described at the beginning of this chapter is, as we said, impossible. But you must strive for it always. There are ways to get closer to your ideal version of yourself.

It starts with setting your intention.[5] Neuroscience indicates that you can positively change your behavior by repeatedly renewing your intention. Your goal is so lofty that you are sure to lose your balance many times and often fail to live up to your extraordinary standards. Don't worry. The point isn't that you lose your balance so much as that you quickly regain it. Radical acceptance is all about being able to keep failing well, and slowly getting better.

Practicing meditation and mindfulness to increase your concentration can also help you continue to become a better version of yourself.[6] When a group of monks were frustrated because they felt their powers of concentration and mindfulness had plateaued even though they practiced nonstop, they approached the Dalai Lama for advice. The Dalai Lama paused for a moment before playfully replying, "I can say that over the past forty years of practice, I have noticed . . . some improvement."

Of course, all the techniques we applied to your other challenges—the Four Stances, the Five Cs—can be applied to your 10x goal of becoming extraordinary.

Watch for Obstacles

Lots of things get in the way of our pursuit of our 10x ideal selves. Primarily, we can use failures and slip-ups as catalysts for wanting to give up or caving to lesser versions of ourselves. Don't shame or blame yourself for being human; just be self-aware and responsible for your behavior.

To live coherently with who you most want to be, you must be able to practice accepting your faults, limitations, and failures even in your toughest moments. Accept that you have a dark side that pulls you away from your ideal self.[7] We encourage you to acknowledge and even befriend it. If you can connect with that part of you and understand where it came from, you can channel it in a positive direction.

All of this is a tall order, but the goal is transcendence—of ego, emotion, and impulse when under stress or attack. Transcendence means you can rise above the fray, and after giving your all, be able to feel equanimity no matter what happens to you and what the outcome of your efforts might be.

You already know the things that threaten to derail you if you can't accept them. They are the same shortcomings you've explored getting past for all your external, internal, and interpersonal challenges. Maybe it's impatience that threatens team unity, lack of empathy that turns away great talent—the things you've spent this entire book learning to recognize and overcome are the things that want to pull you back from reaching extraordinary heights, especially your biggest derailers under stress, such as extreme skepticism or perfectionism. That means when you are working through your day-to-day, real-time challenges, you are working toward that higher version of yourself.

We are all attached to pleasure, averse to pain.[8] Attached to praise, averse to blame. Attached to fame, averse to disrepute. Attached to gain, averse to loss. Even if it's not very likely we will reach a level of enlightenment that allows us to get beyond all this, we can get better at dealing with these forces. Embrace the journey.

Engage Your 10x Self to Effect Changes at Scale, through Culture

What you emanate as a leader as you cultivate your 10x self creates a ripple effect in your environment. You can be a role model, inspiring others to be even better people, increasing your followership as you engage and effect change. In your interpersonal interactions, you will not only be agile in all stances, you will also emanate loving kindness paired with high expectations for others.

Where people are highly engaged and feel their strengths are being fully utilized, they thrive. What a great legacy if others can say they are better for having worked with you.

Just one more Dalai Lama quote, in closing. "Neither a space station nor an enlightened mind can be realized in a day." But the more you practice, the closer you will get. It is our wish that you will join us in practicing. Our hope is that we have been of service to you in helping you rise to any occasion, in real time, and discovering that you can be extraordinary.

NOTES

Introduction

1. V. E. Frankl, *Man's Search for Meaning* (Boston: Beacon Press, 2006).
2. David Noble and Carol Kauffman, "Where There Is a Will: Creating New Pathways to Success," *Egon Zehnder CEO Insights* 21, 2021.
3. Carol Dweck, "How Companies Can Profit from a 'Growth Mindset,'" *Harvard Business Review*, November 2014, 28–29.
4. Dick Patton and German Herrera, "Spanning the Realities of the CEO Role," *Egon Zehnder CEO Insights* 25, 2021.
5. The survey of nearly one thousand CEOs with a combined annual revenue of four trillion dollars yields invaluable insights to all of us interested in leadership: "It Starts with the CEO: A Global Study, 2021," Egon Zehnder, 2021.
6. Kerri Palamara, Carol Kauffman, Valerie E. Stone, Hasan Bazari, and Karen Donelan, "Promoting Success: A Professional Development Coaching Program for Interns in Medicine," *Journal of Graduate Medical Education* 7, no. 4 (2015): 630–637.
7. Kerri Palamara, Carol Kauffman, Yuchiao Chang, Esteban A. Barreto, Liyang Yu, Hasan Bazari, and Karen Donelan, "Professional Development Coaching for Residents: Results of a 3-Year Positive Psychology Coaching Intervention," *Journal of General Internal Medicine* 33, no. 11 (2018): 1842–1844. The program has been adopted by more than thirty of the top medical school teaching hospitals in the United States.
8. Carol Kauffman and Diane Coutu, "The Realities of Executive Coaching," HBR Research Report, 2009; Diane Coutu and Carol Kauffman, "What Can Coaches Do for You?" *Harvard Business Review*, January 2009, 91–97.
9. Carol Kauffman and William H. Hodgetts, "Model Agility: Coaching Effectiveness and Four Perspectives on a Case Study," *Consulting Psychology Journal: Practice and Research* 68, no. 2 (2016): 157.
10. Carol Kauffman, "Positive Psychology: The Science at the Heart of Coaching," *Evidence-Based Coaching Handbook: Putting Best Practices to Work for Your Clients* 219 (2006): 253.

Chapter 1

1. Jon Kabat-Zinn, *Wherever You Go, There You Are: Mindfulness Meditation in Everyday Life* (New York: Hyperion, 1994).
2. John Whitmore, Carol Kauffman, and Susan A. David, "GROW Grows Up: From Winning the Game to Pursuing Transpersonal Goals," in *Beyond Goals* (New York: Routledge, 2016), 277–292.
3. Lisa Feldman Barrett, *How Emotions Are Made: The Secret Life of the Brain* (Stuttgart: Pan Macmillan, 2017).

4. David Noble and Carol Kauffman, "Where There Is a Will: Creating New Pathways to Success," *Egon Zehnder CEO Insights* 21, 2021. Shane and Rick's work is the foundation for "Generating Options," one of the backbone concepts of Shane J. Lopez, *Making Hope Happen: Create the Future You Want for Yourself and Others* (New York: Simon and Schuster, 2013). See also C. Richard Snyder, ed., *Handbook of Hope: Theory, Measures, and Applications* (Cambridge, MA: Academic Press, 2000).

5. Personal communication with General Charles (Chuck) Jacoby (ret.).

Chapter 2

1. Joseph Goldstein, *Mindfulness: A Practical Guide to Awakening* (Louisville, CO: Sounds True, 2013).

2. Shelley E. Taylor, "Tend and Befriend: Biobehavioral Bases of Affiliation under Stress," *Current Directions in Psychological Science* 15, no. 6 (2006): 273–277.

3. Richard C. Schwartz, *Introduction to the Internal Family Systems Model* (Lakewood, CO: Trailheads Publications, 2001).

4. Jose L. Herrero, Simon Khuvis, Erin Yeagle, Moran Cerf, and Ashesh D. Mehta, "Breathing Above the Brain Stem: Volitional Control and Attentional Modulation in Humans," *Journal of Neurophysiology* 119, no. 1 (2018); and Alex Jinich-Diamant, Eric Garland, Jennifer Baumgartner, Nailea Gonzalez, Gabriel Riegner, Julia Birenbaum, Laura Case, and Fadel Zeidan, "Neurophysiological Mechanisms Supporting Mindfulness Meditation–Based Pain Relief: An Updated Review," *Current Pain and Headache Reports* 24, no. 10 (2020): 1–10.

5. Jared B. Torre and Matthew D. Lieberman, "Putting Feelings into Words: Affect Labeling as Implicit Emotion Regulation," *Emotion Review* 10, no. 2 (2018): 116–124.

6. Jon's work is incredible; when he writes a book, buy it. Jonathan Rhodes, John May, Jackie Andrade, and David Kavanagh, "Enhancing Grit through Functional Imagery Training in Professional Soccer," *The Sport Psychologist* 32, no. 3 (2018): 220–225. See also Jonathan Rhodes, Karol Nedza, Jon May, Thomas Jenkins, and Tom Stone, "From Couch to Ultra Marathon: Using Functional Imagery Training to Enhance Motivation," *Journal of Imagery Research in Sport and Physical Activity* 16, no. 1 (2021).

7. Carol Kauffman and Anne Scouler, "Towards a Positive Psychology of Executive Coaching," in *Positive Psychology in Practice,* ed. A. Linley and S. Joseph (Hoboken, NJ: John Wiley, 2004), 287–302. See also Carol Kauffman, "Positive Psychology: The Science at the Heart of Coaching," in *Evidence Based Coaching Handbook: Putting Best Practices to Work for Your Clients,* ed. Dianne R. Stober and Anthony M. Grant (Medford, MA: John Wiley & Sons, 2006), 219–253.

8. Liz Wiseman, *Impact Players: How to Take the Lead, Play Bigger, and Multiply Your Impact* (New York: HarperCollins, 2021).

Chapter 3

1. Lisa F. Barrett and J. A. Russell, ed., *The Psychological Construction of Emotion* (New York: Guilford Publications, 2014).

2. This is just a "starter kit" for thinking about external goals that may be hard to identify initially. There are many additional ways to think about this. For example, you can play offense against a threat; see Leo M. Tilman and General Charles Jacoby (ret.), *Agility: How to Navigate the Unknown and Seize Opportunity in a World of Disruption* (Plano, TX: Missionday, 2019). Also, the Cynefin framework shows how to categorize different situations into simple, complicated, complex, and chaotic categories and identifies actions for each one; see David J. Snowden and Mary E. Boone, "A Leader's Framework for Decision Making," *Harvard Business Review*, November 2007, 68–76.

3. This is illustrative only. Risk is concerned with known outcomes and probabilities, like figure 3-1. In practice, there are relatively few situations we face as leaders where the probabilities are known. Rather, we are primarily faced with uncertainty, which implies that either the range of possible outcomes and/or the likelihoods of outcomes are unknown. In this book we primarily refer to risk for simplicity's sake, but the leadership principles apply to uncertainty as well. To the risk purists who read this book, we ask your forgiveness!

4. Much of the risk and uncertainty literature is focused only on downside risks. But Tilman and Jacoby view risk (and uncertainty) and returns in an integrated way: there is no risk without opportunity and no opportunity without risk.

5. S. D. Kim, "Characterizing Unknown Unknowns" (paper presented at PMI Global Congress, Vancouver, BC, Canada, 2012).

6. For an excellent, practical treatment of how to identify and assess risks and the need to invest in risk intelligence, see Tilman and Jacoby, 106–119.

Chapter 4

1. "It Starts with the CEO: A Global Study, 2021," Egon Zehnder, 2021.

2. Richard E. Boyatzis and Kleio Akrivou, "The Ideal Self as the Driver of Intentional Change," *Journal of Management Development* 25, no. 7 (2006): 624–642. Richard's work is at the core of how we think. His work brings together excellent neuroscience with best practice.

3. Peter F. Drucker, *Managing Oneself* (Boston: Harvard Business Press, 2008).

4. Bill George, *Authentic Leadership: Rediscovering the Secrets to Creating Lasting Value* (Medford, MA: John Wiley & Sons, 2003).

5. Scott Snook, Nitin Nohria, and Rakesh Khurana, *The Handbook for Teaching Leadership: Knowing, Doing, and Being* (Thousand Oaks: Sage Publications, 2011).

6. Carol Kauffman, "The Split-Second Question That Can Change Your Life," Inc.com, January 4, 2021; and Marshall Goldsmith and Mark Reiter, *The Earned Life: Lose Regret, Choose Fulfillment* (New York: Currency, 2022).

7. Richard E. Boyatzis, Melvin L. Smith, and Nancy Blaize, "Developing Sustainable Leaders Through Coaching and Compassion," *Academy of Management Learning & Education* 5, no. 1 (2006): 8–24.

8. Linda Orkin Lewin, Alyssa McManamon, Michael T.O. Stein, and Donna T. Chen, "Minding the Form That Transforms: Using Kegan's Model of Adult Development to Understand Personal and Professional Identity Formation in Medicine," *Academic Medicine* 94, no. 9 (2019): 1299–1304.

9. Lisa Feldman Barrett, *How Emotions Are Made: The Secret Life of the Brain* (New York: Mariner Books, 2017).

10. Christopher Peterson, "The Values in Action (VIA) Classification of Strengths" in *A Life Worth Living: Contributions to Positive Psychology*, ed. Mihaly Csikszentmihalyi and Isabella Selega Csikszentmihalyi (New York: Oxford University Press, 2006). In this little-known book, Chris Peterson anticipates future criticism that positive psychology is too "nice" by showing how strengths can be contorted and lead to lower functioning.

11. James O. Prochaska, John Norcross, and Carlo DiClemente, *Changing for Good: A Revolutionary Six-Stage Program for Overcoming Bad Habits and Moving Your Life Positively Forward* (New York: Avon Books, 1994), 40–56; and James O. Prochaska and Janice M. Prochaska, *Changing to Thrive: Using the Stages of Change to Overcome the Top Threats to Your Health and Happiness* (Center City, MN: Hazelden Publishing, 2016).

12. Abraham H. Maslow, *Toward a Psychology of Being* (Eastford, CT: Martino Fine Books, 2021); and Elizabeth Hopper, "Maslow's Hierarchy of Needs Explained," ThoughtCo.com, February 24, 2020.

13. Edward L. Deci, Anja H. Olafsen, and Richard M. Ryan, "Self-Determination Theory in Work Organizations: The State of a Science," *Annual Review of Organizational Psychology and Organizational Behavior* 4 (2017): 19–43. Deci's and Ryan's work has been replicated hundreds of times, far too many to capture here. The work has many applications on a personal, professional, and organizational level.

14. Jennifer Garvey Berger and Paul W. B. Atkins, "Mapping Complexity of Mind: Using the Subject-Object Interview in Coaching," *Coaching: An International Journal of Theory, Research and Practice* 2, no. 1 (2009): 23–36. See also Robert Kegan and Lisa Laskow Lahey, "The Real Reason People Won't Change," *Harvard Business Review*, November 2001, 84–92; and Robert Kegan, *In Over Our Heads: The Mental Demands of Modern Life* (Cambridge: Harvard University Press, 1998).

Chapter 5

1. Carol Kauffman and William H. Hodgetts, "Model Agility: Coaching Effectiveness and Four Perspectives on a Case Study," *Consulting Psychology Journal: Practice and Research* 68, no. 2 (2016): 157. We believe that no one approach fits all, nor should it. We should assess the usefulness of any framework in context.

2. Dick Patton and German Herrera, "Spanning the Realities of the CEO Role," *Egon Zehnder CEO Insights* 25, 2021.

3. John Paul Stephens, Emily Heaphy, and Jane E. Dutton, "High-Quality Connections," in *The Oxford Handbook of Positive Organizational Scholarship*, ed. Kim S. Cameron and Gretchen M. Spreitzer (New York: Oxford University Press, 2013).

4. Kim S. Cameron, *Positive Leadership: Strategies for Extraordinary Performance* (Oakland, CA: Berrett-Koehler, 2012).

5. Tony Alessandra and Michael J. O'Connor, *The Platinum Rule: Discover the Four Basic Business Personalities and How They Can Lead You to Success* (New York: Grand Central/Hatchette, 1996).

6. These studies are just a few that speak to how our midbrain and limbic system speed-read people and the world around us. See Leanne M. Williams, Belinda J. Liddell, Andrew H. Kemp, Richard A. Bryant, Russell A. Meares, Anthony S. Peduto, Evian Gordon, "Amygdala-Prefrontal Dissociation of Subliminal and Supraliminal Fear," *Human Brain Mapping* 27, no. 8 (2006): 652–661; Dimitri J. Bayle, Marie-Anne Henaff, and Pierre Krolak-Salmon, "Unconsciously Perceived Fear in Peripheral Vision Alerts the Limbic System: A MEG Study," *PLoS One* 4 (no. 12) (2009): e8207; and Mark A. Williams, Adam P. Morris, Francis McGlone, David F. Abbott, and Jason B. Mattingley, "Amygdala Responses to Fearful and Happy Facial Expressions under Conditions of Binocular Suppression," *Journal of Neuroscience* 24, no. 12 (2004): 2898–2904.

7. Carol Kauffman, "Without Compassion, Resilient Leaders Will Fall Short," hbr.org, August 21, 2020; and Richard E. Boyatzis, "Measuring the Impact of Quality of Relationships Through the Positive Emotional Attractor," in *Toward a Positive Psychology of Relationships: New Directions in Theory and Research*, ed. Meg A. Warren and Stewart I. Donaldson (Westport, CT: Praeger, 2017), 193–210.

8. Xiaoyu He, Qinhua Sun, and Cinnamon Stetler, "Warm Communication Style Strengthens Expectations and Increases Perceived Improvement," *Health Communication* 33, no. 8 (2018): 939–945.

9. The power of our belief in another to impact our performance is remarkable. See J. Sterling Livingston, "Pygmalion in Management," *Harvard Business Review*, January 2003, 97–106; and Marlies Veestraeten, Stefanie K. Johnson, Hannes Leroy, Thomas Sy, and Luc Sels, "Exploring the Bounds of Pygmalion Effects: Congruence of Implicit Followership Theories Drives and Binds Leader Performance Expectations and Follower Work Engagement," *Journal of Leadership & Organizational Studies* 28, no. 2 (2020): 137–153.

Chapter 6

1. David Noble and Carol Kauffman, "Where There Is a Will: Creating New Pathways to Success," *Egon Zehnder CEO Insights* 21, 2021; and C. Richard Snyder, *The Psychology of Hope: You Can Get There from Here* (New York: Free Press, 1994).

2. C. Richard Snyder, "Hope Theory: Rainbows in the Mind," *Psychological Inquiry* 13, no. 4 (2002): 249–275. Rick Snyder's work is still the subject of multitudes of dissertations and research studies. It is very sad that he and Shane Lopez both died before their time.

3. Danny Brouwer, Rob R. Meijer, Anke M. Weekers, and Joost J. Baneke, "On the Dimensionality of the Dispositional Hope Scale," *Psychological Assessment* 20, no. 3 (2008): 310; C. Richard Snyder, S. C. Sympson, F. C. Ybasco, T. F. Borders, M. A. Babyak, and R. L. Higgins, "Development and Validation of the State Hope Scale," *Journal of Personality and Social Psychology* 70, no. 2 (1996): 321; Scott C. Roesch and Allison A. Vaughn, "Evidence for the Factorial Validity of the Dispositional Hope Scale: Cross-Ethnic and Cross-Gender Measurement Equivalence," *European Journal of Psychological Assessment* 22, no. 2 (2006): 78.

4. Snyder, "Hope Theory."

5. For scenario planning, refer to Peter Schwartz, *The Art of the Long View: Planning for the Future in an Uncertain World* (New York: Doubleday, 1996). Contingency planning has been mostly applied to downside risks, although it is equally applicable to understanding what leadership actions can be taken to make the most of better-than-expected developments. See Leao J. Fernandes and Francisco Saldanha-da-Gama, "Contingency Planning: A Literature Review" (paper presented at SCMCC-08 Supply Chain Management and Competitiveness, October 2008). For a discussion on how to construct a "risk radar," see Leo M. Tilman and General Charles Jacoby (ret.), *Agility: How to Navigate the Unknown and Seize Opportunity in a World of Disruption* (Plano, TX: Missionday, 2019), 106–119.

Chapter 7

1. Mihaly Csikszentmihalyi, *Flow: The Psychology of Optimal Experience* (New York: Harper Perennial Modern Classics, 2008).
2. Marshall Goldsmith and Mark Reiter, *Triggers: Creating Behavior that Lasts: Becoming the Person You Want to Be* (New York: Currency, 2015).
3. Jose L. Herrero, Simon Khuvis, Erin Yeagle, Moran Cerf, and Ashesh D. Mehta, "Breathing Above the Brain Stem: Volitional Control and Attentional Modulation in Humans," *Journal of Neurophysiology* 119, no. 1, 2018.
4. Goldsmith and Reiter, *Triggers*.
5. Carol Kauffman, Jordan Silberman, and David Sharpley, "Coaching for Strengths Using VIA," in *Psychometrics in Coaching: Using Psychological and Psychometric Tools for Development*, 2nd ed., ed. Jonathan Passmore (London: Kogan Page, 2012): 239–253.
6. Christopher Peterson and Martin E. P. Seligman, *Character Strengths and Virtues: A Handbook and Classification* (New York: Oxford University Press, 2004).

Chapter 8

1. "It Starts with the CEO: A Global Study, 2021," Egon Zehnder, 2021.
2. J. Sterling Livingston, "Pygmalion in Management," *Harvard Business Review*, January 2003, 97–106.
3. Here are simply a few of the representative studies; some of these are meta-analyses with hundreds of studies represented within them: James K. Harter, Frank L. Schmidt, and Corey L. M. Keyes, "Well-Being in the Workplace and Its Relationship to Business Outcomes: A Review of the Gallup Studies," gallup.com, 2003; F. Luthans and C. M. Youssef, "Positive Workplaces," in *The Oxford Handbook of Positive Psychology*, ed. Shane J. Lopez and C. R. Snyder (New York: Oxford University Press, 2009), 579–588; Neal M. Ashkanasy and Claire E. Ashton-James, "Positive Emotion in Organizations: A Multi-Level Framework," in *Positive Organizational Behavior*, ed. Debra Nelson and Cary L. Cooper (Newbury Park, CA: Pine Forge Press, 2007): 57–73; Julia K. Boehm and Sonja Lyubomirsky, "Does Happiness Promote Career Success?" *Journal of Career Assessment* 16, no. 1 (2008): 101–116. Sonya's early work included a meta-analysis of over 300 research studies. See also Sonja Lyubomirsky, Laura King, and Ed Diener, "The Benefits

of Frequent Positive Affect: Does Happiness Lead to Success?" *Psychological Bulletin* 131, no. 6 (2005): 803; and Abraham Carmeli, Daphna Brueller, and Jane E. Dutton, "Learning Behaviours in the Workplace: The Role of High-Quality Interpersonal Relationships and Psychological Safety," *Systems Research and Behavioral Science 26*, no. 1 (2009): 81–98.

4. Rosette Cataldo's "Workhuman" (paper presented at the EVANTA CHRO Meeting, Boston, MA, November 18, 2021) discussed data collected on 6 million workers.

Chapter 9

1. Rosabeth Moss Kanter, "Managing Yourself: Zoom In, Zoom Out," *Harvard Business Review*, March 2011, 112–116.

2. Joseph Luft and Harrington Ingham, "The Johari Window: A Graphic Model of Interpersonal Awareness," Proceedings of the Western Training Laboratory in Group Development, UCLA, Los Angeles, CA, 1955; the four types of knowledge are an adaptation of Johari's window based on what is known and unknown by an individual leader.

3. Carol Kauffman and Tatiana Bachkirova, "The Evolution of Coaching: An Interview with Sir John Whitmore," *Coaching: An International Journal of Theory, Research, and Practice* 1, no. 1 (2008): 11–15.

4. John Whitmore, *Coaching for Performance: The Principles and Practice of Coaching and Leadership*, 5th ed. (London: Hachette UK, 2017). Sir John Whitmore was the first to bring leadership coaching to the United Kingdom. He transitioned from being a Formula One race car driver to a peak performance sports coach to realizing it had a powerful application to the business world.

5. Emily Pronin, Daniel Y. Lin, and Lee Ross, "The Bias Blind Spot: Perceptions of Bias in Self Versus Others," *Personality and Social Psychology Bulletin 28*, no. 3 (2002): 369–381.

6. Dorie Clark, "Simple Ways to Spot Unknown Unknowns," hbr.org, October 23, 2017.

7. We of course cannot do justice to the vast literature on bias in any of its forms. Here are just two of hundreds: Himani Oberai and Ila Mehrotra Anand, "Unconscious Bias: Thinking without Thinking," *Human Resource Management International Digest*, October 2018; and Sarah Fiarman, "Disrupting Inequity, Unconscious Bias: When Good Intentions Aren't Enough," *Educational Leadership* 74, no. 3 (2016): 10–15.

8. Nikolaus Franke, Marc Gruber, Dietmar Harhoff, and Joachim Henkel, "What You Are Is What You Like: Similarity Biases in Venture Capitalists' Evaluations of Startup Teams," *Journal of Business Venturing* 21, no. 6 (2006): 802–826; and Sebastian M. Barr, Kate E. Snyder, Jill L. Adelson, Stephanie L. Budge, "Posttraumatic Stress in the Trans Community: The Roles of Anti-Transgender Bias, Non-Affirmation, and Internalized Transphobia," *Psychology of Sexual Orientation and Gender Diversity* (2021).

9. Daniel Kahneman, *Thinking, Fast and Slow* (New York: Farrar, Straus & Giroux, 2011).

10. Philip E. Tetlock and Ariel Levi, "Attribution Bias: On the Inconclusiveness of the Cognition-Motivation Debate," *Journal of Experimental Social*

Psychology 18, no. 1 (1982): 68–88; and Matthew T. Billett and Yiming Qian, "Are Overconfident CEOs Born or Made? Evidence of Self-Attribution Bias from Frequent Acquirers," *Management Science* 54, no. 6 (2008): 1037–1051.

11.   Maria Kozhevnikov, "Cognitive Styles in the Context of Modern Psychology: Toward an Integrated Framework of Cognitive Style," *Psychological Bulletin* 133, no. 3 (2007): 464; and Richard Riding and Indra Cheema, "Cognitive Styles—An Overview and Integration," *Educational Psychology* 11, no. 3–4 (1991): 193–215.

12.   Kahneman, *Thinking, Fast and Slow.*

13.   C. Sandler, "The Emotional Profiles Triangle: Working with Leaders Under Pressure," *Strategic HR Review* 11, no. 2 (2012): 65–71.

14.   Daniel Goleman, *Emotional Intelligence: Why It Can Matter More Than IQ* (New York: Random House, 1997). It's hard to believe that people did not recognize the importance of emotions in the business world until Dan Goleman brought the work to the world in 1997. See also Carlton Brown, "The Effects of Emotional Intelligence (EI) and Leadership Style on Sales Performance," *Economic Insights–Trends & Challenges* 66, no. 3 (2014): 177; and Peter Hills and Michael Argyle, "Emotional Stability as a Major Dimension of Happiness," *Personality and Individual Differences* 31, no. 8 (2001): 1357–1364.

Chapter 10

1.   Leo M. Tilman and General Charles Jacoby (ret.), *Agility: How to Navigate the Unknown and Seize Opportunity in a World of Disruption* (Plano, TX: Missionday, 2019), 130–131, 137, 139, and 212–219; and personal conversations.

2.   Deborah Ancona, Elaine Backman, and Kate Isaacs, "Two Roads to Green: A Tale of Bureaucratic Versus Distributed Leadership Models of Change" in *Leading Sustainable Change: An Organizational Perspective*, ed. Rebecca Henderson, Ranjay Gulati, and Michael Tushman (New York: Oxford University Press, 2015), 225–249.

3.   Boundary conditions are the guardrails that you set for your team or organization. These include, but are not limited to, behavioral guidelines such as the need to live the organization's values and ethical standards; methods that can be used or not used to achieve the goal such as organic or inorganic (M&A) growth; and constraints related to time and resource availability.

Chapter 11

1.   Personal communication with Chuck Jacoby.

2.   That is, decisions reserved for the leader alone to make, with input from others.

3.   "It Starts with the CEO: A Global Study, 2021," Egon Zehnder, 2021.

4.   Horowitz, Ben, *What You Do Is Who You Are: How to Create Your Business Culture* (New York: Harper, 2019).

5.   For a fuller treatment of culture, see Terence E. Deal and Allan A. Kennedy, *Corporate Cultures: The Rites and Rituals of Corporate Life* (New York: Basic Books, 2000), and Charles A. O'Reilly and David F. Caldwell, "People and Organizational Culture: A Profile Comparison Approach to

Assessing Person-Organization Fit," *Academy of Management Journal* 9 (1991).

6. Daniel Goleman, Richard E. Boyatzis, and Annie McKee, *Primal Leadership: Unleashing the Power of Emotional Intelligence* (Boston: Harvard Business Review Press, 2013); Barbara L. Fredrickson, "Leading with Positive Emotions," *Organisational Science* 5 (2016): 1–3; and Lori Desautels, "Emotions Are Contagious," *Scholarship and Professional Work–Education* (2014).

7. Charles Duhigg, "What Google Learned from Its Quest to Build the Perfect Team," *New York Times Magazine*, February 25, 2016. Amy's body of work on psychological safety began decades before Google's famous "Project Aristotle" blasted it into the mainstream; see Amy C. Edmondson, *The Fearless Organization: Creating Psychological Safety in the Workplace for Learning, Innovation, and Growth* (New York: John Wiley & Sons, 2018); and Chen Ming, Gao Xiaoying, Zheng Huizhen, and Ran Bin, "A Review on Psychological Safety: Concepts, Measurements, Antecedents, and Consequences Variables" in *Proceedings of the 2015 International Conference on Social Science and Technology Education* (Pleasantville, NJ: Atlantis Press, 2015).

8. Róisín O'Donovan, Desirée Van Dun, and Eilish McAuliffe, "Measuring Psychological Safety in Healthcare Teams: Developing an Observational Measure to Complement Survey Methods," BMC Medical Research Methodology 20, no. 1 (2020): 1–17.

Chapter 12

1. Marshall Goldsmith and Mark Reiter, *What Got You Here Won't Get You There: How Successful People Become Even More Successful* (New York: Hyperion, 2007).

2. Steven Markham, Ina S. Markham, Janice Witt Smith, "A Review, Analysis, and Extension of Peer-Leader Feedback Agreement: Contrasting Group Aggregate Agreement vs. Self-Other Agreement Using Entity Analytics and Visualization," *The Leadership Quarterly* 28, no. 1 (2017): 153–177.

Chapter 13

1. Michael D. Watkins, *The First 90 Days, Updated and Expanded: Proven Strategies for Getting Up to Speed Faster and Smarter* (Boston: Harvard Business Review Press, 2013).

2. Mark Byford, Michael D. Watkins, and Lena Triantogiannis, "Onboarding Isn't Enough: Newly Hired Executives Need to Be Fully Integrated into the Company's Culture," *Harvard Business Review*, May–June 2017.

3. IDEO, *The Field Guide to Human-Centered Design* (Cambridge, MA: IDEO.org/Design Kit, 2015).

4. John J. Gabarro and John P. Kotter, *Managing Your Boss* (Boston: Harvard Business School Press, 2008).

5. Philipp Koellinger, Maria Minniti, and Christian Schade, "I Think I Can, I Think I Can: Overconfidence and Entrepreneurial Behavior," *Journal of Economic Psychology* 28, vol. 4 (2007): 502–527.

6. This remarkable work looked at four kinds of responses in interaction: Active/passive constructive and active/passive destructive. The findings surprised the authors. Shelly L. Gable, Gian C. Gonzaga, and Amy Strachman, "Will You Be There for Me When Things Go Right? Supportive Responses to Positive Event Disclosures," *Journal of Personality and Social Psychology* 91, vol. 5 (2006): 90.

7. Richard E. Nisbett and Timothy DeCamp Wilson, "The Halo Effect: Evidence for Unconscious Alteration of Judgments," *Journal of Personality and Social Psychology* 35, vol. 4 (1977); and W. Wen, J. Li, G. K. Georgiou, C. Huang, and L. Wang, "Reducing the Halo Effect by Stimulating Analytic Thinking," *Social Psychology* 51, no. 5 (2020): 334.

Chapter 14

1. Linda A. Hill, Greg Brandeau, Emily Truelove, and Kent Lineback, *Collective Genius: The Art and Practice of Leading Innovation* (Boston: Harvard Business Review Press, 2014). Greg collaborated on several engagements related to team and organizational innovation.

2. Mark Bonchek, "How to Create an Exponential Mindset," hbr.org, July 27, 2016.

3. We are indebted to Rob Nail, a cofounder and ex-CEO of Singularity University for sharing his practical approach to Exponential Thinking. See www.robnail.com.

Chapter 15

1. Leo M. Tilman and General Charles Jacoby (ret.), *Agility: How to Navigate the Unknown and Seize Opportunity in a World of Disruption* (Plano, TX: Missionday, 2019), 19–22; and General Stanley McChrystal and Anna Butrico, *Risk: A User's Guide* (New York: Portfolio/Penguin, 2021).

2. For a treatment of the Detect Assess Respond (DAR) framework, see McChrystal and Butrico, *Risk*.

Chapter 16

1. Frédéric Laloux, *Reinventing Organizations: A Guide to Creating Organizations Inspired by the Next Stage in Human Consciousness* (Millis, MA: Nelson Parker, 2014).

Conclusion

1. Brian K. Cooper, James C. Sarros, and Joseph C. Santora, "The Character of Leadership," *Ivey Business Journal*, May/June 2007.

2. Christopher Peterson and Martin E. P. Seligman, *Character Strengths and Virtues: A Handbook and Classification* (New York: Oxford University Press, 2004).

3. Nick Craig and Scott A. Snook, "From Purpose to Impact," *Harvard Business Review*, May 2014, 104–111.

4. Craig and Snook, "From Purpose to Impact."

5. Richard E. Boyatzis and Kleio Akrivou, "The Ideal Self as the Driver of Intentional Change," *Journal of Management Development* 25, no. 7 (2006).

6. Joseph Goldstein, *Mindfulness: A Practical Guide to Awakening* (Louisville, CO: Sounds True, 2013).

7. Jeremy D. Mackey, B. Parker Ellen III, Charn P. McAllister, and Katherine C. Alexander, "The Dark Side of Leadership: A Systematic Literature Review and Meta-Analysis of Destructive Leadership Research," *Journal of Business Research* 132 (2021): 705–718.

8. Goldstein, *Mindfulness.*

INDEX

ACKNOWLEDGMENTS

Our gratitude starts with all the leaders who have entrusted us to work with them. We hope we have been of service to you. In turn, we want to let you know that we have learned so much from you and will continue to pass on your collective wisdom.

Thank you to Scott Berinato, our amazing editor and alchemist, who truly can turn lead into gold. Your near immediate and then steadfast belief in us, and your capacity to lean back and not lean, allowed us to lean in and keep writing. Most of all, thank you for leaning with us when we needed it.

Whitney Johnson, words cannot express how your deep faith, coaching, and occasional prodding helped start and then kept the ball rolling. Thank you for all of the Friday afternoon calls. Connecting us with Scott was a wonderful gift.

Dr. Marshall Goldsmith, thank you for "Marshalling" us along with humor, challenge, and caring. Your support got us from a 10 to 10x.

Mark Thompson, without you this book would not exist. Thank you for supporting both of us.

We are delighted to make a special acknowledgement of German Herrera. German exemplifies extraordinary leadership: crystal-clear goals along with four or more ways to achieve them; humble, confident, collaborative, and generous; and interpersonally agile. He paved the way for our first two-on-one coaching engagement by introducing us to one of his most important client relationships. German has been a constant supporter since, including providing insightful comments on the first draft of this book, which immeasurably improved it.

Emily Loose, thank you for helping us organize our thinking and getting our first draft worthy of being read.

Thank you to our HBR peer review readers, who gave us incredible advice, guidance, and feedback, including Edilson Camara, Darleen Caron, Jonathan Isaacson, Penny James, Jim Jirjis, Jonathan Isaacson, Dave McKay, Ikdeep Singh, Ramez Sousou, and Nick Studer.

It takes a village to create a book. We are so grateful to our HBR team. Melinda Merino, senior director and associate publisher, for her oversight and guidance throughout. Stephani Finks, bless you for all of your iterations of our cover, which went far beyond the call of duty. Felicia Sinusas and Sally Ashworth, thank you for your major efforts helping the book get attention around the world; your help has been invaluable. Jordan Concannon, Lindsey Dietrich, Brian Galvin, Erika Heilman, Alexandra Kephart, and Jon Shipley gave us invaluable advice and support in the tricky world of sales and marketing. Allison Peter, thank you for getting all of the trains to run on time. Rick Emanuel, Josh Olejarz, and the entire production team, your indefatigable help kept improving the book. Thanks to the entire HBR community. You have supported us and had our backs throughout the process. We could not have asked for more.

Thank you to our Life Plan Review group members. Our weekly meetings for our six-month-plus stints were instrumental in helping us think bigger, holding us accountable, and galvanizing us into action. Special thanks to Marcia Blenko, Magda Mook, Sanyin Siang, Michael Bungay Stanier, Gabriela Teasdale, and, of course, Marshall Goldsmith and Mark Thompson.

To our brilliant friends, who have been our eyes and ears to help guide us.

To John-Paul Pape, for your warmth and insight, not to mention your amazing sense of fashion! We have so appreciated your sponsoring and working with us for years on the trickiest and most interesting team and organizational effectiveness issues.

To Julia Nenke, who worked with us side by side with senior leadership teams, whose great warmth and support inspired us, and whose insight helped refine our thinking.

Jill Ader, your steadfast commitment to leadership advisory work has been an inspiration. Dorie Clark, your advice on how best to reach leaders has been invaluable. Laine Joelson Cohen, your sense of joy and love of coaching is vital and viral. Douglas Choo for your thought partnership, insights, and being willing to read so many versions of our drafts. Nancy Glynn, thank you for being a thought partner and for teaming up with us to work with leaders. Hubert Joly, a true sage, we appreciate you sharing your experiences with us. Mark Patricof, for paving the way for us to work with amazing athletes.

And to our trusted and supportive associates. Thank you for being with us every step of the way, for years! Karl Alleman, Govind Ayer, Ian Bolin, Francesco Buquicchio, Jon Carter, Alyse Forcellina, Namrita Jhangiani, Martha Josephson, Toru Kaihatsu, Martin Knudsen, Martin Kramer, Brigitte Lammers, Fiona McGauchie, Yasushi Maruyama (an exemplar of the Four Stances!), Koshiro Miyake, Yoshiaki Obata, Dick Patton, Kati Najipoor-Smith, Greig Schneider, Carol SingletonSlade, Trent Aulbaugh, Valerie Spriet, Ashley Summerfield, Calvin Yee, and Elaine Yew, who are all outstanding players in the leadership advisory space.

We are indebted to our friends and thought partners and major influencers. Thank you to Richard Boyatzis for intentional change theory, Greg Brandeau and Owen Rogers for innovation and creativity, Amy Edmondson for bringing psychological safety front and center to leadership, General Charles (Chuck) Jacoby (ret.) for commander's intent, Rob Nail for 10x, Dick Schwartz for internal family systems and the Five Cs, and Leo Tilman for risk and agility.

• • •

David has the following individuals to thank.

Douglas Choo for your total trust and belief in me and your thought partnership. You helped me find an inner light when I most needed it, and I am grateful that you express *mudita* whenever I experience success or a happy moment.

Once again, all the leaders I have been blessed to work with—you know who you are!

Jon Aaron for being my teacher and guide to meditation and mindfulness. Ray Bingham for entrusting me multiple times to work with leaders who were under your wing. Alisa Cohn for your zest and savvy. Vincent Dominé and Rolf Frey, dear friends for two decades who are also best-in-class coaches. I am particularly grateful to you for my very first coaching referral. Alan Hilliker, you're one of the best search professionals on the planet, and I'm so grateful that you "discovered" me and helped to launch my career in leadership advisory. Chuck Jacoby, your character strengths and wisdom are so dazzling that I have never taken a single note from you; our discussions are imprinted immediately in my head. Christoph Knoess, Janice Fukakusa, and Scott McDonald for believing in me, opening your hearts as well as game-changing leader referrals, and patiently seeing me through my various incarnations from banker to strategist to leadership adviser. Ana Lueneburger, another top coach, I am grateful for our lasting friendship, your kindness and insight, and your introduction so many years ago to Carol Kauffman, which led to a wonderful creative partnership and friendship. Christoph Lueneburger, you and Ana truly are family. Beyond that, I have always admired your strength of intellect and clarity of thought. And I'm grateful for you blasting open the doors to the world of private equity for me and trusting me with your most important relationships. Joan Mohammed, who started as a colleague and became my closest friend, thank you for your loyalty, encouragement, and caring. Mary Ann Ochs, you have taken care of me for over a decade. Thank you for your friendship, thank you for your excellence, and what would I do without your memory?! Scott Osman, we have collaborated on some complex and nonlinear engagements, and I am always grateful for your steadiness, constant curiosity, and integrity. Ashley Stephenson, what can I say? You brought me along the curve, first on how to assess top leaders and then on how to develop them. I've been lucky to have had many mentors in my career, but you are the only role model I've ever had. And you still are. Henry Topping, I appreciate your friendship and will never forget that you gave me my first big coaching break. I am still working on how to return the favor.

To my parents—you told me since I was a child that I would write a book. I wish you could have been around to see this one get published.

• • •

Carol has the following individuals to thank.

To Mark Goldblatt for your patience and steadfast support in more ways than I can count as I have disappeared into the book, you've kept me grounded in the real world.

My band of special leaders, I won't name you, but thank you from the bottom of my heart for being wonderful humans and letting me into your lives.

Marshall Goldsmith, you have been unbelievably generous for years on end, from our very first encounter when you saw me as a kindred spirit before I did. Mark Thompson, I am eternally grateful for your rock-solid belief in me that exceeded my own. Thank you for calling me over and over telling me that I need to write a book, and then helping me along the way. Ruth Ann Harnisch, you were the single most powerful force that launched my coaching career. This was as important to me as The Harnisch Foundation's gift of $2 million to start the Institute of Coaching; your capacity to be caring and challenging in a way I'd never seen before has informed my coaching. Phil Levendusky, few people have had someone like you shepherding their career, from my first year as intern at

McLean Hospital, a Harvard Medical School Affiliate, when I was twenty-five, supporting my faculty appointments at HMS up till the present day. Margaret Moore and Susan David, true partners as we built the Institute of Coaching from just the three of us to a dynamic, global organization, funding education and research and a community of over twenty thousand. The two of you, soon joined by Jeff Hull, have been fountains of knowledge and the bedrock of the field. Nick Craig, thank you for dragging me forward and throwing me into deep waters. Our six years of continuous Authentic Leadership Programs around the world, and the hundreds of leaders I coached, helped forge me into who I am today. Your introduction to Dick Schwartz and our years working together are core to all I do.

Thanks to my ESMT colleagues (European School of Management and Technology) for bringing me back so many years. Manfred Kets de Vries, Elizabet Engellau, and Kostya Korotov, thank you for teasing my brain, and Andreas Bernhardt, thank you for meeting me all over the world at a drop of the hat for incredible conversations. Thanks also to my fabulous APA Div 13 (Consulting Psychology, American Psychological Association), Bill Berman, Dick Kilburg, David Peterson, the smartest coaches I've had the pleasure to know. To Anne Scoular and Meyler Campbell for giving me the honor of being their chief supervisor for many years, and for the dozens of excellent coaches you sent my way. To my "tiny team," Jaime Banks (my boss), Missy Chabot (psychological twin), and Tiffany Dally (ever steadfast), and Paul Nunez. Thank you for years of support and keeping me on track.

As I embarked on the journey with David to write this book, many of you have made this possible. Our journey as part of the MG 100 has been amazing. Again, Whitney, thank you thank you, from the first moment you approached me and said, "I just know we are going to be friends," I could not have imagined how rewarding a relationship was waiting for us. You keep amazing me! Liz Wiseman, your counsel, breathtaking intelligence, and joy have been wonderful. Asheesh Advani, for being an inspiration with your work at Junior Achievement. Safi Bahcall, for your wit and wisdom, contagious humor and energy, and Loonshots. Tal Ben-Shahar, for being a great role model and helping me see what kind of leader I was—way back when you taught the most famous course at Harvard. Peter Bregman, for lending me some of your emotional courage. Ayse Birsel, thank you for your work in designing the life you love. Bill and Julie Carrier, your tenacious support and enthusiasm are wonderful. Herminia

Ibarra, thank you for your invaluable advice and practical support, which made a huge difference. Martin Lindstrom, marketer extraordinaire, thank you for being such a light and guide. Garry Ridge, your goodness and enthusiasm as a CEO and great human is contagious. Thank you for putting "Who do you want to be right now" in huge letters on the wall. Diane Ryan, for being the embodiment of courage under fire (literally). Brian Underhill, for fifteen years of encouragement and valuing the work.

Thanks to my lifelong friends Elizabeth Murphy, Dorothy Bennett, Michael Cusumano, Caroline McCabe—all super smart, super loyal, lucky to have you in my life. Charlie, you are in a category all your own. Sasha and Michael—amazing to have grown-up offspring who are fun, interested in the field and are thought partners. Yay!

David—you are the best business partner, brother, and friend I could ever wish for.

• • •

Again, most of all, we would like to thank our spouses for their rock-solid encouragement, patience, and suggestions! Thank you for all the dinners that allowed us more time to write. You are our shining lights.

ABOUT THE AUTHORS

David Noble is the founder of View Advisors, a consulting firm that works globally with CEOs, their teams, select C-suite leaders, boards of directors, investors, and star athletes on leadership and strategy. He also serves as a senior adviser to Egon Zehnder, the Institute of Coaching, and Oliver Wyman Group and was previously on the management advisory board of TowerBrook Capital Partners, the first B Corp private equity fund. In 2021 Noble was named by Thinkers50 as one of the world's top coaches. He is also a member of the Marshall Goldsmith 100 Coaches community of leaders and coaches.

Noble brings a rare combination of leadership, strategic, and operating lenses to his advisory work, based on over three decades of experience as an operating executive, as well as a consultant to senior leaders. He has been a senior executive at RBC and Morgan Stanley, two of the world's best-run financial institutions, holding positions as varied as head of strategy, assistant chief economist, corporate banker, and CEO of the world's first digital retail bank, as well as head of the world's first digital brokerage. Subsequently, he spent several years on the executive committees at two global strategy consultancies: as a global practice leader at Kearney and as head of Asia Pacific at Oliver Wyman.

He became business partners with Carol Kauffman in 2015 when they began the novel "two-on-one" coaching method. Their goal was to bring their complementary experiences and approaches to the most complex leaders, who are often facing near-impossible goals and challenges. They have also worked together extensively at the top of the house with CEO team coaching, workshops, and leader-as-coach programs. The aim varies from increasing alignment and driving step changes in team dynamics to developing exponential thinking for innovation.

Noble is married and is based in Miami Beach, Florida, where he loves to swim as often as possible, and Hudson, New York, where he tends to his vegetables, berries, and orchard. He is also active in the not-for-profit world, supporting the arts, environmental advocacy, and land preservation.

Carol Kauffman is an international leader in the field of coaching and has more than 40,000 hours of practice. Her clients primarily comprise C-level leaders and their teams or elite athletes and creatives. She has been described as a lateral thinker who pushes the edges with a sense of humor and can disrupt someone out of their comfort zone. She was shortlisted by Thinkers50 as one of the top eight coaches around the globe for her thought leadership, entrepreneurial spirit, and contribution to coaching best practices. She is a founding member of Marshall Goldsmith 100 Coaches and ranked the number one leadership coach in the world. She founded the Institute of Coaching with a $2 million gift from the Harnisch Foundation.

Carol is an assistant professor at Harvard Medical School, a visiting professor at Henley Business School, and a senior leadership adviser at Egon Zehnder. At Harvard she launched the annual Coaching in Leadership and Healthcare Conference, one of the most highly attended events at HMS. Her professional development program, Leader as Coach, won Harvard's inaugural Program Award for Culture of Excellence in Mentoring and has been rolled out throughout the United States. She was also the founding editor in chief of *Coaching: An International Journal of Theory, Research and Practice*, the first peer-reviewed coaching journal published by a major house.

Carol's unparalleled expertise in the art and science of coaching combines uniquely with her business savvy, high energy, and appreciation for the absurd. It is easy for Carol to speak the truth to the powerful in a way they find intriguing, informative, and enjoyable. She brings this energy to her keynote addresses, master classes, and town halls, which are high-impact and memorable.

David Noble and Carol teamed up in 2015 and have worked extensively at the top of the house with team coaching, workshops, and leader-as-coach programs. Together they are an unstoppable force, working with nearly any business coaching challenge and bringing to an engagement remarkable and complementary skill sets. The strength of their partnership creates a safe and enriching environment that fosters trust, growth, and innovation. For the most complex leaders, Carol and David developed their unusual "two-on-one" coaching model to unlock the most difficult and often paradoxical challenges.

Carol is married with two children and based outside of Boston. She and her husband love prehistoric art, safaris, and anthropology and travel the world to follow their diverse interests.

Learn more at CarolKauffman.com.

Learn more at www.view-advisors.com.